Henry James Coleridge

The nine months

The life of our Lord in the womb

Henry James Coleridge

The nine months
The life of our Lord in the womb

ISBN/EAN: 9783743336476

Manufactured in Europe, USA, Canada, Australia, Japa

Cover: Foto ©Lupo / pixelio.de

Manufactured and distributed by brebook publishing software (www.brebook.com)

Henry James Coleridge

The nine months

THE NINE MONTHS

THE LIFE OF OUR LORD IN THE WOMB

BY

HENRY JAMES COLERIDGE

OF THE SOCIETY OF JESUS

LONDON
BURNS AND OATES
GRANVILLE MANSIONS W
1885

✠

VIRGINUM CUSTOS ET PATER
SANCTE JOSEPH
CUJUS FIDELI CUSTODIÆ
IPSA INNOCENTIA CHRISTUS JESUS
ET IPSA VIRGO VIRGINUM MARIA
COMMISSA FUIT
TE PER HOC UTRUMQUE CARISSIMUM PIGNUS
JESUM ET MARIAM
OBSECRO ET OBTESTOR
UT ME AD OMNI IMMUNDITIA PRÆSERVATUM
MENTE INCONTAMINATA
PURO CORDE ET CASTO CORPORE
JESU ET MARIÆ
SEMPER FACIAS
CASTISSIME FAMULARI

PREFACE.

THE present volume, like that which preceded it, is so far complete in itself, that it embraces a distinct and separate stage in the history of the Incarnation. Our Lord's Life in the womb of His Blessed Mother is a part of His Infinite condescension which has more than one characteristic of its own, and which calls for a corresponding and particular devotion on our part. As the present volume reaches from the Annunciation itself to the Eve of the Nativity, it covers the whole of this unborn Life of our Lord. It is enough for devout Christians that there exists this separate portion of our Lord's human existence, the period of His greatest humiliation and self-abasement. It is only natural that this should at once attract our adoring homage, and that those who give themselves to the special devotion which it suggests should find themselves consoled and assisted in a wonderful degree by the practices and contemplations which belong to that devotion.

There are many reasons which may be assigned

as special incentives to this devotion, besides the simple truths that our faith teaches us concerning it. In the first place, it sets before us the complete interior picture of the Sacred Humanity itself, the immense treasures which constitute that fulness of grace of which we all receive, and the intense activity of the Heart and Mind of our Lord at the time of all others when no other activity was possible to Him, in the arrangements of Providence. It was a Life almost entirely addressed to God, and the object of His infinite complacency and delight. Moreover it was the true foundation of all that followed afterwards, and on this account we find those Christians who entirely ignore it, very generally wanting in an intelligence of the simplest truths of faith concerning the Incarnate Son of God. The Babe of Bethlehem is like any other child to them, as He was to the people of Bethlehem itself, or even to the Egyptians among whom He dwelt for a time. The misconception leads on to others, and extends to an inadequate idea of the whole Life, office, and work of our Lord, Who He is, and what He came to do.

Again, our Lord's Life in itself, at this time, reveals the work and office which He at once gave Himself to discharge towards His Father. The created existence which began at the moment of the Incarnation was the greatest of the works of God.

It may be considered as the crown and completion of the former great work of the creation of the universe, with all its marvellous orders of natures in various degrees of elevation and perfection in their reflection of the attributes of God. Holy Scripture speaks of our Lord as the Head and consummation of the whole creation. He was sent indeed on earth for the redemption of mankind, and for their instruction in the manner of serving God perfectly, but as it is implied, His presence as Man added the crowning dignity to the creation as it was originally left. Only through Him could there be that perfect intelligent and worthy service to the Creator, which no one could give to Him but a Divine Person. God's greatness and goodness and power and beauty and majesty, as displayed in the Creation, required as their correlatives, so to speak, the most perfect intelligence, appreciation, gratitude, praise, and these had never been rendered to Him adequately, nor could they ever be so rendered, until the moment of the Incarnation. The Life which then began paid this homage and tribute to the immense glory of God from the very beginning, in a thousand acts of adoration and self-abasement, oblation, and thanksgiving. The Soul of Jesus Christ was a living mirror which gave back to God the perfect representation of His glories and wonders and benefits, in an adoration of reverence, joy, and delight and gratitude which was of infinite merit and worth, because it was the homage of a Divine Person. In this consisted the gain to the glory of God which came about at the moment of the Incarnation.

We may represent this truth to ourselves in this way. Let us suppose that, in the original creation, there had been no orders of spiritual beings superior to man in intelligence, nobility, and capacity. Let us suppose that then, at a certain moment in the history of creation and the world, God had created the Holy Angels with their wonderful nature and gifts, and that they had burst suddenly into existence to give Him homage, glory, service, and gratitude, such as had been impossible for Him to receive from our feebler and narrower intelligences, our less powerful wills and duller affections. That would have been a wonderful change, and an advance in the glory received by God from His Creation, to which nothing else could compare in its history. But it is plain that the difference between the spiritual creation of God, with or without the whole innumerable host of the Angels in all their various ranks and hierarchies, would have been as nothing in comparison to the difference between the Creation of God without the Incarnation and the same Creation after our Lord had become a Creature. And the difference would come to this, that now at length God could be understood and worshipped, and thanked and honoured in an ineffably adequate manner, by a created intelligence and will united to a Divine Person, and that thus at last He could have from His Creation a worship worthy of Himself. Our faith teaches us that it was this that was brought about by the Incarnation, and that this work was complete from the very first instant of the Divine Union. This was the occupation and Life of our Lord during these nine months, when He did not begin as yet to redeem, or to atone, or to teach, in the ordinary way, as He did afterwards, but when He began from the very first moment to devote Himself to honouring and glorifying His Father by the most intense acts of love and adoration. The eye of faith can see, in the circumstances of this stage of His Life, many holy and tender lessons of humility, obedience, silence, recollection, dependence, and other virtues. We may gather also that at the first moment of this adorable Life was made the great oblation of Himself, of which the Scripture speaks, to undergo all that had been decreed for Him to suffer in order to repair the sins of all the world before the justice of God. But the occupation of the Sacred Heart during these long months, an occupation never since intermitted and never to cease for all eternity, was the employment of all His faculties of intelligence and affection upon the greatness and loveliness and majesty of God.

These nine months are the time in our Lord's Life

which seems most entirely given up to this employment. God was all in all. Out of this life in the womb, which had no external manifestation at all, there sprang all the beauties and charities of the after stages of the Holy Infancy, the Childhood, the Hidden Life at Nazareth, the Public Ministry, the Passion, the Risen and Sacramental and Glorious Life. It is this Life which continues now in Heaven where He sits at the right hand of God, and, in order that earth may not be without this continual and most perfect worship, He remains among us on the altar, not only to be the food and consolation of the devout souls who receive Him and live by Him, but also that from Him may rise up, day after day and night after night, as long as the world lasts, His own most loving adoration, most powerful intercession, and most intelligent praise. In the Blessed Sacrament He lives indeed for us, but His Life there is a return to His former existence in this stage of His Infancy, only that He has added to it, in His infinite tenderness and most ingenious and long-suffering love, the marvellous communication of Himself which embodies all the choicest fruits of His Life and Passion.

We may understand in this sense also the words of our Lord in His last prayer to His Father before the Passion, "I have glorified Thee upon earth, I have accomplished the work which Thou gavest Me to do, and now glorify Me, O Father, with Thyself with the glory which I had with Thee before the world was"[1]—that is, give to My Humanity the glory which belongs to Me as Thy Only-Begotten Son. For the perfect glorification of the Father, of which our Lord speaks, must certainly include the utter self-abasement with which He began, humbling Himself even to the condition of a babe in the womb of a woman, the nearest approach to utter annihilation of self that can be conceived, as well all the other service and homage and obedience and praise and worship of which His life was made up as it advanced. Thus our Lord as the second Adam was able to humble Himself before His Creator even more than was possible to the first Adam, who came into the world a full grown man and had no mother or father. It would not have seemed to us strange if it had been recorded of Adam, that when he first woke up into consciousness, and found himself in presence of his Creator and all the wonderful works in which his Creator chose to reflect His own greatness and power and goodness, he had been entranced in ecstatic contemplation of the marvellous world before him, and of God as revealed thereby, for the intelligence of all which he had been so wonderfully armed by the special gifts of grace with which he was endowed. It would not have been wonderful, if long days had passed before he had been able to think of anything but God, to do anything but

[1] St. John xvii.

give Him homage and glory. The intelligence and affections of the second Adam were far keener and intenser than anything that could have had place in the first father of mankind. And moreover, His soul had, from the first moment, the fulness of the Beatific Vision. It cannot surprise us that He should have found an intense delight in this noblest occupation of His created faculties, before proceeding, when the appointed time came, to make Himself visible to mankind as the Child of Bethlehem. What but the union with a Divine Person could have borne His Humanity up in so great a contemplation?

Another and very momentous fruit of an intelligent devotion to this part of the Sacred Infancy is to be found in the light which it throws on the position of the Blessed Mother of our Lord in the Kingdom of her divine Son, His dependence on her and union with her in the natural order, the immensity of her graces and the supreme perfection of her virtues. His dependence on her as her Child was different from that which is ordinary, on account of His full consciousness and perfect possession and use of all His faculties of intelligence and will. It is during this period of the Nine Months that He was hers and hers alone, and that she fulfilled, if not entirely alone, at least in a supreme degree which no one could approach, the duties of the whole human race in regard of the honour and service due to Him. St. Joseph and St. John Baptist share this office in some measure. But it is now that the preeminent greatness of the Mother of God seems to dwarf the magnificent perfections even of the highest of other saints, on account, in the first instance, of her unapproachable nearness to our Lord, her incomparable dignity as His Mother, and her unexampled faithfulness to the graces which she received, while all the time she is almost as hidden and silent as our Lord Himself. Again, the devotion which is fed on the contemplations which belong to this stage of the history involves a constant exercise of the highest faith, and is rewarded by a great increase and deepening of that most precious virtue.

I trust that no one will blame me for having given so large a part of the present volume to an attempt to unfold the meaning of the two first Evangelical Canticles, especially the Canticle of our Blessed Lady. This may be considered as, in one sense, the first utterance of our Lord Himself, as well as a revelation of the thoughts and affections of His Blessed Mother which has no parallel at all in the rest of Sacred Scripture. A great part of the commentary, in an earlier chapter, on the privileges of our Blessed Lady, will not be new to those who are acquainted with the treasures of Marian devotion to be found in the writings of St. Antonine and the Blessed Albert the

Great, which contain stores of this kind which are not sufficiently resorted to in our own time. The other chief subject contained in the present volume is the Preparation of St. Joseph for his high and peculiar office in the accomplishment of the decree of the Incarnation and all that followed on it. It has always seemed to me that the careful consideration of the scope and object of the first Evangelist in his short narrative, was quite sufficient to explain whatever appears obscure in the Scriptural statement on this great subject.

In order to help somewhat to the increase of devotion to our Lord while yet unborn, I have added as an Appendix a number of very short heads of meditation on His Life in the Womb, which may perhaps serve for the use of persons who are in the habit of developing for themselves subjects set before them in this concise way. I would gladly have made these longer and more complete, but I was anxious that this volume should be in the hands of the public before the beginning of the nine weeks before Christmas, which are often devoted to these considerations by way of preparation for the better celebration of the great Feast. They are abridged from the meditations of Father Spinola, a writer who is remarkable, among others of his class, for the fulness of his meditations on the Holy Infancy in general. For the same reason I have anticipated the publication of this volume, which was originally intended to appear simultaneously with the third and last part of this work on the Infancy. That is now passing through the press, and will I hope, be published before the Advent season of the present year is over. May the Blessed Child of Mary vouchsafe to accept this most imperfect offering in His honour and in that of His Immaculate Mother!

H. J. C.

31, Farm Street, Berkeley Square:
Feast of St. Michael, Archangel, 1885.

CONTENTS.

	PAGE
PREFACE . .	ix—xix

CHAPTER I.

The Salutation of the Angel.

St. Luke i. 26—28; *Vita Vitæ Nostræ*, § 4.

	PAGE
St. Gabriel in Scripture .	1
The light at his presence .	2
Words of the Evangelist .	3
First words of the Salutation	4
Fulness of grace . .	5
Three kinds of fulness .	6
Our Lady's plenitude .	7
Three kinds of effluence .	8
Grace of winning favours for others . . .	9
Increase of grace in our Lady	10
Sacramental graces . .	11
Gifts of the Holy Ghost .	12
Commentary of St. Antonine	13
Cardinal and theological virtues	16
The privileges of our Lady	17
Freedom from sin . .	17
Impossibility of sinning .	17
Constant meritoriousness .	18
The highest purity . .	18
Virgin and Mother . .	18
Mother of God . . .	19
Virgin of Virgins . .	19
Mother of all the redeemed	20
Gate of Heaven . . .	22
Queen and Mother of mercy	23
Communication of the Passion	25
Exaltation above all creatures	27
All these graces founded on her elevation to the Divine Maternity . .	28
Next words of the Angel .	33
Lord rather than God .	36
The Lord with thee ! .	38
Blessed among women .	38

CHAPTER II.

The Trouble of Mary.

St. Luke i. 29; *Vita Vitæ Nostræ*, § 4.

Our Lady understanding the message . . .	40
Accustomed to the visits of Angels	41
Maidenly fear . . .	42
Various kinds of trouble .	42
Explained by Toletus .	42
Probable privilege of Mary	44
Her trouble voluntary .	45

	PAGE		PAGE
Her humility . . .	46	Fervour and Divine Love .	70
Purpose of Virginity . .	46	Our Lady's faith . .	71
Perfection of her silence .	47	The key to unlock God's treasures. . . .	73

CHAPTER III.

The Son of David.

St. Luke i. 30—33; *Vita Vitæ Nostræ*, § 4.

Answer of the Angel . .	48
Our Lady's intelligence .	49
Allusion to prophecy . .	50
Emmanuel	50
Scriptural language . .	51
The Divine Maternity .	53
Heresies destroyed by the Angel's words. . .	55
Perfection of our Lady's Maternity . . .	56
The Son of the Most High	57
Greatness of our Lord's Person	58
His office	59
The Incarnate Son . .	60
Our Lord's Kingship. .	61
Universal extent and duration.	64

CHAPTER IV.

"How shall this be done?"

St. Luke i. 34; *Vita Vitæ Nostræ*, § 4.

Prudence of the Angel .	65
Mode of the execution of the promise . . .	66
Our Lady's surmise . .	67
Reticence of St. Gabriel .	67
Our Lady had no doubt .	68
Her love for purity . .	69

CHAPTER V.

The Conception by the Holy Ghost.

St. Luke i. 38; *Vita Vitæ Nostræ*, § 4.

The answer of the Angel a demand on fresh faith .	74
Heresies cutting down the truth	75
The full truth conveyed by the Angel . . .	76
Coming of the Holy Ghost	77
For the purpose of the mystery	78
Special action of the Holy Ghost	79
Sanctification of Mary .	79
Of the Conception itself .	80
Preparation of the substance	82
Why attributed to the Holy Ghost	82
Union of the Divine Person	83
The Power of the Most High	85
The Son of God. . .	86
'The Holy Born in thee' .	87
Other holy conceptions .	88
Our Lord as Man, Son of God	89
Connection of the words .	89
The words about St. Elisabeth	90
A confirmation of the truth	91
Suggestion of charity .	93

	PAGE
'No word impossible'	94
Our Lady grasping the mystery	95
Greatness of her faith	96
Immensely pleasing to God	97

CHAPTER VI.

The Fiat of Mary.

St. Luke i. 38; *Vita Vitæ Nostræ*, § 4.

No delay in our Lady's intelligence	99
Gabriel's three words	100
Answer of Mary	102
Virtues manifested in it	103
It reveals her desire	104
Departure of the Angel	105
Contemplation of the Incarnation	105
Advance in Mary's sanctification	109
St. Thomas and Suarez	110
Mary and Eve	111
Their names	112
The two messengers	113
Manner of reception	114
Obedience and disobedience	115
Comments of the Fathers	116

CHAPTER VII.

Our Lord's Life in the Womb.

God made an Infant	119
Analogy to the Blessed Sacrament	120
The secret worshippers	121
Mary's office	121
Homage due to our Lord	123
Body and Soul of Jesus	124
Excellencies of the Sacred Humanity	125
Knowledge and wisdom	125
Gifts of the Holy Ghost	126
Complacency of God	127
Joy of the Three Divine Persons	128
The Life of our Lord in the womb	128
Interior work for God	129
Vision of God, and all things	129
Special virtues at this time	130
Obedience	130
Humility	131
Meekness	131
Patience	132
Prayer and silence	133
Our Lady adoring	135

CHAPTER VIII.

The Visitation.

St. Luke i. 39—56; *Vita Vitæ Nostræ*, § 5.

Dealings of God with souls	137
With each singly	138
Joseph and Mary	139
Omission of guidance as to St. Joseph	140
Designs of God	141
Silence as to His favours	142
Delays of God	143
Narratives of St. Matthew and St. Luke	143
What St. Luke omits	144
What St. Matthew omits	145
Narrative of the Visitation	146

	PAGE		PAGE
St. Joseph with our Lady	147	The two clauses.	174
At the Temple	147	Creator and Redeemer	174
House of St. Zachary	148	Habitual thoughts of our Lady	175
Mary's intention and God's design	149	*Mater Creatoris, Mater Salvatoris*	176
Salutation of our Lady	149	Mary, Queen of Angels	177
State of St. John	150	Magnification of God	178
Effect of our Lady's voice	151	'*Gloria in excelsis*'	179
Sanctification of St. John	152	Affection of joy	180
Illumination of St. Elisabeth	152	Mary in possession of her joy	182
What she knew	153	Personal blessings to Mary	183
Details of the Annunciation	154	'Humility'	184
Words of St. Elisabeth	155	Contrast with God	185
Leaping of the child in her womb	156	His handmaiden	185
		How He 'regards'	186
Blessedness of Mary	157	All generations to call her Blessed	187
Elisabeth's prophecy	158	Prophecy in her words	188
Connection of the mysteries	158	Foreknowledge	189
Confirmation of faith	159	'All generations'	190
		Three attributes of God	191
		God's three gifts	192
		His power	192

CHAPTER IX.

The Canticle of Mary.

St. Luke i. 46—56; *Vita Vitæ Nostræ*, § 5.

	PAGE		PAGE
		Holiness	193
		Mercy	194
		From the beginning	195
Our Lady obliged to speak	161	Wide range of the blessing	197
Inspired by our Lord	162	Mary speaks for all	198
The *Magnificat* and the New Testament	163	Her personal connection with the blessings	199
Subjects of the Canticle	164	Reference to canticle of Anna	200
The canticle of Anna	165	Typical character of Old Testament events	201
Compared with the *Magnificat*	166	Deliverances of the holy people	202
General correspondence	169	Rule of God's action	203
Old Testament canticles	170	Love of humility	204
First word of the Canticle	171	Who are 'the mighty'?	205
Soul and spirit	172		

	PAGE		PAGE
The rebel Angels	206	Probably after the Birth of St. John	236
Their fall	207	Order of the Church.	237
Conceit of their hearts	207	Birth of St. John	237
Passages of St. Paul.	209	His circumcision	238
Other illustrations	211	The name 'John'	239
'Filling the hungry'.	213	St. Zachary speaking.	240
Three judgments of God	213	Spread of the wonder	241
Successive stages	214	Joyousness of these mysteries	241
Loss of power and dignity.	215	Fulfilment of the words of St. Gabriel	242
Angels and men.	216	Crown to the mystery	243
Exaltation of the humble.	218	Spiritual joy	244
Rich sent away empty	219	The *Benedictus*	245
Feeding on good things	220		
Contrast between the treatment of Angels and of men.	221		

CHAPTER XI.

The Canticle of Zachary.

St. Luke i. 67—80; *Vita Vitæ Nostræ,* § 7.

The world yearning for our Lord.	222		
The saints and the effects of grace.	223	Divisions of the canticle	246
Emptiness of the lost	224	Our Lady's words taken up	247
The enemies of our Lady.	225	'Visitation' of God	248
Faithfulness of God.	226	Kingdom of the Messias	249
Meaning of 'received'	227	Dispensation of Redemption.	250
God chose a Mother.	228	A visible Kingdom	251
Thankfulness of our Lady.	229	The Horn of David	251
Fulfilment of promises	229	The holy prophets	252
Summary of the Canticle.	230	A chain of predictions	253
Its use in the Church	232	Restoration of the throne.	254
She rests on God's faithfulness	233	Characteristics of the Kingdom	255

CHAPTER X.

The Nativity of St. John.

St. Luke i. 59—80; *Vita Vitæ Nostræ,* § 7.

		Salvation from enemies	256
		Mercy with our fathers	257
		Saints still in need of mercy	258
Silence of the Gospels	234	Covenant of God	258
Presence of our Lady	235	Oath of God	259
Her return.	235	The three bonds	260

	PAGE		PAGE
Thoughts of St. Zachary .	261	St. Matthew's account .	289
Serving God without fear .	263	His words guarded . .	290
Tyranny of the devils .	264	Conception by the Holy	
New service to God . .	265	Ghost	291
Holiness before God . .	266	Subject of the revelation .	292
Blessings commemorated in the canticle. . .	267	Quotation from Isaias .	293
Address to St. John . .	268		

CHAPTER XIII.

The Trial of St. Joseph.

St. Matt. i. 18—25; *Vita Vitæ Nostræ*, § 6.

To go before our Lord .	269		
Knowledge of salvation .	270		
Immense mercy of God .	271		
The Orient from on high .	272		
Twofold image . . .	273	Silence of the Gospels as to interior acts . .	295
Enlightenment . . .	274	Close of the Visitation .	296
The shadow of death. .	275	Separation of Joseph and Mary	297
Gentiles and Jews . .	276	Ended after the Visitation.	298
Growth of St. John . .	277	Our conceptions as to our Lady and St. Joseph .	299

CHAPTER XII.

The opening of St. Matthew's Gospel.

St. Matt. i. 18—25; *Vita Vitæ Nostræ*, § 6.

We must be consistent .	299
Immense glory to God at this time. . . .	300
St. Joseph's part . .	301

God dealing with St. Joseph	278	Silence after the Annunciation . . .	302
We now leave St. Luke for St. Matthew . .	279	Enlightenment after the revelation . . .	303
Particular object different in each . . .	279	What was St. Joseph's office ?	304
St. Luke's object . .	280	His hesitation . . .	305
St. Matthew's object .	281	" Putting away privately "	305
Sections in his Gospel .	281	Carefulness of St. Matthew	305
Apologetic manner .	282	The Holy Ghost mentioned	306
Questions answered . .	283	Various interpretations .	306
Objections	284	St. Joseph's "ignorance" .	306
Difficulty about St. Joseph	285	A possible fear . . .	307
Answered by St. Matthew.	285	Contemplated withdrawal .	308
Witness of St. Joseph .	286	St. Jerome's opinion . .	309
Natural meaning of the narrative. . . .	287	Humility of St. Joseph .	310
Christian view of St. Joseph	288	This hypothesis adopted .	310

	PAGE		PAGE
Fourth conjecture of the truth	311	Time of great peace and grace	333
Use of the delay	311	New Presence of God	334
St. Matthew's language	312	Immense spiritual gifts	335
Injunction to St. Joseph	313	Mary's titles in the Litany	336
Virtue exercised.	314	Grace of St. Joseph	337
Charity of Judgment.	314	Their neighbours at Nazareth.	338
Humility	315		
No sign asked for	316	Bethlehem in Prophecy	339
God's way the best	317	How were they to be there?	339
St. Joseph's trial	318	Difficulty solved by God	340
Analogy to the trial of Mary	319	Decree of Augustus	341
His presence at the Visitation.	320	Our Lord to obey the law.	341
		The enrolling	342
St. Joseph in the Holy Family	321	Quirinus	343
		Longing for the Birth	344
Our Lord's true obedience	322	Mary's desire	345
St. Joseph in the spiritual kingdom	323	St. Joseph's	346
		The Nazarenes	347
Experiences of the spiritual life	323	Hardships of the journey.	348
New relations between St. Joseph and our Lady	324	Yearning of the Creation in St. Paul	349
Elevation of Mary	325	The physical creation to be made perfect	350
Their union made more indissoluble	326	The human world, and the Saints	350
Perfection of both	327	Desire for the Nativity, as an onward step	351
Immense supplies of grace.	328		
Workings of grace in St. Joseph	329	Joy of the first Christmas.	353
		Our Lord's Heart	354
Saints ignorant of their own future	330	Compassion	354
		Good and evil in man	355
God's plan the best	331	Workings of the Good Spirit	356
CHAPTER XIV.		Prayers of the Saints	357
The Expectation of the Nativity.		Our Lord before the Passion.	358
St. Luke ii. 1—15; *Vita Vitæ Nostræ,* § 8.		So also now	358
		Completion of the work in the womb	359
Interval after the Visitation	332	The worship of God	359

	PAGE		PAGE
The work of Redemption	360	§ 6. The Revelation made to St. Joseph by the Angel	365
Work in the souls of Mary and Joseph	361
All now ready	362	§ 7. The Nativity of St. John, the Forerunner of our Lord	366

Harmony of the Gospels.

APPENDIX.

§ 4. The Conception of our Saviour Jesus Christ	363	Heads of meditation on the Life of our Lord in the Womb	369
§ 5. The Visitation of the Blessed Virgin Mary	364

CHAPTER I.

THE SALUTATION OF THE ANGEL.

St. Luke i. 26—28; *Vita Vitæ Nostræ*, § 4.

THE sacred narrative tells us nothing as to the time or place at which the Annunciation occurred, except that it was at Nazareth. The words of St. Luke, about the Angel entering in, seem to imply that it was in the house that the message was delivered, and thus to overthrow the not very probable story of our Lady having been by the side of a well to draw water when the apparition occurred. The apparitions of St. Gabriel in the Sacred Scriptures are more than once connected with the time of the offering of the evening sacrifice in the Temple, a time which may very naturally be supposed to have been, to all the devout Jews, whether at Jerusalem or elsewhere, a time of adoration and prayer. It was at this time that St. Gabriel appeared to Daniel to give him the famous prophecy of the seventy weeks, and it was at this time also that he had appeared in the Temple itself to the holy Zachary. Thus the devotion of the Church, which keeps the *Magnificat* of our Blessed Lady for the Vesper service, would have a kind of foundation in the history of the Annunciation.

Some of the liturgical books give us the idea that it was either evening or night when St. Gabriel appeared, and they speak of the great light which accompanied the Angel as startling our Blessed Lady. The Greek text, instead of the word which has been rendered by our version, 'when she had heard,' has another word, 'when she saw' him. All the details of the scene are veiled from us in the simple brevity of the Gospel words. But we are not forbidden to fill them up for ourselves, out of the contemplations of the saints. We may well suppose that Mary was praying earnestly for the fulfilment of the promises made to the holy nation, now that the time seemed to have come. They occupied her thoughts day and night, and her desire for herself, as we have seen, was that she might live when their accomplishment came to pass, and perhaps be the servant of that blessed Virgin who was to be the Mother of the Divine Child. "I saw" she said to her devout servant St. Bridget, in the place already quoted, "a star, but not such as shines from heaven, I saw a light, but not such as shines in this world. I perceived a sweet odour, but it was not of herbs, or anything of that sort, wonderfully sweet and such as cannot be described. It filled everything, and I was exulting with joy on its account. And then immediately I heard a voice, but not from human mouth. On hearing it I was much afraid, thinking in myself, whether perchance it was an illusion. And immediately there appeared to me an Angel of God as a most beautiful man, but not clothed in human flesh."[1]

[1] St. Bridget, *Rev.* i. 10.

But it is time for us to give the simple words of the Evangelist, in which the history of the Annunciation is related, probably, as has more than once been hinted, from the statement of our Blessed Lady herself. St. Luke has just told us that St. Elisabeth hid herself for five months after the conception of her son. The narrative of the Annunciation, is a continuation of the same record. "And in the sixth month the Angel Gabriel was sent from God into a city of Galilee called Nazareth, to a Virgin espoused to a man whose name was Joseph, of the house of David, and the Virgin's name was Mary, And the Angel, being come in, said unto her, Hail, full of grace, the Lord is with thee, blessed art thou among women. Who having heard, was troubled at his saying, and thought within herself what manner of salutation this should be. And the Angel said to her, Fear not, Mary, for thou hast found grace with God. Behold thou shalt conceive in thy womb, and shall bring forth a Son, and thou shalt call His Name Jesus. He shall be great, and shall be called the Son of the most High, and the Lord God shall give unto Him the throne of David His Father, and He shall reign in the house of Jacob for ever, and of His kingdom there shall be no end. And Mary said to the Angel, How shall this be done, because I know not man? And the Angel answering said to her, the Holy Ghost shall come upon thee, and the power of the most High shall overshadow thee, and therefore also the Holy One which shall be born of thee shall be called the Son of God. And behold, thy cousin Elisabeth, she also hath conceived a son in her old age, and this is the sixth month with her that is called barren, because no word shall be impossible with God. And Mary said, Behold the handmaid of the Lord, be it done to me according to thy word. And the Angel departed from her."

We must first consider the opening address of St. Gabriel to our Blessed Lady. "Hail, full of grace, the Lord is with thee, blessed art thou among women." The word Hail is the common salutation, wishing joy and happiness, implying respect and good will, but not, of necessity, adoration or worship. The word which our version most rightly renders, 'full of grace' is the perfect participle passive of the Greek verb formed from the word which is always translated by our word grace. The Greek verbs of this formation imply that the quality or thing, represented by the substantive from which they are formed, is conveyed and given to the subject of the verb to which they are applied, somewhat in the same way as we in English use the noun itself as a verb, when we speak of persons being 'graced' or 'gifted' and the like, using the noun grace or gift in the sense of a verb. The perfect participle implies that the action is completed, and the words might have been rendered Hail, graced one, or fully graced one, and the meaning would then have been conveyed that the person to whom the words were applied was endowed with grace in its fulness, that the process, so to say, of her endowment with grace was as complete as it could be. This sense is expressed in the Latin versions, both the Vulgate and the old Italic, by the words 'gratia plena,' and our English words 'full of grace' express the same meaning, while they convey most perfectly the theological truth also, that grace is a quality or substance which is in the soul itself, not merely the favour with which the soul may be regarded, without any actual possession of the quality signified by the word. This is the great defect of the common Protestant version, in which the Greek word is rendered 'highly favoured,' and which on on this account is liable to grave censure. The revised English version recognizes this to some extent, by placing in the margin, 'endowed with grace.' The words of the Angel imply, by their own force and weight, that the soul of Mary was at this moment already filled with grace.

We have already had to speak of the fulness of grace which is thus brought before our minds, for we have had to interpret the great words of St. John in the opening of his Gospel, in which he tells us that the Incarnate Word of God dwelt among us, full of grace and truth, and that of His fulness we have all received, and grace for grace.[2] The plenitude of grace, therefore, of which the Angel now speaks, in the case of the blessed Mother of our Lord, must be considered as the fullest and highest possible participation of the fulness of the grace of the Incarnate Word, although, at the moment at which these words were uttered to Mary, the Divine mystery of the Incarnation had not yet taken place. But all the graces of Mary were for the sake of her Son, all given to her out of regard

[2] St John i. 16.

to His ineffable merits, all with the view of fitting her for the supreme honour of becoming His Mother. We may therefore speak, in commenting on these words of St. Gabriel, of the graces of the Sacred Humanity of our Lord, although they did not at this precise moment as yet exist. Those who have written on this great subject tell us that there are three kinds of plenitude of grace. The first is in God, in Whom alone are all good things, all gifts, all graces, essentially and infinitely perfect. God can receive no grace, for He is the one full and inexhaustible fountain of grace, a fountain which may give out countless treasures of the highest graces to His creatures, and which yet remains infinite and undiminished in its own fulness.

The next kind of fulness or plenitude is that which belongs to Christ as Man, the Sacred Humanity of our Lord. It is this of which St. John speaks in the words just now quoted. It is of this fulness that we have all received. The fountain and source of all the graces of the Sacred Humanity is the Union with the Divine Person of the Word of God, and it is from the One Godhead, which He possesses in common with the Father and the Holy Ghost, that our Lord as Man receives infinitely and without measure, as the same Evangelist says, every kind of grace. As His grace is without measure, He cannot be said in the strict propriety of the words to increase in grace. His works were all of infinite merit, all proceeding from infinite and most perfect charity, and by them He merited indeed, though not for Himself, but for us. Thus indeed He is full of grace, He has as Man by grace what He has as God by nature, and no grace in Him was ever wasted or idle, or liable to any diminution or failure. This is the fulness of grace which belongs to our Lord as Man.

These two great plenitudes of grace might be said to have been in Mary in a certain way, because she had within her, after the Incarnation, God Himself to Whom the first plenitude belongs, and our Lord also as to His Humanity, to Whom belongs the second. But speaking strictly, Mary cannot have either the fulness which is infinite and which sheds itself on all creatures without exhausting itself, nor can she have the imparted grace of the fulness which was in our Lord as Man, in Him alone without measure. In the same way she could not have been so full of grace as not to be able to receive more, or to increase in grace, nor, with regard to the fulness of truth of which St. John speaks, could she in her mortal life, have had that in such a manner as to know all things, nor did she behold God as He is, in the way in which the saints in glory behold Him. Her plenitude of grace was the plenitude of a pure creature, and therefore immeasurably distant from that which is in God and in our Lord. When the Angel addresses her as full of grace, he must be understood as implying that she was as full of grace, in that way which was possible to her, as she could be full. And the Saints and Fathers tell us that she was thus so full of grace, as that she could have had no greater fulness, unless she had been herself united to the Godhead, as was the Humanity of her Son. The reason for this is the simple principle, to which we have already referred the immense treasure of grace which Catholic teachers tell us to have existed in Mary, namely, that she had been raised, or was to be raised, to a dignity than which no higher, under God, can possibly be conceived, the dignity of the Mother of God.

It falls within the range of this created plenitude, so to speak, that our Blessed Lady should have been so full of grace, as that her grace made her so pleasing to God that all her works were most perfect and meritorious of eternal life through her Son. This kind of fulness of grace, flowing over, so to say on all that is said or done by the person who possesses it, is thought to have been in the holy Apostles, and in others, as St. Stephen, of whom is said that he was full of grace and fortitude. But it must have been in our Blessed Lady in a higher degree than in any of the saints, for a good theological reason which is given by St. Antonine. In proportion as any thing or any one that receives, for instance, grace, from another, is more close and near to the person or principle from which or from whom the gift or the grace imparted proceeds, in the same proportion is the reception of the gift received more complete and perfect in degree and in kind. Our Blessed Lady was far closer and more united to her Divine Son than any of the saints could be, and therefore she must have received from Him the treasure of which we are speaking far more perfectly and largely than any other. The writer whom we are following distinguishes three degrees in which the grace which sanctifies the soul may shed itself, so to say, outwardly. The first is when the interior grace sanctifies also the exterior works and acts, and so makes them edifying and helpful to others. The second is when the external influence extends itself, not simply to edification, but also to instruction and teaching. And the third is when the Saint, who has this abundance of interior grace, goes so far as to lay down his life for others, as was the case with St. Stephen.

The same writer speaks of a further effluence of grace, in the case of those who are so full thereof and so pleasing to God, that they have the power granted to them of winning from Him favours and graces for others as well as for themselves, in the way of merit, and this may be either partially or more largely, according to the degree of the grace with which they are full, and the power granted to them by God. We have but very few incidents of the life of our Blessed Lady to judge from as to this, but we may fairly take the two first miracles in the life of our Lord as instances of this kind of grace in her. These two are the sanctification of St. John in the womb of his mother, and the change of the water into wine at the marriage of Cana. The words of St. Elisabeth at the Visitation seem to attribute the leaping of the babe in her womb, in which we understand the sanctification of St. John to be included, to the salutation of Mary. The miracle of Cana was certainly wrought out of regard to her intercession. Here then would be instances of the grace that was in our Blessed Lady, winning from God graces both of a spiritual and temporal kind for others besides herself. This is enough to have said as an explanation of the words of the Angel as far as regards the plenitude of grace imputed to Mary.

We must add a further thought. The graces of our Blessed Lady, wonderful as they were even at the very outset of her life, when the privilege of the Immaculate Conception was bestowed on her —for this very purpose, as we may surely think, among others, that it might be the foundation on which the great treasure of gifts and graces, which belonged to the position of the Mother of God in the kingdom of the Incarnation, might be raised— were nevertheless always such as admitted of growth and increase. We believe that she did continually advance and increase in grace, from moment to moment, with a swiftness and ease and invariable continuity of growth of which there is no other instance in the whole Creation, as her dignity as Mother of God has no parallel therein. The writers whom we have hitherto followed in this short account of her graces, do not pause to distinguish those graces which she received at the outset of her life from those which may have been afterwards added. They speak rather theologically than historically. It is thus we find St. Antonine discussing the question about her reception of the Christian sacraments, at the time that he is commenting on this salutation of the Angel of which we are now speaking. It csnnot be doubted that the continual growth of Mary in every grace was a special subject of delight to God, distinct from her simple possession of so many graces, and from her practice of the highest virtues, interior and exterior, from the moment when she became capable of such exercise of her gifts. But this peculiar beauty of the unfolding, before the eyes of God, of this most beautiful flower of Paradise, is something which it is beyond our power to draw out in our present exile from heaven. It is natural that the theological writers of whom we speak should treat of the graces of Mary rather in general, without reference to the order in which they were developed and manifested.

St. Antonine divides what he has to say on this great subject into several heads, which correspond to the various divisions of grace with which our divines are familiar. He speaks first of the graces of the Sacraments, then of the graces of the virtues, then of the graces which he calls *nominales*, that is, the graces contained in the gifts of the Holy Ghost properly so called. Then he passes on to the graces which are known by the names of graces *gratis datæ*, and he ends by a catalogue of personal privileges of grace bestowed on Mary on acconnt of her Maternity. In a later chapter he gives an account of the fruits of the Holy Ghost in our Blessed Lady.

The saint has some beautiful contemplations on the sacramental graces, but, as the sacraments could not have been instituted or received at the time of the Annunciation, we may pass over those for the present. The graces of the gifts of the Holy Spirit do not fall under the same category. As the Holy Ghost is the Divine Person to Whom in a special manner is attributed the carrying out of the Incarnation, it is reasonable to suppose that His gifts were most fully and lavishly bestowed upon Mary from the very moment at which her soul became capable of receiving them, and that He ever afterwards took a special delight in increasing them, in their beauty and efficacy, more especially as the great stages of her life succeeded one another, whether before the moment of the Incarnation or after it. Indeed, short as the records are which remain to us, they seem not to be too short to show us the continual exercise of these gifts. It is indeed most important for us, in our considerations of the mysteries of the Incarnation, not to have any limited or jejune estimate of the amount of the graces possessed from the very first by her, who was so chief an agent in them all. It would take us a long time to write out all that St. Antonine tells us concerning the gifts of the Holy Ghost in this royal soul, but the general principle which guides him in his estimate cannot be forgotten, if we are to understand rightly the history before us. The gifts of the Holy Ghost are usually divided into two classes, according to the faculties of the soul which they affect and elevate and, as it were, transfigure, with new powers. Four of the gifts affect the intelligence. These are the gifts of wisdom, of understanding, of counsel, and of knowledge. The remaining three, the gifts of fortitude, piety, and fear, perfect the will and make its action noble and lofty. In the possession of each of these classes of gifts our Blessed Lady was unique among pure creatures. The first class she did not possess in the same measure which she now possesses them in heaven, but she possessed them in one sense in a higher way still, in that she possessed them in a way which made their use meritorious in her. She had them in a degree which is unexampled and singular, as to the perfection of the acts which she elicited by them. As regards the other gifts, whose perfection consists in action rather than in intelligence, these she had as highly as was possible, as to the perfection of her acts, and also as to the immense meritoriousness of those acts.

St. Antonine has many beautiful thoughts in his account of these gifts in our Blessed Lady. He takes, for instance, the definition of the gift of wisdom, as being a kind of taste and intense relish of God in His goodness, and lays down that in this kind of taste or relish there are three things to be distinguished, the touch, the discernment, and the delight which is the result of both. The imagery is taken from our reception of some exquisite food, which we first receive by the sense of touch, then discern and distinguish by the delicacy of the palate, and then relish or enjoy with a delight in proportion to our capacity, and to the intrinsic sweetness of the viand. As to the first, Mary was immensely more near to God than any one else could be, her charity, which was the uniting principle between Him and her, was such as to bind her closer to Him than any but she could be. As to her power of discerning and distinguishing the true savour in spiritual things, here again she was far above all others, and by no means could she either be deceived as to what was the true good, or fail in appreciating the good which she tasted to the very utmost of its capacity. And as to the delight which this relish would produce in her, here again she surpassed all. The just in this life are said to hunger and to thirst after God, and the blessed in heaven to be satiated with the possession of Him. This hunger and thirst on the one hand, and this satisfaction on the other hand, represent the two stages of the workings of this gift of wisdom in their souls. In our Blessed Lady the result of this gift was something which raised her above the state of hunger and thirst, because she had the perfect cognisance of God in the Sacred Humanity of our Lord, and yet she could not have as yet the full satiety with which her soul was to be flooded in heaven.

St. Antonine here quotes the Blessed Albert the Great concerning the gift of understanding or intelligence as possessed by our Blessed Lady. He tells us that, with regard to this gift, she had certain privileges of her own. She had by grace, even in this life, a very perfect knowledge of the Divine Trinity, and in the same way, of the mystery of the Incarnation, though in this case her own long familiarity with it and with our Lord was, in part, the ground of her privilege. Her own predestination was revealed to her. She had a marvellous intelligence of her own soul, and a singular knowledge of the souls of other, of angelical and diabolical spirits. Her grace also included a wonderful knowledge of all things that belonged to her conduct in her mortal life, which included the understanding of the Sacred Scriptures, and of all she had to do and to contemplate, and this extended itself, by a special revelation, to future things concerning herself, to the state of heaven, and the like.

The gift of counsel, according to St. Thomas, is

that by which the Holy Ghost directs us in all things which are ordained to the end of our eternal life, whether they are commandments necessary to salvation or not. . . . "But Mary was a most perfect observer, both of the commandments and of the counsels of God. She had beyond all, therefore, the knowledge of His counsels by this gift of counsel. She was also most dear to and familiar with God above all others, and so instructed even in the greatest secrets. Among the other counsels of God are poverty, virginity, and obedience, and she observed these in their highest perfection. She was most poor," as we see in her offering in the Temple. . . . "She was the first to make the vow of virginity, which she always observed without the slightest contrary movement, and she was most obedient," as we see in the mystery of her Purification, to which she was not bound, in her journey to Bethlehem, in her visit to Jerusalem, for the feasts and the like.

We pass over for the present what the saint tells us about the gifts of fortitude and knowledge. He makes the gift of piety consist in three acts, in disposition for works of mercy, in perfect obedience to the Sacred Scriptures, and in due honour to holy persons and things. He has little difficulty in showing the perfection of these acts in our Blessed Lady. She was moved to works of mercy by considering all men, not only as the images of God, but also as representing Him in a new way in consequence of the Incarnation. The simple words of the Angel were enough for her to ground on them her stupendous act of faith, when she said, "Behold the handmaid of the Lord, be it done to me according to thy word." She was in her life time the pattern of veneration for all holy things and places, feasts and the like, and we probably owe to her the first example of the veneration which has always been shown in the Church to the special objects of Christian devotion, such as the Holy Cross, the Holy Sepulchre, the Way of the Cross, relics, and the Blessed Sacrament. Lastly, the saint comes to the holy gift of fear. There are, he says, three kinds of fear. There is the fear of servants, which consists in the apprehension of punishment for disobedience, there is the chaste fear, of which the Psalmist speaks, and this has two acts, the fear of separation from God, like the fear of a pure spouse lest she should lose her beloved, and the fear of reverence, which consists in a very humble veneration, mixed with love of the thing or the person venerated. It was this last which was so excellent in Mary. She could not fear chastisement, who had no sin, nor could she seriously fear to be separated from God, who was confirmed in grace. But she was overwhelmed with the thought of the magnificence and greatness and mightiness and majesty of Him Who had lavished His choicest blessings on her, and raised her to a height unparalleled among His creatures.

St. Antonine has a long chapter on the cardinal and theological virtues as possessed by our Blessed Lady. As the incidents in which their presence in her soul are chiefly manifested belong to later periods of our history, or at least to the narrative

[3] Psalm xviii.

of the Incarnation itself, it may be well to refrain here from entering on this delightful subject. Lastly, he treats at considerable length of what he calls her special privileges. These, as has already been said, are in truth so many natural and reasonable deductions, from her one fundamental grace of the divine Maternity. Although in this case also the saint anticipates the historical order in the unfolding of these privileges, it may be well summarily to mention them now, inasmuch as they were already conferred on our Lady potentially and in their germs.

The first privileges in this series need not detain us long, for something has already been said of them. These are, her perfect freedom from all sin, whether original or actual, mortal or venial, and even beyond this, the kind of impossibility of sinning in her which has been explained above. The saints in glory cannot sin, because they are absolutely united to God, in Whom there can be no sin, by a means which precludes their ever being separated from Him, which is the state of glory. In this sense Mary was not incapable of sin, because she was not as yet united to God in the state of glory. But she was united to Him by the plenitude of her grace, and although grace is in itself a thing that may be set aside, yet there was in her condition nothing at all by means of which it could be set aside, nothing at all that could bring about a separation from God, and in this sense her plenitude of grace was incompatible with sin. Her third privilege has already been spoken of, namely, that all her acts of free will were meritorious. The fourth privilege was that she was the expression of the highest purity. The purity of which the saint speaks is not simply freedom from what is impure, but the closest possible approximation to the supreme purity which is in God, and to this privilege our Lady attained by four steps or stages, in each, as they succeeded, deriving greater and higher grace from the bounty of God. These four stages were, as St. Antonine tells us, her sanctification in her mother's womb, that is, her Immaculate Conception and the graces received therewith, her practice of virtue as her years went on, the coming on her of the Holy Ghost for the accomplishment of the Incarnation in her, and her Virginal Conception of the Son of God.

The next of the privileges of Mary was that she was at once Virgin and Mother. This must not be considered a simple prodigy of nature, in the physical order, uniting in her, so to say, the beauty of Maternity and the pure and incorrupt splendour of Virginity. For both Maternity and Virginity have a kind of natural glory of their own. But in Mary both were meritorious and deliberate, meritorious because so deliberate. Her Virginity was the most perfect purity of mind and body, springing from her consummate charity and love of God, and her Maternity was accepted and willed, merited, as it is said, *de congruo*, by her faith, her hope, her charity, and especially by her incomparable humility. And her fruitful Virginity and most pure Maternity made her the Mother of God. Under this privilege is included the whole of her wonderful relations with our Lord, from the moment when

He became her Son in her most chaste womb, her intercourse with Him during the nine months, the thirty years after His birth, and throughout all the ages which have since passed, throughout all eternity. Thus the woman who lifted up her voice out of the crowd proclaimed her blessed, "blessed the womb that bare Thee and the breasts which Thou hast sucked."[4] And if the privilege of being made His Mother at the moment of the Incarnation was so ineffable, it has lasted on in ever increasing glory and magnificence, and will last on for ever.

But if the Maternity of Mary was thus a privilege which cannot be measured in its fruits and results, a privilege which is as fresh and fruitful in heaven at this moment as it was at the first instant of the Incarnation, so also is the Virginity of Mary a privilege which lasts on and is continually most fruitful. For she is called in the Litanies sung in her honour "Sancta Virgo Virginum," and she deserves this title on two accounts. In the first place, as has already been said, she was the first, without any commandment of God, or any counsel of God made known to men, and without any example in the ancient saints, to discern, so to say, the inappreciable treasure of Holy Virginity, and to raise its honour in the world, to the immense glory of God and benefit of mankind. And, in consequence, she is the mother of all holy virgins, a countless throng of both sexes, who have served God faithfully in this holy state. She may truly be called also the Mother of all the good works and great achievements which have become possible

[4] St. Luke xi. 27.

to men in consequence of the honour in which Virginity has been placed by her, and which have ever been the strength of the whole Church, the glory of our Lord and the sources of infinite blessings to mankind. And in the second place, Mary is the Virgin of Virgins, because she is the one most perfect and incomparable instance of Virginity. For her Virginity was not, as in others, a crown which had to be defended against the assaults of internal concupiscence, for in her the root of evil concupiscence was destroyed, and it was in itself of a purity which has no peer, even in the most spotless. It has also the unattainable glory of fertility, fertility of that unapproachable dignity which belongs to the fruitfulness which generates the Son of God in human nature.

These last privileges in the list of St. Antonine are clearly the issue of the Maternity of Mary. He follows them up by three privileges which do not at first sight seem to belong so much to the present stage of the story of her life, but which nevertheless may most properly be here considered, for they are in truth, contained in the decree whieh made her the Mother of God Incarnate for the redemption of the world. It is thought by some theologians that the Incarnation might have been, even if Adam had not fallen, and that thus there might have been a Divine Maternity which would not have been that which made Mary the mother of the Saviour of the world. Even in this case, it cannot be doubted that our Lord would have been the head of the whole universe by virtue of His Incarnation, and that all the elevation of which creatures might have been made partakers would have come from and through Him. If so, Mary would still have had that relationship to all those who are members of our Lord and who are united with Him in the nature which He has assumed through and from her, which she actually has, a relationship which is involved in the Divine Maternity bestowed upon her, and without some account of which that Maternity cannot be fully understood. It is essential that this thought should be included in the idea of her Maternity, and our grasp of this truth is confirmed by the position which she occupies in the sacred scroll of prophecy, as the second Eve, by the truth that she was not an involuntary or unconscious instrument of the Incarnation, and by the fact that, as we are told by some of the Fathers, she merited, in the only way in which a creature could merit such a grace, that she should be made the Mother of God.

St. Antonine tells us that she is the Mother of all those who have a share in the new creation which has been the work of her Son, in various ways. She bare Him for us, Who created us and regenerated us all virtually by His Passion, which confers the power of grace on the Sacraments, and she merited congruously by her virtues that she should bring forth Him as her Son. It was from her most pure flesh and blood that the Holy Ghost, by her own consent, took the flesh which He transformed into the Body by which our Redemption and new Creation were effected. Moreover, our Lady, by her wonderfully godlike conversation, was to us the pattern and example of our turning away from darkness to light, and our perfect conversion unto the vision of the primeval light. And lastly, he says that the whole work of our redemption and new creation was ordered by God to her glory and honour. Thus the vision of the Apocalypse represents the elders in heaven casting their crowns down before the feet of the Lamb,[5] as if to acknowledge that they owe all to the humiliation of our Lord and the Sacred Humanity which He took of Mary. And he says that this truth of the Maternity of Mary over all who are redeemed by her Son, is touched on in her own words in her Canticle, where she says that from henceforth all generations shall call her blessed. For the regeneration and re-creation of all things by means of the Incarnation make her in this sense the Mother of all.

It is a part of the same truth that Mary is called the Gate of Heaven. It is the function of a gate that through it everything must pass which enters or comes forth from the city of which it is the gate. This name has sometimes been applied to the saints, as it is used in the Apocalypse of the Apostles, and it is sometimes applied to the holy Cross. Its application to Mary represents the truth that we have through her the whole of the blessings which come to us by means of the Incarnation, because we have through her her Divine Son. It means also that as we all enter heaven through her Son, we enter heaven through her, whose Son He was. It is well known how some of the fathers and saints have insisted on the

[5] Apoc. v. 8.

doctrine that all graces pass through the hands of Mary to us, by the special disposition of God, and it would not be easy to see how the denial of this truth can be altogether consistent with the true appreciation of the Incarnation, when those other truths are remembered of which we have made mention, her being the conscious and deliberate instrument of that Divine mystery, and of the part which she had in meriting its accomplishment.

The third privilege of this class in our Blessed Lady is that she is the Queen and Mother of mercy. Although so many of the great attributes of God are manifested in the Incarnation, still it is true to say that His mercy is therein manifested more than all others, and that it is, in itself, the greatest of all the manifestations of His mercy. St. Antonine tells us that there is glory in heaven alone, that there is grace on earth alone, but that in heaven, and even in hell, as well as on earth, there is always mercy. For the blessed in heaven are rewarded beyond their strict deserts, and the enemies of God in the place of torment are punished less than they deserve. The Incarnation was beyond everything else a work of mercy, and its effects reach throughout all the Kingdom of God. Thus our Lord is the embodiment of the Divine mercy, and it is but right that Mary should have a great position in this kingdom of mercy, as she has so large a part in the administration, so to say, of all that her Son has wrought. She is herself the greatest instance of His mercy, because she has received therefrom more than all others, she has a larger share in the benefits of His Redemption than others, and from this it is only congruous to reason that she must have an immense share and power in turning His mercy on others by means of her intercession. For we can trace the working of this principle in the special powers and offices allotted to the saints in the Kingdom of Heaven, which seem constantly to have reference to the graces and works for which they are distinguished in their earthly course.

It may here be repeated that we must constantly remind ourselves, in considering these privileges of our Blessed Lady, that she was not an unconscious or involuntary instrument in the Incarnation, nor was she an unwilling victim of all the agony she had to undergo when she stood by the foot of the Cross. She freely was made the Mother of the Redeemer, and she freely gave Him up for us all on the Cross. She had thus much to do with the carrying out of the Divine mercy on the human race, and it is not a farfetched thought that she stands, and always stood, before God, as the representative of His counsel of mercy, the counsel which set aside for the moment the strict rights of His justice, and by virtue of which the claims of His mercy are always to be urged on Him, notwithstanding all the provocation which He receives from the sins of mankind. Thus she is the Queen of mercy, with a nobler right to the title than her famous prototype Esther, who obtained by pure favour, and the influence of the affection which she had inspired in the King, the pardon and deliverance of the whole nation to which she belonged. Mardochai told Esther that she might have been raised to the kingdom for that very purpose in the Providence of God, that she might use her influence in the great need and danger of her nation.[6] In something of the same way Mary may have been raised so high and granted so much power, with the especial design that she should always plead for mercy, even when the justice of God might well have its course, if it were not for her office of asking again and again for pardon for sinners.

There remain, according to St. Antonine, two more of these privileges of Mary to be considered in our present short view of this great subject. The first of these two is that to her was communicated the Passion of our Lord. He founds this statement on the common interpretation of the prophecy of holy Simeon, on the occasion of her Purification, and he quotes St. John Damascene, who says that the pangs of childbirth, which she did not undergo at the Nativity, were reserved for her in the Crucifixion of her Son. St. Antonine explains his meaning in this way. The privilege of the communication of the Passion implies two things, her faith in the Crucified as God and Man, and the suffering which was occasioned by her sympathy for His sufferings. Our Lady, as he shows, was the only one who had both these in full measure, that is, whose faith was entirely unshaken and unclouded, and whose compassion was intense to the fullest measure of intensity. Her Son, he says, desirous of giving her the reward involved in such a privilege, chose to communicate to her the merit of His Passion, that He might

[6] Esther iv. 14.

make her a sharer in the benefit of redemption, inasmuch as that as she had helped in the work of redemption by her Compassion, she might also become the Mother of all in the New Creation resulting therefrom, and, as the whole world is under an immense debt to God for His Passion, so also it might be the debtor of our Lady for her Compassion.

St. Antonine adds that it is said of our Lord that He had in His Passion the height of sorrow and the height of joy, sorrow in the sensitive part of His Humanity, and joy in the intelligent part of the same Humanity. So it is also true to say of our Lady, that she then had the extreme of compassion from His sorrow, and the extreme of sympathy in His joy. Her soul regarded the death of her Son as the extreme of pain to its nature, and in this way she felt the extreme of sorrow, and at the same time she knew that that death was the remedy by which mankind was redeemed, and so she felt the highest joy. Again, her love for our Lord is the measure of her sorrow at His sufferings, and as her love was in every way most intense, so also her sorrow for His sufferings was in every way most intense. This was the cause, then, of the immeasurable height of her sorrow, and at the same time, as she loved God and her neighbour in the highest degree, and as from the Passion was to come the immense glory of God and the immense advantage of her neighbour, the Passion was on this account the cause of the most intense joy to her.

The last of these twelve privileges of our Lady

is her exaltation above all creatures. St. Antonine proves this by various theological reasons, and by quotations from works attributed to St. Augustine and St. Jerome. He goes on," Our Blessed Lady, therefore, is not rashly spoken of so devoutly as exalted above all the choirs of the Angels, and it is believed that the Saviour of all things by Himself, came to meet her in her Assumption, all full of joy, and placed her with delight by Himself on His throne." Between God and Creation, there is something intermediate, that is the Creature who is united to God. And between the simple creature and the created nature united to God, there is something intermediate, that is the creature from whom that united created nature is taken and born in the world. Thus there is something intermediate between the Incarnate Son and simple creatures, and this is Mary, whose place, therefore, is above all creatures, and therefore above the Angels. And in the second place, this devout doctor applies to our Lady the rule of our Lord, that whosoever humbleth himself shall be exalted, and the more any one humbles himself, the more he shall be exalted by God in the realms of bliss. St. Paul speaks of the humiliation of our Lord in His human nature as being the cause of His exaltation above all in that nature, and in the same way, as Mary was the humblest of all except her Son, so in heaven is she the highest of all after her Son. And so he concludes his chapter on the fulness of grace in Mary, by saying that she was full of grace in four ways. First, she had all the graces, general and special, of all creatures in the highest degree. Secondly, she had those graces which other creatures had not. Thirdly, she had grace in so great a degree that a simple creature was not capable of more. Lastly she had in herself the uncreated grace Himself, that is God.

If we consider these privileges one by one, and also as a complete series, we shall be able to understand easily, as has been said, how they are all founded on the supreme grace which none but Mary can receive, the grace of the elevation to the Divine Maternity. They are not the simple exaggerations of devotion, endeavouring to heap up at haphazard an immense mound of graces and gifts, without reason and without connection, for the sake of making the honour of the Mother of God more conspicuous and more prodigious. That God should do everything great in the order of grace for her whom He chose to make His own Mother, is an axiomatic truth. Axiomatic truths do not need positive assertion or accumulated evidence. Such supports are out of place with them. The whole of Scripture may witness to the truth in question, but it rests primarily on a true conception concerning God. We are able to separate these privileges into certain classes and, by doing this, the truth now asserted will become more plain. Let us take the four first in the catalogue of St. Antonine, and we shall see that they are simple corollaries from the fact of the Divine Maternity in itself.

It stands to reason that the Mother of God could never be allowed to be stained by sin. The theologians of the school to which St. Antonine belonged had not the same ideas with regard to the moment of Conception which now prevail, and in consequence they spoke of the sanctification of our Lady in her Mother's womb, rather than of her Immaculate Conception. But it is not difficult to see that they meant the same thing with the modern Church. They also included in the sanctification of which they spoke so large a dowry of graces and spiritual aids to the will and the intelligence, that it was easy for them to conclude that our Blessed Lady was incapable of sin, not, as has been already said, by the destruction of her liberty, but by the overwhelming abundance of her grace. Is it to be said to be impossible with God, thus to preserve His creature from the actual possibility of sin, without taking away her freedom? If this is not impossible, it must be said that this grace was the grace of Mary. In the same way as to the third privilege. Neither in reason, nor in deference to our experience in the history of the dealings of God with His servants, can it be said, that it is not possible for Him to grant to any one of His reasonable creatures the power of continual capacity of meriting. Adam and Eve could merit, from the first moment of their creation, and we have evidence in Scripture of the anticipated use of the reasonable and affective faculties for this very purpose in the case of some of the saints. Therefore this privilege would be found in its highest expression in the Immaculate Mother of God herself. Nor can this seem strange after she has been acknowledged as dowered with the graces already mentioned, which were not given her in her Conception or original sanctification to remain idle and unfruitful. And in the same way the fourth privilege, that she is the highest expression and loftiest instance of all purity in the true sense of the word, is a compendious way of summing up the workings and fructifications of grace in her soul by virtue of the exercise of the privileges already enumerated. It claims for her simply the highest grace that can be conferred, for instance, by the reception of the Christian sacraments, worked and wrought out by the constant and most perfect exercise of all virtues, increased by the full collation of the gifts of the Holy Ghost and after that, by His fruits and the beatitudes. The absolute freedom from sin of every kind, orignal, actual, venial, and even every possible imperfection, is the beginning of this chain of graces, which is completed by the consummate purity of this final grace made as high and as fruitful as possible.

If these first privileges in the list given by St. Antonine are simply corollaries from the fundamental truth that our Blesed Lady is the Mother of God, the three which follow next in the same list hang together as being connected with that great privilege of the manner of her Maternity, according to which she was to be at once the most fruitful of Mothers and the most pure and unsullied of Virgins. It seems to the Christian intelligence impossible to conceive that Mary could have been a Mother otherwise than by remaining perfectly a Virgin, that any one but God and herself should have any part in the generation of the Incarnate God. It is hardly possible to think that those who speak otherwise can have any real belief in the Divinity of our Lord. The Virginal Conception of our Lord does not seem a very stupendous miracle, when we consider Who it was that was to be conceived in her most chaste womb. But if this fundamental privilege be once understood, the other privileges of which we are now speaking follow almost as a matter of course, namely, that she was most truly and perfectly Mother, and the Mother of the Divine Person Who took flesh in her, and, again, that she is preeminent among virgins, the Virgin of Virgins, as the Church calls her, having thus the perfection and unattainable grace of having as a Mother God Himself for her Son, and as a Virgin, the singular dignity of uniting this inconceivable fruitfulness with her Virginity, of being the Mother of God, and of being also the Mother of thousands on thousands of virgins among the children of Eve, wto have followed her in her holy counsel and resolution of chastity. Thus by adding the simple truth of her Virginal Maternity to the other of the dignity of her Maternity itself, we find explained the greater part of these privileges set forth by the saintly doctor of Florence.

There remain five more of these privileges, all of which are most naturally connected with the object in the Divine counsels for which the Incarnation took place. The object of the Incarnation was the Redemption of the world. It was to provide the race of mankind with graces and aids which might enable them to win the eternal rewards, to fill the places which had been left empty by the fall of the evil spirits, and for this purpose the Incarnation resulted in a great store and armament of means of grace most powerful and most multifarious. If Mary the Mother of God was raised so high in the favour of God in order that she might be fit, so to say, to be the conscious and willing instrument of this great work of the Incarnation, it stands to reason that her influence and power with God, which of necessity correspond to her graciousness in His sight, must be exercised in favour of those for whom He became her Son, and that she must have the office of being the patroness and advocate of all those for whom He was to die, and this not occasionally or accidentally, but officially and by virtue of a Divine appointment. As our Lord made Himself our Brother by taking flesh in her most pure womb, our relation to her as His brethren must be that of children, and thus the holiest and tenderest of ties that can exist between creatures, that of Motherhood and Sonship, binds us to her and her to us by a bond that nothing can sever. When she ceases to be the Mother of Jesus Christ she will cease to be our Mother through Him.

From the same consideration of the object of the Incarnation which was carried out in her womb, we arrive at the reasonableness of the other two privileges mentioned by St. Antonine, that she is the Gate of heaven and the Queen of mercy. Heaven is opened to us by our Lord, and our Lord is what He is to us through her, and thus she is the Gate of heaven by the decree of God which gave Him to us through His Mother. Unless we are to make a stop in the Divine mercies and draw a line where we see no line drawn by God, it is natural to think that she has an office connected with the distribution of all the graces which flow to us from her Son. This is, after all, a less wonderful privilege than that we should have Him in all His infinite condescension and beneficence through her. For the fountain of all graces is itself something more than the application of those graces to individual souls one by one. We have said that the Incarnation itself is supremely and above everything the exhibition of the fulness of the infinite Mercy of God. No doubt it displays His Power, His Wisdom, and a number of His other attributes, in a marvellous manner, but still it is pre-eminently the realm of the Mercy of God. The Redemption that was wrought on the Cross was exacted, so to say, by the Justice of God, but the Incarnation, which is the field of the action of Mary, is pure Mercy. And thus we may understand the contemplations of those saints who speak of our Blessed Lady as having the special office of pleading, with all the intensity of her Maternal intercession, the interests of mercy and of mercy alone, as representing, if we may so speak, the Mercy of God and nothing else before His throne in heaven, not urging His Justice or rousing His indignation against sinners, as the Guardian Angels of the little ones may perhaps do when their charges are led astray or scandalised. It is as if that original act of mercifulness, which made God conceive the design of the salvation of the world by the Son of Mary, were now enshrined in her, the purest and the most holy and the most powerful of creatures, using her influence in that royal way which becomes a Queen, who has a right to the Heart of the King, and has nothing to do with His vengeance, but only with His compassionateness and clemency. In this sense we rightly speak of her as the Queen of Mercy.

The next privilege which we have had to explain above touches on a different point in the execution of the great counsel of the Redemption of the world, namely, the execution of that counsel by the particular means of the Passion of the Son of God. It is conceivable, as has already been said, that the Incarnation might have been granted without the necessity of redemption thereby, and the redemption of the world might have been granted on some other condition than that of the Passion. If the work of our Lord had taken some different method in the counsels of God, we cannot doubt that His Blessed Mother would have had her share, as near as possible to that of her Son, in that dispensation, whatever it might have been. For, after all the privileges of which we have spoken, it becomes impossible, if it could ever have been possible, to separate the action of Mary from that of Jesus, where there is no separation between them by the necessities of the case. Thus it is impossible to suppose that Mary had not the fullest participation of the Passion of our Lord which it was possible for her to have,—in its intelligence, in its pains, in its fruits, in its merits, in the application of its graces to others and in the enjoyment of them in herself. It takes but a moment to write these few words, but it will take all the years of eternity for the illuminated minds and inflamed hearts of the blessed in heaven to comprehend their full meaning. And again, after this consideration of the reasonableness, or rather the necessity, of this privilege of the communication of the Passion to Mary, it is very little to add the last privilege on the list, that she is exalted above all creatures in heaven, both on account of her personal nearness to our Lord, and on account of her perfect following of Him in the one pre-eminent virtue on which all exaltation depends, the virtue of humility.

The next words of the Angel, "the Lord is with thee," may be understood either as an assertion of the presence of God with our blessed Lady, or as the expression of a desire or prayer that He may be with her. Thus the priest in the holy Mass frequently prays that the Lord may be with the people, when he invites them to pray, and in this case the words are the expression of his desire that so it may be. But, in the greater number of cases in which these words occur in Sacred Scripture, it appears that they are the assertion of a truth, namely that God is with the person to whom they are addressed, in some special manner and for some special purpose. Thus it is said, more than once, of some saint or servant of God, that God was with him, that is, that God assisted him in some work or office with which he was charged. This seems to be the meaning in this place. The Angel has already asserted the most glorious things of this Blessed Maiden, and if she were already full of grace, it is almost a superfluous prayer to ask that God may be with her. But it was not superfluous to assert that God was with her at that particular time, and for the particular object which was before the mind of the speaker. The Angel has to announce the greatest work of God's power and wisdom as about to be accomplished in Mary, and he begins, after his first salutation, by declaring that God is with her, in this new and wonderful way. Some writers have thought that the words convey the truth that God is with her, by having taken flesh already in her most chaste womb. But this would be to anticipate her consent before it was given, and would be inconsistent with her own words, when she presently enquires about the manner in which the great mystery is to be accomplished. It remains therefore for us to understand the words in the way already indicated, namely, as an assurance to our Blessed Lady that God was with her in a peculiar and special manner, for the perfect accomplishment of the great work of the Incarnation, to which she was invited by the mission of the Angel who speaks.

It is remarkable that the Angel uses the word 'Lord' rather than the name of God, following in this the common practice of Sacred Scripture. The use of the word is thought by some of the Christian writers to have a special purpose, of a twofold kind. In the first place, it was the object of the Angel to make the great mystery which he was announcing easily acceptable to the marvellous faith of the Blessed Virgin, and for this it was well that, by the very name of the 'Lord,' he should remind her of the immense majesty and power of God, and of all the wonders which He had already wrought for

His people, whose Lord in particular He was. In the second place, the name Lord expresses the sovereign dominion of God over His creatures, and it was therefore an appeal to the obedience of the Blessed Virgin, as well as to her faith. Thus the blessing which was offered to her came from Him Whose servant she was and delighted to call herself, and this would add a new element of delight and joy to her in surrendering her own will to His, in a matter so highly conducing to His glory, as well as to her own exaltation. It was a great thing to be so exalted, but, as we see from our Lady's own Canticle of joy, she rejoiced especially in the truth that all this was done for her by God her Lord and Master. He was with her, then, it is implied by the Angel, for no less a work than the formation in her womb by His own Almighty power of the Body of our Lord, of the creation of the Soul by which that Body was animated, and of the accomplishment of the pre-eminent wonder of the personal union of the human nature thus formed with the Divine Son. He was with her for the purpose of making her in this stupendous way the Mother of God, and bringing about all the consequences of the Incarnation, the Redemption of the world, the glorification of her Son Jesus Christ, and the elevation of the whole human race and the whole creation by means of Him. All this is contained in these words of the Angel as their legitimate meaning.

This meaning was not plainly expressed to the Blessed Virgin at first, but it is clear that her trouble at the words of St. Gabriel, of which we shall presently speak, was occasioned in great measure by her deep knowledge of the Scriptures and of the ways of God, and probably also by her very enlightened intelligence of what might be expected when the promised Incarnation took place. But the words contained all these Divine blessings and actions under their meaning, as the words of God, at the moment when they were used and when they sounded in the ears of Mary. She was full of grace, and the fulness of her grace was what it was, in the counsels of God, in order that she might receive fitly, if so it could be, the dignity of the Divine Maternity. And now, having made her fit to receive that ineffable dignity, God is with her for the accomplishment of His purpose in the Incarnation, and whatever belongs to that accomplishment, on His part, is an element of the special assistance to and presence with her which the great words, "the Lord is with thee," are intended to convey.

But the Angel has other words still to add, words also eminently Scriptural, and intended probably to revive in the mind of the Blessed Virgin the long train of prophetic anticipations of which, as she well knew, the future Mother of God had been the subject. "Blessed art thou among women." The words are most probably taken from the song of triumph of Debbora and Barac,[7] after the defeat and destruction of Sisera and his host. They are there applied to Jael, whose hand had been the instrument of the death of the dreaded champion of the enemies of the holy people. But

[7] Judges v. 24.

they were probably applied to her, by the composers of the song of victory, not without a reference to her typical representation of the Woman who had been promised from the beginning as the great enemy of the spiritual foes of mankind, the one by whose means the head of the serpent was to be crushed. Or, if this had not been in the mind of the first composers of the song, it may at least be considered certain that it took its place as the record of an action of deliverance of the people, in which a woman was the chief agent, and which consequently became prophetical and typical of the great future deliverance. But the words signifying blessing must have been naturally connected in the minds of the devout Jews with the great blessing which had been promised to Abraham and the other Patriarchs after him, and then to David and his race, and this again, as has been seen, was but a repetition and confirmation of the original promise on which all the hope and faith of the whole human race rested, the promise in which the figure of the Mother was so closely associated with that of her Son. Thus it is not too much to say that, to a mind so stored with Divine intelligence and with knowledge of the prophetic writings as that of our Blessed Lady, the words of the salutation of Gabriel must have awakened at once the thought that the Divine message which they conveyed was of the very highest import indeed. What more could be said to the chosen Mother of God herself, than that she was full of grace, that the Lord was with her for the purpose of the accomplishment of some most Divine work, and that she was blessed among women?

CHAPTER II.

THE TROUBLE OF MARY.

St. Luke i. 29. *Vita Vitæ Nostræ*, § 4.

WHAT has already been said is enough to make it appear to us very probable that our Blessed Lady may have divined the meaning, or at least suspected the meaning, of the words of the Angel, and have already, from the first, seen in them the full revelation, at least in germ, of the will of God as to her own elevation. The words of St. Gabriel which follow presently are, as we shall see, the unfolding more clearly of that which is wrapped up, as it were, in the original salutation of which we have now spoken. When he tells our Blessed Lady that she has found grace with God, he unfolds more fully the meaning of what he has already said in the words, the Lord is with thee. When he goes on to speak of her conceiving in her womb, and bearing a Son Whose Name she is to call Jesus, he unfolds again what he has already hinted in the salutation by which he hailed her as the Blessed among women. Thus it is very probable that our Lady understood the salutation as containing in itself what might involve the great and unique privilege of the Divine Maternity, notwithstanding her own resolution and vow to remain for ever a pure Virgin. It is not necessary to suppose that she did not understand that the Mother of God was to be such a Virgin. But as yet nothing had been said by the Angel on this point, even in the most obscure way, unless it were contained in the simple title of Blessed among women, inasmuch as the highest of all blessings of which women are capable is that of the most fruitful Maternity united to most pure and unsullied Virginity. This then may have been the effect of the salutation of the Angel on the enlightened mind of the Blessed Virgin. It was a message of the highest dignity, speaking of the loftiest graces and the most wonderful elevation.

This may account for the next incident in the narrative, of which we are now to speak. This is the trouble of the Blessed Virgin at the words of the Angel. "Who having heard, was troubled at his saying, and thought within herself what manner of salutation this should be." We have already mentioned the Greek reading, according to which the words should be "having seen" rather than "having heard." But the rest of the context shows us that the trouble of Mary was occasioned by the words of the message, and not by the appearance of the messenger. It is highly probable that our Blessed Lady was well accustomed to visits from the Angels, and in any case it was one of her great privileges to have a marvellous knowledge and intelligence of the Angelic creation, and a great discernment of spirits. Thus it is not likely that she would be simply frightened at the appearance of St. Gabriel, in the way in which St. Zachary had been frightened. Some writers have thought that she might have been alarmed at his appearance in the form of a man, on account of her singular modesty and virginal bashfulness, especially as the visit seems to have been made when the shades of night were falling or had fallen, and when she was altogether alone. In this way, as she is the supreme example of all maidenly perfection, God may have wished to place on record this act of modesty in her trouble at the visit of the Angel. But it must be remembered that there can never be anything in the visions of Angels that can be in the least degree suggestive of danger to the extremest perfection of purity, and that, on the contrary, such appearances must be as productive of the purest and holiest thoughts as if those to whom they are vouchsafed were already in the society of heaven itself, which will be full of the greatest, most enchanting, and at the same time most pure, beauties. It is therefore better to look elsewhere for the cause of the trouble of the Blessed Virgin of which the Sacred narrative now tells us.

The great commentator Toletus shall explain to us the manner in which it seems right to understand this trouble. He begins by laying down for us the various kinds of trouble of which we find mention in the Gospels, for the sake of illustrating this passage. He takes in the first place the trouble of St. Zachary at the appearance of the Angel to him in the Temple. In the second place he puts this trouble of our Blessed Lady. In the third place he speaks of the trouble of our Lord Himself, of which mention is made in three separate places of the Gospel of St. John, once in the account of the raising of Lazarus, where it is said that "He troubled Himself," again in the next chapter, where we have the account of the Gentiles who wish to see Him, when our Lord said " now is My soul troubled," and again in the history of the Last Supper, where He is said to have been troubled in spirit before He spoke about the treason of Judas.[1] In all these cases, whether in our Lord, in our Lady, or in St. Zachary, the trouble was not simply in the mind, but must have to some degree affected the body also, as is usual when mental trouble takes place.

The difference discernible between the effects of the trouble in these various cases is great. In the case of St. Zachary, we see that the trouble went so far as to disturb his mind, and to some extent interfere with the perfect rule of reason, inasmuch as he was led to give in to a kind of doubt, even as to the truth of the Angelic message which was delivered to him. The trouble which affected our Blessed Lady could not go so far as this. For all the movements and affections in our Blessed Lady were fully under the control of reason, they could not either lead her mind away or even rebel against its dominion. Even in the saints of God these affections can rise up against the rule of reason, as St. Paul speaks of the law in his members contrary to the law of his mind. In the case of the saints and servants of God the grace of God supplies the power of quelling this rebellion. But in the Blessed Virgin it was different, for it was one of her privileges that she had no such unreasonable affections or movements.

---

[1] St. Luke i. 12. St. John xi. 33; xii. 27; xiii. 21.

Her mind and reason were not only not liable to be overpowered by them, but they could not even be assailed by them. The privilege of our Lord went beyond this, for in Him every affection was voluntary and fully deliberate. This is indeed witnessed to by the language of St. John, who speaks of Him as troubling Himself, and thus whenever He felt trouble, or distress, or fear, or sadness or sorrow, it was because He chose at that time to admit such affections to His soul, and exactly as far as He chose to endure and have experience of them.

Thus there are three degrees in our experience of such movements as that here spoken of in our Blessed Lady. They arise without our will and against our will, they rise up against our reason and assail its dominion and empire in the soul, and sometimes they are so powerful as to overcome our reason, although they cannot do this altogether against our will. Of these three degrees none were to be found in our Lord. These passions or affections could not arise in Him without or against His will. They could not assail and rebel against reason, nor could they in any way overcome it. In our Lady they could neither assail the dominion of reason nor could they triumph over it. Whether they could arise in her mind without her own will and consent, may not be quite certain. At least, Toletus says, we have not on this point any certain doctrine of the Fathers. But he says that it is highly probable and reasonable that she should have had this privilege also, that the Mother might be like the Son in this also, though she would not have had it in the same perfection and excellence, nor for the same cause.

Our Lord would have it because He was the Divine Person of the Word. But our Lady would have had it by a special privilege and gift, just as we say that neither of them had any sin, though not from the same cause. And Toletus adds that he is inclined to this opinion, because the power which our passions and affections have, of out-running reason and taking possession of us involuntarily, comes from the original sin which we all inherit, and from which our Blessed Lady was altogether free.

This then being the case in general with the movements and affections which passed over the soul of the Blessed Virgin, we must answer any questions which may arise concerning the trouble of which we are now told by the Evangelist in accordance with this general doctrine. Thus we may begin by saying that it is most highly probable, if not certain, that the trouble of which we now hear was a voluntary movement of her mind, acting under the command of reason, and occasioned by something that was contained, or which she felt might be contained, in the message of St. Gabriel. If we ask what this was, we can find at least two things in the message. or in what it implied, which may have been the cause of this voluntary trouble. The first would be that the message was beyond all doubt one that presaged her elevation to some very high dignity in the kingdom of God. It may not be certain to all minds that she at once perceived that this dignity was no other than that of the Divine Maternity. It is very likely that this explanation will not approve itself to all. But it is certain that the words of St. Gabriel foreshadowed some very high dignity for her to whom they were addressed, and this would be enough to alarm seriously the intense and most profound humility of the Blessed Virgin. It must have been at once certain to her that the message of the Angel involved a destruction of her own chosen station in entire obscurity, with the hope and prayer that she might live in the days of the Messias, and perhaps have the happiness of being the handmaid of His Mother.

This was one thing in the words of the Angel, and in the simple fact of his appearance, which may have been a legitimate source of fear on the part of this blessed soul. Another point as to which she might have been alarmed may have related to her purpose of Virginity. She was already a married wife, though by the great grace of God her spouse had the same holy resolution with herself, and there was no fear on her part that he could ever place any hindrance in the way of the perfect execution of her holy and cherished purpose. But she could not but know that the embassies of Angels in the Sacred history were frequently connected with the miraculous or marvellous births of children, designed for some high office in the kingdom of God, and perhaps the Divine counsels might require on her part, as on the part of St. Joseph, the sacrifice of this purpose of immaculate purity.

These are the two points in the Angelic message which may have struck our Blessed Lady with some kind of alarm and made her proceed to examine in her own thoughts, as the Evangelist tells us, what sort of salutation this might be. It might almost be rendered, where this salutation could be from, to what class of salutations did it belong. These words of the Sacred text seem to point to the magnificence of the language as a kind of shock to her intense humility, in the first instance, as furnishing her with the ground of her voluntary trouble and of her careful pondering of the words of the Angel before making any answer on her own part. Thus the greatness of the blessing which seemed to be held out to her made her pause and consider it, in the interests of her own incomparable humility. On the other hand, her vow or purpose of Virginity rose up as another reason for deliberation in the interests of her purity. No definite proposal had been made to her, no direct injunction had been given to her, and she was therefore left in her own intense prudence, to ponder over the words, consider their full meaning, and then make her own blessed choice in accordance with the will of God as it might be declared to her. There is something here like that of which St. Paul speaks in our Blessed Lord Himself, that He did not snatch at and grasp as a prey the dignity of His Divine Nature, but humbled Himself and made Himself low, being made obedient unto death even the death of the Cross.[2] Thus this first response on the part of our Blessed Lady to the message as sent her by God, the response of silence and deliberation, was the most perfect choice which she could have made under the circumstances of her great probation.

[2] Philipp. ii. 8.

CHAPTER III.

THE SON OF DAVID.

St. Luke i. 30—33. *Vita Vitæ Nostræ*, § 4.

"AND the Angel said to her, fear not, Mary, for thou hast found grace with God." The Angel, as a messenger of God, may have been Divinely illuminated to understand the causes of the timidity of the Blessed Virgin, and he proceeds at once to remove them. The causes, as we have seen, may have been two, her great humility and the plan of life in perfect virginity which she had resolved on for herself as her special service to God. Both of these causes are met by the assurance that she is not to fear, for she has found grace with God. For those who have found grace with God need not fear any elevation to which He may raise them in His Divine counsels, seeing that, if He is with them, no work can be too great for them, no position too sublime. For those whom He exalts will always have His support in their exaltation as in their abasement. And if she has found grace with God, this is an assurance, like that given to St. Zachary that his prayer was heard, that she might rest in peace as to the accomplishment of the holy purpose for the glory of God with which He had Himself inspired her. As Abraham was assured by his immense faith that

God could fulfil his promises through Isaac, at the very time that He gave him the command to sacrifice that same beloved son on Mount Moriah, so Mary might be assured by her far loftier faith, that if she was to be a Mother, it would still be without the slightest detriment to her Virginity. She has found grace with God, and therefore her resolution will remain intact and inviolate, even though she is to be a Mother. For God Who could raise up Isaac from the dead, if so He had willed, is able also to give the grace of fecundity to a Virgin, and to preserve the unsullied purity of a Mother. Therefore there is no need for fear.

Our Blessed Lady, without any special or direct revelation, might have thought these great things of God. For she could not doubt in any way of His supreme and infinite power. But the words of the Angel convey to her what she could not have received on faith, without some assurance on the part of God, stating that it would be so in the present case. She had found grace with God, the special grace required for the accomplishment in her of the mystery of the Divine Maternity, with the perfect preservation of her immaculate purity. God had accepted her beautiful offer of herself in the holy estate of continence, and whatever He might afterwards ask her to do or to become would not be a violation of that which He had so graciously sanctioned, and with which He had been so well pleased. Nay, it may be said, as has been already hinted, that her humility and her love of purity, the graces in her which now caused her fear and trouble, were the very graces above all others which had secured to her the ineffable privilege of becoming the Mother of God. She had found by them the grace which was now offered to her, and which was their fruit, and so could not be contrary to them.

Having thus calmed the trouble of which the Evangelist has spoken, the Angel goes on to unfold to our Blessed Lady the particulars of the divine message committed to him. He does this in the language of prophecy, though, as in the case of the prophecy of Malachias which he had used in his address to Zachary, he does not exactly follow the words of the prophet whom he quotes. Isaias had said, "Behold, that Virgin that is with child, and bearing a Son! and they shall call His name Emmanuel," "which being interpreted," St. Matthew adds, "is God with us." The words of the prophet had spoken of the Virginal Conception and Childbearing, and he had said that the name of the child should be Emmanuel, that is, that He should be spoken of as God with man, the Incarnate God. St. Gabriel in these words to our Blessed Lady begins with the very words of Isaias, applying them to her. He does not address her as the Virgin, for the thought of her Virginity was the thought which had created her trouble. But the assurance of the preservation of her Virginity is conveyed in the allusion to the prophecy itself as a whole, the very point of which was the Virginal Conception and parturition. His words have the same meaning which would have been conveyed if he had said, Behold, thou art to be that Virgin of whom the prophet speaks when he says that a Virgin shall have in her womb and bear a Son, Who shall be the Incarnate God.

But at the same time he varies the name given by the prophet, for the personal name of our Lord was to be Jesus, and not Emmanuel. He was to be Emmanuel, God with us, but He was to be known as Jesus, and she His Mother was to give Him this Name, not men in general. And in the holy Name which she was to give to her Divine Son was to be contained the whole of His office and work for the honour of His Father. He was to save His people from their sins, as it was afterwards said when this same charge, belonging to the true parental character, was also given to St. Joseph. He shall save His people from their sins, according to the meaning of the Name Jesus, because He shall be that which is signified by the name mentioned by the prophet, because He shall be Emmanuel, God with us. Thus the words of the Angel at once send the thoughts of the Blessed Virgin back to the great prophecy by which the former promises made from the beginning of time were confirmed to the house of David, in the dark and disastrous days of the wicked and feeble king Achaz, and by this very reference she was also reminded of the whole chain of the predictions from the beginning, relating to the promised Mother of God, the Woman between whom and the serpent God was to place enmities.

The Angel goes on to describe the greatness and other characteristics of the Child Who was to be born of Mary, in language continually taken from the prophecies. This is the chief reason, we may suppose, why the language in this great message is what it is. It is natural that the fulfilment of the well known predictions should be announced in the words of the predictions themselves. The language of Scripture constantly uses the words "shall be called" in the sense of 'shall be.' The name "Son of the most High" is used several times, as in the Psalms and elsewhere, for the saints of God, but the most direct reference in this passage seems to be to the great prophecy which is found in the 88th Psalm with reference to David, "I have found David My servant, with My holy oil I have anointed him.... He shall cry out to Me, Thou art My Father, my God and the support of my salvation. And I will make Him My first born, high above the kings of the earth. I will keep My mercy for him for ever, and My covenant faithful with him, and I will make His seed to endure for evermore, and his throne as the days of heaven."

We also find it an expression used in the prophets, "the king that sitteth on the throne of David"[1]— "a throne shall be prepared in mercy and one shall sit upon it in truth in the tabernacle of David,"[2] and the covenant was spoken of as the "faithful mercies of David" that is, promised to David. The great Psalm says "For Thy servant David's sake, turn not away the face of Thy anointed. The Lord hath sworn truth unto David, and He will not make it void, of the fruit of thy womb I will set upon thy throne."[3] In the same way the expressions of the kingdom lasting for ever, of reigning over the house of Jacob, of there being no end of the kingdom, are all scriptural and prophetical. Perhaps the most direct reference in the latter words of the Angel is to the famous prophecy

[1] Jer. xxii. 2.   [2] Isaias xvi. 5.   [3] Ps. cxxxi. 10, 11.

of the Child to be born, and the Son to be given, in
the ninth chapter of Isaias, where the prophet winds
up by saying, " His empire shall be multiplied, and
there shall be no end of peace, and He shall sit
upon the throne of David and upon his kingdom, to
establish it and strengthen it with justice and with
judgment, from henceforth and for ever."[4] By selec-
tions taken from this treasure of prophetical language, the blessed Gabriel was guided to frame his
announcement of the dignity and greatness of the
Child Whose Conception he was now setting before
His destined Mother. "He shall be great, and
shall be called the Son of the Most High, and the
Lord God shall give unto Him the throne of David
His Father, and He shall reign in the House of
Jacob for ever, and of His kingdom there shall be
no end."

The first words of the announcement with which
we are concerned leave no doubt at all as to the
office to which our Blessed Lady was now called.
The dignity of the Divine Maternity may have
been veiled in the earlier words, in which she was
saluted as full of grace. It may have been contained in those which followed, in which she was
told that the Lord was with her. It may have been
all but expressd in the others, in which she was
hailed as "blessed among women." For the fulness
of grace was the appointed and legitimate preparation for the work of being the fit Mother of God.
The Lord being with her, implied that He had
chosen her for some very lofty and unique position,
and, if there was to be a Mother of God, the pre-

[4] Isaias ix. 7.

paration which had been accorded to her was such as might make her able to bear the weight of so great a dignity. And who could be in so unique and unrivalled a degree the Blessed among women, but the Woman chosen from all eternity to carry out the great counsel of the Incarnation as its conscious and willing instrument? But what was before veiled and hinted and implied, what perhaps our Blessed Lady herself divined as the probable meaning of a salutation so august, was, now that the fear of that Blessed Mother had been removed by the words of the Angel,—words fraught, no doubt, with divine efficacy, to produce what they signified,—openly declared without any ambiguity or reserve, excepting only as to the manner in which the mystery was to be accomplished, that is, by the operation of the Holy Ghost. The revelation of this was to be kept for the second part of the Angelic salutation, which was to come as an answer to the most prudent and humble question of our Blessed Lady.

"Behold, thou shalt conceive in thy womb, and shalt bring forth a Son, and thou shalt call His Name Jesus." The assurance to our Blessed Lady that she had found grace with God, coming after the great words with which the Angel had begun his salutation, would be enough to make her secure that her purpose of virginity was not to be surrendered in consequence of the new dignity to which she was to be raised. The words before us seem to contain a direct allusion to the great prophecy of Isaias, to which reference has already been made, and thus to suggest to our Blessed Lady that she was to be the Virgin spoken of in that prophecy, which was, in truth, a confirmation and assertion, for the particular purpose of the encouragement and consolation of the house of David at that time, of the original promise made in Paradise. The word "behold," seems to convey this allusion; and as the Virgin spoken of by Isaias was to conceive and bear a Son, so our Blessed Lady is told that she is to conceive in her womb and bring forth a Son. The language is precise, and may be considered as adopted for the purpose of making it clear that the conception spoken of was not to be a spiritual or figurative conception, but a natural conception, in the ordinary way, in the womb and of the substance of His Blessed Mother, only without any share of man therein.

Thus, as the Catholic commentators remark, the heresies which denied the reality of our Lord's flesh, or that He was of the same substance with us, or that Mary is not truly the Mother of the Divine Person, and the like, are all destroyed or excluded by those simple and plain words of the Angel. There is no loophole left for any denial of the Catholic truth in all these matters. Our Lord is most truly the Son of Mary, and Mary is most truly the Mother of God. He did not even choose to become man as Eve was made out of a part of the substance of Adam, for in that case Mary would not have been His Mother. He chose to be the Son of a woman, as St. Paul says, of the seed and lineage of David, and thus our Brother by the closest of ties. He chose to cleanse and sanctify by His own touch and presence all that had been corrupted by the fall of Adam, conception, childbirth, infancy, the miseries and weaknesses of our gradual growth, our years of helplessness. He chose to be as truly the Son of man by a true generation, as He is the Son of God by a true generation, and to win for us that adoption as the children of God which is connected in Sacred Scripture with His own condescension in truly and perfectly becoming a child of Adam. The greatness of His love for us required that He should humble Himself as far as was possible to all the lowliness of our natural condition. This would not have been His, if He had not chosen to be an infant for nine months in His Mother's womb, and to undergo all the humiliations and restraints and dependencies of our childhood and youth.

Moreover, it was an essential feature in a part of the Divine Counsel that our Blessed Lady should be His Mother in all the perfection of Maternity, and this includes all that utmost intimacy of union between Him and her, and of dependence of Him on her, which is involved in her discharge towards Him of the full functions of His only parent in His infancy and childhood and ever after. She was to conceive Him, and bear Him, and nurse Him, and suckle Him, and watch over Him, and by this relationship be raised to the incommunicable honour and power which she possesses by right in His Kingdom. Her honour in heaven is ours also, because she is of our race and family. She has taken away the disgrace which clung to her sex, because through that sex sin began, as she has raised the fallen race to which she belongs. And her power also is for us, for the intercession of a Mother must avail more with a Son than the prayers of all beside, and for this very reason she has been so highly exalted by God, that we might have all the power of her prayer on our side, winged by her intense love for our salvation, as that of those for whom the precious Blood of her Son was shed. All this is included in the words of the Angel, that she shall conceive in her womb and shall bring forth a Son.

And, as the crown to all that he has hitherto said, St. Gabriel adds that she shall call His Name Jesus. In this, as has been noticed, he departed from the direct letter of the prophecy which he was, more or less closely, following, in order to give the precise and personal name of the Child of Mary. She could not have been ignorant of the depths of meaning contained in the Holy Name now mentioned to her, especially when it came as the crown and consummation of the great prediction now delivered. This Divine Son, Who was to be conceived in her womb and born in so marvellous a manner, Whose Conception and Birth were to be the fulfilment of the great promises of God made from the beginning, was to be called Jesus. The simple injunction that such a name should be given to Him was enough to show that God intended that He should be all that was signified thereby. Thus our Blessed Lady is at once assured that her Child is to be the long foretold and anxiously expected Saviour of the whole world.

"He shall be great, and shall be called the Son of the Most High." The passage which thus begins is the description by the Angel, in language chiefly taken from the prophetic writings, of the Sacred

Humanity of our Lord. He is the promised Seed of the Woman, God made Man, great from all ages with the greatness and perfection of the Divine Nature, and great, from the moment of His Conception, when His Human Existence in body and soul began, with the greatness belonging to Him by virtue of the Hypostatic Union. It is this latter greatness which the Angel now sets forth, reserving the manner and method of the accomplishment of the Hypostatic Union for a further communication, and indeed keeping it, as it seems, in the back ground, as if out of deference to the extreme humility of her whom he was addressing. Thus we may divide the great truths concerning our Lord's Incarnation into two parts, the first of which is contained in the declaration of the Angel now before us, while the second is conveyed in his answer to the question of our Blessed Lady herself of which we shall presently speak.

The first quality which the Angel attributes to our Lord is greatness, and this, not in any single or particular manner, but generally and perfectly. He was to be great on account of His Person, the Person of the Son of God in Human Nature. From this greatness of His Person, flows the greatness of His Sanctity and of His Power. And moreover as He has come on earth for a certain definite purpose and on a particular errand, His greatness must be such as belongs in a special manner to the perfect accomplishment of that work. His work involved the revelation of His Father and the declaration of the truths of salvation and faith by word of mouth, and thus He is great in word. No man ever spake as He spake, as was said of Him by those who were sent to apprehend Him. He was to teach the greatest and most sublime truths in the most efficacious and marvellous manner. Moreover, He was to confirm His words by works. In the first place, His works were to go before His words. That is, the example of every most perfect virtue which He taught was to be preceded by His most perfect practice of that virtue. In the second place, He was to confirm His words by showing the Divine authority with which He spoke, both by the inherent majesty of His teaching, and by the marvellous miracles by which that teaching was authenticated. "No man," said Nicodemus to Him, "can do the works which Thou doest, unless God be with Him," and the disciples with whom He conversed on the road to Emmaus spoke of Him as a man mighty in work and in word.

We see the same character of greatness when we turn to consider the office which our Lord filled in the Providence of His Father. He was the Redeemer and Saviour of the world, the Good Shepherd Who was to gather into one Fold the children of God that were scattered abroad, and Who was of His own freewill to lay down His life for the sheep, and to take it again. He was the great High Priest of the New Covenant, offering to God the one perfect adorable Sacrifice of infinite efficacy. He was the great Prophet Who was to come into the world. He was the King of Kings and Lord of Lords, and all the nations were to be given to Him as His inheritance, and all were to bow down before Him. He was to set up a religious empire which was to reach from one end of the world to the other, and to last as long as time remains.

Of these elements of greatness the Angel touches mainly on those which are sufficient to mark out our Lord as the great subject of prophecy. In the first place, he says that He shall be called the Son of the Most High. For the foundation of the greatness of our Lord in prophecy lay in the truth that He was to be the Incarnate Son of God, God made man, and this, as it is implied, not by any adoption or grace, as if He had become the Son of God by virtue of the Incarnation, not having been so before. And again, when it is said that He shall be called the Son of the Most High, it is signified that He is truly what He is called, and moreover, that He shall be known and acknowledged all over the world as the Son of God. Thus the words of the Angel seem to convey the same truth which is set forth by St. Paul in the opening of the Epistle to the Romans, where he says of our Lord that He was the Son of God, made to Him of the seed of David according to the flesh, and predestinated (or declared and shown) to be the Son of God in power, that is, by the stupendous power of all kinds which He displayed, including His miracles, " according to the spirit of sanctification," by His own intrinsic and manifest sanctity, and by His power of imparting holiness to others, and finally, " by the resurrection of our Lord Jesus Christ from the dead," which was the crowning proof and demonstration that He was the Son of God.

The next words of the Angel speak especially of the Kingship of our Lord, in which characteristic are summed up all the other excellencies predicted concerning Him, and which was the last most conspicuous and most permanent result of the mission on which He was sent. For He came not only to redeem the world, to open Heaven, and to win for man the thrones therein, but to do this by the application of His merits and the carrying on of His work, age after age, by means of the Church, the kingdom which He was to found as the inheritance of the throne of David. "And the Lord God shall give unto Him the throne of David His Father, and He shall reign in the house of Jacob for ever, and of His kingdom there shall be no end."

It is said here that the Lord God shall give to Him the throne of His Father David, because it is as Man that our Lord receives this kingly power, and whatever He has as Man He receives from the Father as His Lord and God, to Whom it belongs to distribute and allot all that is great, royal, and powerful, in the world. The kings, the ancestors of our Lord, who succeeded one after the other to the throne of David, received it simply by the right of human inheritance, but our Lord received it by virtue of a Divine appointment. The throne of David had passed away from the eyes of men, for its power was gone after the Captivity of Babylon. But it was revived for our Lord by the Providence of His Father, and bestowed on Him in fuller right and power than ever it had been held before. For the rod was to spring up out of the root of Jesse, the trunk which had been, as is were, cut down, was to become again productive, and send forth its shoot, the new kingdom was to be a sign to all people, and all nations were to serve it. Thus our Lord's title to the throne was far higher truer, nobler, than that of any of the kings who had reigned before Him. As the Incarnate Son of God, He was by right King of the whole creation, which was all summed up in Him and made for Him. As Redeemer of the world, again, He was King of heaven and earth, for all power was given to Him, as He said after His Resurrection, in heaven and on earth. Again, as the Son of the Father, the Lord of all, He has the possession of all the world as His inheritance, a title which is often insisted on in Sacred Scripture. Again, the dominion over all things was given to Him as a gift from His Father, as St. John says that He knew that the Father had given all things into His hands. Again, His great humiliation unto death, even the death of the Cross, is mentioned by St. Paul as the cause of this exaltation to the rule and dominion of all things, and that at His Name every knee is to be bent, of those in heaven, and on earth, and under the earth.

Moreover, the Christian writers tell us that as our Lord's titles to His Kingdom were so far higher than those of any other sovereign, so also was His dominion and kingly power more complete and perfect than those of any other. For earthly sovereigns, even the most despotic, have no right to command their subjects as if they were slaves, the property of their masters, whereas our Lord's dominion extends so far that there is no part or element in our body and soul which is not absolutely His. Again, all earthly sovereignty is limited as to those who are its subjects, but our Lord's kingdom embraces all things whatsoever. No earthly king is anything more than a delegate and a subordinate to God, whereas our Lord is God Himself. All earthly reigns are necessarily limited, at least by the limits of human life and existence, but the reign of our Lord is the reign of an immortal King, Whose power can never be shaken or fail. As this royal dignity of our Lord is grounded, in the first instance, on the Hypostatic Union, it follows that He possessed it by right from the moment of that Union. The Wise kings who came from the East to adore Him in His cradle bore solemn witness to this as the burthen of prophecy, and from time to time, during His earthly life, our Lord allowed His royal dignity to be disclosed, as in His entrance into Jerusalem on the day of Palms, and, even when He stood as a condemned prisoner before Pilate, the representative of the highest of earthly monarchies, He bore witness to this truth that He was a King. So His Father, in His Providence, would not allow His title of King to be blotted out from the title on the Cross. But He did not exercise His royal right or authority, ordinarily, while He was on earth, in order that He might suffer, and leave us the example of His humility. But His exercise of dominion and authority, as in the case of the herd of swine, of the ass's colt on which He rode into Jerusalem, and some others, showed that He still preserved the right of a sovereign, although it did not suit the counsel of His wisdom to use them. It was after His Resurrection and Ascension that the continual exercise of His royal Power was to begin.

"And He shall reign in the house of Jacob for

ever, and of His Kingdom there shall be no end." These words, few and short as they are, sufficiently indicate the universal extent and endless duration of the Kingdom of our Lord. The words, "the House of Jacob," signify that it extends to the whole people of God, the true Israel, whereas the rule of the House of David, in the history of the holy nation, had been limited, after the death of the first successor of David, to the two tribes of Juda and Benjamin, which alone remained faithful after the revolt of Jeroboam, while the remaining ten were never again brought under the sceptre of the royal house. Again, the dynasty founded by David had lost the throne altogether, after the lapse of comparatively few generations, by the conquest of the whole land by the kings of Babylon. It is not so to be with the Christian Kingdom of our Lord. It is to be universal in the extent of its dominion, embracing all peoples and nations and languages. It is to last upon earth as long as the world lasts, and, when the history of earth is closed, it is to continue throughout all eternity in heaven.

CHAPTER IV.

"HOW SHALL THIS BE DONE?"

St. Luke i. 34—*Vita Vitæ Nostræ*, § 4.

THE Angel Gabriel had proceeded with the utmost gentleness and prudence in his disclosure to the Blessed Virgin of the great office to which she was called by God. He had spoken chiefly in the words of the prophets, and had confined himself, if we may thus speak, to the glories of the Sacred Humanity of our Lord as set forth in Scripture. To one so enlightened as our Blessed Lady in the intelligence of the Scriptures and of the ways of God, it could not be a matter of doubt that the promised Child of the House of David was to be the Incarnate God Himself. But this had been implied, rather than openly stated in so many words, by the Angel, except that he had said that her Child was to be called, and therefore to be, the Son of the Most High. It yet remained to set forth the most marvellous and magnificent part of the truth concerning this great mystery. For nothing had as yet been said by St. Gabriel, concerning the Conception by the Holy Ghost, and the whole manner in which this Divine Birth was to be brought about. It may also be said with much truth, that this part of the great mystery had not been spoken of prominently by the prophets themselves. There were words in the prophecies of Isaias and Micheas which implied that the words "Son of God," "Son of the most High," and the like, were not used of the promised Messias in any ordinary way, in which they might be applied to men as the adopted children of God or as His special favourites. It was also clear from the faith which had been in the world since the first promise made to our first parents in Eden, that the Redeemer of the world must be more than man. In the same way the Virginal Conception of the Divine Child was plain from the prophecy of Isaias and Jeremias. Still nothing had been said as to the precise agency by which it was to be brought about.

Our Blessed Lady may have had an intelligence of the secrets of God of which we have no idea, because she was so singularly prevented and favoured by His graces, both of the understanding and of the will. But the saints of God do not trust their own surmises or thoughts. Thus, even if the illuminated intelligence of Mary had been made acquainted, in some marvellous way, with the ineffable condescension by which the Holy Ghost was Himself to work out the mystery of the Incarnation, nothing had been said to her on this matter, and therefore it was left for her to enquire in her humble and most modest manner, how this thing was to de done? As to this she was much in the same position as that in which her Spouse St. Joseph was left, after the Incarnation, until the moment came for him to have the mystery, and his own office with respect to that mystery, revealed to him by a special vision from heaven. That he was so left was the essence of the trial to which he was put. We may trace something of the same kind in the Divine dealings with Mary herself.

There had hitherto been one singular reticence in the words of St. Gabriel. In ordinary communications of the kind to which this belongs, namely, communications made with regard to the birth and conception of some saint of God, it had usually been said that the wife was to conceive and bear a son to the husband. We have seen how the thought of the hindrance which her virginal vow might possibly present to the carrying out of the mystery, may have been the cause, or one of the causes, of that fear of our Blessed Lady which had been removed by the last words of the Angel, following on his first great salutation. His words assuring her that she had found grace with God, would have been equivalent, in her mind, to a promise that that which she feared as possible would not be. But nothing had been added as to the actual manner in which the Divine counsel was to be brought to its accomplishment. Thus when the Angel ceased speaking, Mary, who had not interrupted him in his message, was left without further positive assurance, except that she had found grace with God, and was to be the Mother of the Messias. This great work might, perhaps, have been wrought in various ways by God, but there was as yet no distinct intimation what the particular way was to be which He would choose. It was therefore a most prudent question for her to ask, how it was to be done? and it gave her the opportunity of pleading her devotion to the purity which she had vowed to God, and so of making herself more fit and worthy to receive the ineffable grace of Conception by the operation of the Holy Ghost.

Thus we see that these words of our Blessed Lady do not in any way imply a doubt of the truth of the message which the Angel had delivered to her. One who asks how a thing is to be, or to come about, implies that it is to be done in some way or other. As it was to take place in herself, it was the most natural and right thing for her to ask for directions how to act. This might have been the case, even if Mary had not had the Virginal vow binding on her of which we have already spoken. But as this bond lay on her, it was only right and natural that she should refer to it, and refer to it in such a way as to show that she considered that way at least to be excluded which would have involved a violation of her vow. She was precluded from becoming a mother in the ordinary way of women. We may well think that, if she divined that the Mother of God must be a mother in some more sublime and heavenly manner than the rest of mothers, still she might be kept by her own deep humility from imagining that she could be raised so high as to conceive by the operation of the Holy Ghost.

The distinct words of the Angel, about her conceiving in her womb, excluded any thought of the formation of the Body of our Lord from her in the manner in which Eve had been formed from the side of Adam, and thus the only manner of which there was any example of generation other than in the ordinary way was shut out. Moreover, the words of our Lady's question show her intense love for purity, and her fixed resolution not willingly to sacrifice her virginal dignity, even for the sake of the blessing held out to her. The words show unmistakably that she was bound by an irrevocable tie. It is unreasonable to interpret the words as simply meaning that, up to the time of the Annunciation, she had remained a pure Virgin. They must signify that she was so to remain for ever, and this by an obligation from which she could not free herself if she would, and from which she would not free herself if she could. Thus it is quite true to say, as is said by some of the Catholic commentators, that these words show us quite plainly that our Lady remained as untouched after the birth of our Lord as before, and thus they supply, if any such confirmation can be needed to Catholic and Christian minds, a commentary on the account given in the first chapter of the Gospel of St. Matthew, of her virginal Conception, in which words the Evangelist simply asserts her purity before the Nativity of our Lord, without adding anything more about the rest of her life. It would have seemed to him superfluous and insolent to suppose any such question possible.

This then seems to be the meaning of the words before us, in which our Lady draws out from the messenger of God the great and most wonderful truth concerning the manner of the Conception of her Divine Son. Instead of showing any incredulity or any hesitation as to the truth of the message which had been delivered to her, our Lady shows, by her question, the strongest and most lively faith. Soon after this we find St. Elisabeth, speaking, no doubt, under divine guidance, calling our Lady by the name which signifies this her singular and transcendent faith. "Blessed thou that didst believe!"—almost as if the saint had had in her mind the incredulity of which her own husband Zachary had been an instance, and for which he had been signally punished by the justice of God by a chastisement under which he was still suffering when his wife thus spoke.

Moreover we may see in the question of which we are speaking a great fervour and strength of divine love. The words are those of one who welcomes the message, and is most desirous to know how its behests are to be executed. We have already mentioned also the singular prudence of the question, which asks for the information as to the will of God which is necessary for her at the time, in the simplest, shortest, and most submissive way. It is in this respect like the question of St. Paul on his conversion. "Lord, what wilt Thou have me to do?" and if in the case of our Blessed Lady it is not a perfectly unconditional surrender of her will, this is because that will was already bound by a pledge to God against one possible alternative as to the manner of the fulfilment of the command. And this again, certainly shows us the character of the bond by which Mary was bound to Virginity. If it had been only her own desire, or resolution, or purpose, the question would have been whether she was to carry out that intention or purpose. She could not plead the difficulty which she does plead, unless she had been certain that what God had inspired He would not call on her to sacrifice, and that His will could not be the violation of the solemn vow by which she was to remain a Virgin for ever.

It has been thought by some writers that the words of which we are speaking may be considered as implying that our Blessed Lady was so firm in her love for Virginity that she would not have consented to become the Mother of God if her cherished virtue and crown had been endangered. But it is quite needless to suppose that this alternative was ever present to her mind. She was before all things the handmaid and servant of her God and Lord, and whatever choice she might make, or whatever desire she might conceive, was made or conceived, out of regard to His supreme will and out of obedience to Him. Her heroic faith made it easy for her to believe that He would find a way of His own for the accomplishment of both of His decrees concerning her, just as the faith of Abraham made it easy for him to think that God could still give him the promised seed in his son Isaac, even though He commanded him to offer him in sacrifice on the mountain. It was not to Abraham a choice between foregoing the promises which had been made to Him, and disobeying the command to slay Isaac. He believed that what God had promised He was able to perform. So with Mary, it was not that she felt obliged to choose between the preservation of her promise to God, inspired by Himself, and the acceptance of the glorious dignity and lofty service to Him now held out to her by the Divine Maternity. She could believe as Abraham believed, though the thing which she had to believe was the more difficult of the two.

Our Blessed Lady could believe that if God willed her to be the Mother of the Incarnate Word, He could and would provide some way by which this purpose of His could be brought to its full execution, without the necessity of her sacrificing that which she had promised to Him to maintain. The supreme faith of our Blessed Lady saved her from having to balance in her heart between two things which might be incompatible in the thoughts of men, but which were not incompatible in the decrees and unto the power of God. She does not express any preference in her words for one of these alternatives over the other, because they were not, to her enlightened mind and marvellous faith, irreconcilable. But it is natural to suppose that her Virginal purpose was very dear to her. It was the choice she was inspired to make, the first of all the servants and children of God. It was her treasure, as it were, her discovery under the guidance of the Holy Ghost, like the treasure in the parable, her darling plan for her life, her glory, in the sense in which St. Paul speaks of his own special sacrifice, in his work for God, of not living at the expense of the Churches to which he preached, while other Apostles did this without blame or hesitation. In this sense of her intense love for the beautiful grace of Virginity, we may understand the sayings of some of the Christian writers of whom we are speaking.

And again, if the question of our Blessed Lady

was so perfectly prudent, so full of faith and love, displaying so entire a submission to the Will of God, and so lofty an intelligence of His ways and of His power, it was also, as we shall see, most fruitful, in the great revelation to which it led. It was the key which unlocked the secret treasures of God, and brought to light the ineffable condescension which He was preparing for the carrying out of the promise of the Incarnation. It has already been said that this part of the great counsel of God had not been as yet revealed. It was not told to prophet or seer, nor had it been written in the pages of revelation, nor divined by the contemplations of the saints. It was naturally reserved for the Blessed Mother herself to know first how the Incarnation was to come about. There was something wanting in the fulness of this great revelation until Mary unlocked this its last treasure. It was not known before the time. When the moment came for the chosen Virgin to ask this question, then at last the final word was spoken by the mouth of Gabriel, and the Angels who hung around him in eager expectation might rejoice over this clear manifestation in its minutest details of the beautiful design on which their contemplations had so long fed with ecstatic delight. "How shall this be done, seeing that I know not man?" The future Queen of Heaven and earth, the humblest and most docile of God's creatures, whose will was so entirely His that the slightest intimation of His desire was her law, was thus the appointed person to bring out, by her question, the mystery concealed from the foundation of the world.

CHAPTER V.

THE CONCEPTION BY THE HOLY GHOST.

St. Luke i. 38. *Vita Vitæ Nostræ*, § 4.

It has been said that the faith of the Blessed Virgin had already soared so high, as to find no difficulty in the great announcement which had been made to her by the Angel, while she had most prudently enquired what was to be the manner in which the mystery was to be carried out. The answer which the Angel was now to give her was to rise to the full height of the most marvellous of the works of God, the Conception of our Lord in her womb by means of the operation of the Holy Ghost. Thus it could not but involve a fresh demand on her incomparable faith, a demand to which she was enabled by the grace of God to respond, with the same perfect docility and ready intelligence as in the former case. We live on the mystery of the Incarnation, and we are so familiar with its details as they are set before us by the teaching of the Church, that we do not comprehend the immense act of faith which was now required of Mary, and which was made by her, as it seems, without any strain or effort.

The long history of the Christian Church informs us of the many various devices which have been adopted by those who have not been made able to receive the great truth, even after it has been made certain by Divine revelation. Some of the heresies on the subject of the Person of our Lord are very grotesque, while others show us how the human mind shrinks back from the full apprehension of so wonderful a truth as that of the Incarnation carried out as it actually was. We see the malignity of Satan in the many attempts made by the heresiarchs to pare down the Divine truth, so as to deprive man of the full benefit of the infinite condescension of his God. But we may also see, in the same false systems, the perversity of the human mind, taking refuge in any imagination which may give it an excuse for not believing that God has done for us all that He has done. Men have tried to believe that our Lord was a simple man, conceived and born as such, to whom the Divine Person of the Word was united for a time, and not by an absolute and indissoluble identity. They have imagined that the Union might have taken place at some time subsequent to the Conception of her Son by Mary, that it did not last beyond the time of the accomplishment of the work of Redemption, that the Christ was a different person from the Son of God, and the like.

Thus, in every imaginable way the great mystery has been cut down, and explained away. And it is very probable that, outside the Catholic Church, this process is still constantly gone through in the minds of thousands who consider themselves Christians, mainly on account of the feebleness of the human mind to grasp the full truth, because it is so great and magnificent and complete on the part of God. It must be remembered that many of the ways, in which heretics have supposed the union to have taken place, may have been in themselves possible, if God had so chosen, though they would not have brought about an Incarnation in the true Christian sense of the word, they would not have given to us a Saviour in the sense of the prophecies and promises of God from the beginning of time. The full truth was now conveyed to the chosen Mother by the next words of the Angel, without any reticence or concealment, as to one whose faith could not be too severely taxed by the magnificence of what she was asked to believe on his simple word. "And the Angel said to her, the Holy Ghost shall come upon thee, and the power of the Most High shall overshadow thee, and therefore also the Holy which shall be born of thee shall be called the Son of God." Our Blessed Lady's own words had already excluded the possibility of the ordinary mode of Conception in this case, and the Angel seems to take her words up, and to supply what she could not have known without the special revelation now made to her, that the Conception was to be brought about by the action of the Holy Ghost Himself. She was to conceive as a pure Virgin, but not by any simple act of her own will alone, for the Holy Ghost was to bring about the formation of the body of her Child from her most pure flesh. She was to be the sole parent of the Child, but the Conception was to be the work of the Holy Ghost. This is the great mystery which we must now endeavour to explain in accordance with the Catholic teaching on the subject of the Incarnation.

In the first place, some of the commentators insist upon the word used in the Gospel before us, which is translated in the Vulgate *superveniet*, shall come upon thee. In the Greek, the preposition with which the verb "come" is combined hardly signifies all that is conveyed by the Latin word *super*. But these writers, insisting on the full meaning of the Latin preposition, suppose the word to signify that the Holy Ghost would come to our Lady in a new manner, having been already with her, as He was certainly with her, in the plenitude of His graces. This doctrine is perfectly true, and it belongs to the intelligence of the mystery to remember it. But it is not precisely conveyed by the original words of the Evangelist. These words are almost equivalent to a simple assertion that the Holy Ghost would come to our Blessed Lady. This does not in any way imply that He was not already with her. It means that He will come to her in a new and special manner, for the purpose of which the Angel is speaking, that is, for the purpose of bringing about in her, without the intervention of man, the miraculous Conception of her Divine Son.

This is the general meaning of Scripture, when it speaks of the coming or the presence of the Holy Spirit, namely, that He comes to the person who is the subject of the discourse for some particular purpose, and to produce some particular effect or influence. Thus the Holy Ghost is promised to the Apostles by our Lord, just before His Ascension, where He tells them that they shall receive the power of the Holy Ghost coming upon them,[1] al-

[1] Acts i. 8.

though we know that they had the gift of the Holy Ghost bestowed on them in a solemn manner on the day of His Resurrection, when He gave them the power to forgive sins. On that former occasion the Holy Ghost came to them for the purpose of making them efficient ministers of the Sacrament of Penance, and He was to come to them on the day of Pentecost in a new manner, for the purpose of arming them with all the powers and graces which were required for the due discharge of their great work of preaching to the whole world. In each case the gift or presence of the Holy Ghost is something new, though He was with the Apostles before, and for other purposes, especially of sanctification, and this new presence or power of the Holy Ghost corresponds exactly to the designs of God in sending the Apostles on a particular mission or employing them for a special work.

This then is the meaning of the coming of the Holy Ghost to our Blessed Lady. He is to come to her, for the purpose of accomplishing in her the work of the Conception of her Son, and of fitting her for the part which she herself was to have in that Conception. Thus the work of the Holy Ghost is summed up by the theologians under four heads, two of which have reference to the order of grace, and two of them to the completion of the work of nature in conception. In the first place, the Holy Ghost was to come to her, to confer on her a new and great increase of sanctity, that she might be fit to give of her substance that of which the sacred Body of our Lord might be formed. In the second place, He was to make the Conception itself perfectly holy and worthy of the Son of God. In the third place, He was to supply and make perfect the work of nature in the process of Conception, making perfect that which our Lady was naturally to perform on her part, and supplying what would have been the effect of the action of the other parent in cases of ordinary conception. In the last place, we are told that He was to bring all this about in a most perfect and instantaneous manner, whereas in an ordinary conception there might be delay, or slowness, or some lapse of time. We must say a few words as to each of these heads.

In the first place, then, it is undoubted that our Lady was already full of grace, but this did not exclude the special action of the Holy Ghost for this particular purpose. He was to come upon her with a fresh abundance of graces and gifts, now that the message of the Angel had been delivered to her so far, and she had so far corresponded in perfect faith and ready docility and obedience to the designs of God. He was now to dispose her finally, by His sanctifying power, that she might be worthy to conceive the Son of God, and that He might fully sanctify that body of hers from which was to be taken the substance of the flesh which was to be that of the Incarnate Word. This is that operation of the Holy Ghost of which the Church constantly sings, when she prays to Almighty God, "Who with the cooperation of the Holy Ghost didst prepare the body and soul of the glorious Virgin, that she might merit to be made the dwellingplace of Thy Son." This fresh and final sanctification of our Lady, in body and soul, is the first effect to be produced by the coming upon her of the Holy Ghost of which the Angel speaks.

In the second place, the Holy Ghost was to come upon her for the purpose of making the Conception itself, which was to take place, perfectly holy. This is something different from the former sanctification of the body and soul of Mary. To explain this we need only follow the doctrine as it is laid down for us from the Fathers by Toletus. If Adam had not sinned, he would have been holy himself, and not only so, but he would have communicated his holiness to the children born of him. In this case, not only would the offspring have been holy, but the act of conception would have been holy also, and a kind of means by which the holiness of the parent would have been handed on and communicated to the children. The sin of Adam changed all this. Instead of the children being holy, they are born in sin, and their conception itself is infected and corrupt, for by it the sin of the parent is derived to the children, for the very reason that they are born of Adam. Of course in the Conception of our Lord there could be no question of sin, for He was Himself the Fountain of all sanctity, not only ineffably holy Himself, by virtue of the Divine Union, and nothing could either take away from or add to His sanctity, but also the source of all grace and holiness to others. But yet it was befitting that His Conception should be holy in itself, and for this end the Holy Ghost was to come upon the Blessed Mother, and make the Conception in her womb such, that nothing but what was most holy could proceed from thence.

This is the second reason for the coming of the Holy Ghost to our Blessed Lady, when she was about to conceive her Son. This truth is illustrated by some examples and reasonings. For instance, if a child of Adam, at the moment of his conception, were endowed and flooded with grace, so that the soul then joined to the body should be perfectly holy, that child would be born in perfect sanctity, but still his conception would have been in sin, on account of the infection which the sin of Adam has entailed on all conceived from him in the natural way. This child would escape the contagion of sin on account of his sanctification in the womb at the moment of conception, and it would be by virtue of the hindrance opposed to sin by the grace of that particular sanctification. Again, if Adam had not been elevated by grace at the time of his creation, and if he had begotten a son in the state of innocence, this child would have been conceived and born in innocence, but not in sanctity. The effect of the coming of the Holy Ghost on our Blessed Lady was to make her holy for this especial purpose, and to make her Conception holy in itself. Not that the grace of this Conception was the cause of the sanctity of her Son, but that her Son, before He was conceived in her womb, merited and won for her by anticipation the grace that sanctified her for this purpose, that she might holily conceive the Holy of Holies.

These are the effects the production of which, in the order of grace, was the Divine reason for the supervention of the Holy Ghost on our Blessed Lady, for the purpose of her Conception. The other effects already mentioned belong rather to the order of nature, and consist in the action of the Holy Ghost in bringing about the completion and perfection of the Conception of our Lord in His Mother's womb, in taking, moulding, disposing, quickening, and organizing the substance which she contributed to the body of our Lord, and in supplying all that is naturally dependent on the action of the father in such cases for this purpose. All that is required for the preparation of the substance for animation, for the infusion of the soul, and the like, was supplied in this miraculous Conception by the operation of the Holy Ghost, and, as has been said, if we suppose, as was of old thought, that some time must of necessity elapse before the process of animation is completed, this delay of time also was anticipated and cut short by the Divine power of the Holy Ghost.

The reasons which have been now, however shortly, given, sufficiently explain why the Conception of our Lord in the womb of His Mother is a Divine work specially attributed, as we say, to the Holy Ghost, although all the works of God outside Himself are the works of all Three Divine Persons equally. The reason is, because this Conception of our Lord had so much of the character of sanctification, not only in that the Holy Ghost formed and prepared, and brought about the animation of, the body of our Lord, but also because He exercised His special function and office of sanctification, by His operation in preparing our Blessed Lady, body and soul, for this Conception and by making the Conception itself intrinsically holy. Another reason is also given for this attribution, namely that the gift of the Incarnation of the Son of God was something entirely gratuitous and unmerited by man, a pure act of the most infinite mercy. Now the gifts of God of this kind are usually in Sacred Scripture attributed to the Holy Ghost. Moreover, the end and object of this Conception was the sanctification of the whole world, and this is a work which especially belongs to the Holy Ghost.

The Angel next goes on to complete his message. He has spoken of the action of the Holy Ghost in the sanctification of our Blessed Lady for the special purpose of her Conception, and in the preparation and animation of the substance which was to become the Body of our Lord. But this work might have been conceivably done with a view to the Conception of some one who was not in Himself Divine, whereas in the Conception of our Lord there were further mysteries and marvels to take place beyond this action of the Holy Ghost, limited as it might possibly have been to a merely human birth. The Child Who was to be conceived in the womb of Mary was indeed to have a perfect human Nature, but He was to be at the same time a Divine Person. He was to have no personality or subsistence except a Divine Personality. For this it was necessary, in the designs of God, that the Person of the Word should be united to the Human body formed in the womb of Mary, and to the soul created and infused into that body by God, and that thus the Child should be at once God and Man, " God of the substance of the Father, Begotten before the worlds, and Man of the substance of His Mother born in the world." The words of the Angel of which we have already spoken, "The Holy Ghost shall come upon thee," describe the formation of the human Body out of the substance of Mary, and out of her substance alone, and also the preparation of that Body for the reception of the Soul created by God for it. The words which follow describe the Divine operation by which the Person of the Son of God was to be united at the instant of the Conception to the human nature, the Body and the Soul thus prepared for this ineffable union. And thus they complete the description of the Incarnation, in the fewest and simplest terms, making indeed a great demand on the wonderful faith of the Blessed Mother, but still not a demand too great for that stupendous faith. "The Holy Ghost shall come upon thee, and the power of the Most High shall overshadow thee." These last words, as has been said, complete the revelation in the manner now stated.

The formation of the Body of our Lord, and its conjunction with its Soul, are thus prior, in order of thought, in the history of the Incarnation, to the union with the Person of the Son of God of which these last words speak. But it must always be remembered that, in point of fact, the whole of the great mystery was carried out instantaneously, and in the same moment of time, and thus it is that the human nature of our Lord had never for one moment a Personality of its own, distinct from that of the Son of God. This truth is necessary for the intelligence alike of the mystery of the Incarnation, of the Personality of our Lord, and of the Divine

Maternity of Mary. In the formation of the Body of our Lord, our Blessed Lady had her part as Mother, contributing of her most pure blood for the substance necessary for that purpose. The creation and infusion of the Soul was the work of God the Creator alone, in this case as in all others. The Holy Ghost supplied by His action, as has been said, all the effects that would in ordinary conceptions be produced by the father of the child. The Union of the Person of the Word to the human nature thus formed and created, formed as to the Body and created as to the Soul, was the work also of God alone, and, like the other works of the Ever Blessed Trinity of the same order, was wrought by all Three Persons equally and in common. But, as it is a work of the most stupendous and marvellous power, it is one of those Divine works which are particularly attributed, as theologians speak, to the Eternal Father.

This, then, is the meaning of these words, "the power of the Most High shall overshadow thee." The Eternal Father is spoken of as figuratively overshadowing the Blessed Mother, that she may become the Mother of His Son, covering her with His infinite power that so great a Conception may take place in her womb as that of His own Only-Begotten Son, Whose sole parent, in His Divine Nature and Person He, the Father, is. And thus the Three Divine Persons have each one His proper work in the execution of the mystery. The Father works the work of power in the Union of the Person of His Son to the Human Nature, the Holy Ghost works the work of goodness, beneficence, mercy and sanctification in the preparation of that Human Nature, and the Divine Son Himself becomes Incarnate, and takes to Himself, for ever and for ever, the Human Nature, the Body and the Soul conceived in the womb of Mary.

"And therefore also the Holy which shall be born in thee shall be called the Son of God." These words form the conclusion of the direct message in which the mystery of the Incarnation is explained to the Blessed Mother. The Angel tells her that, because of the two truths which he has revealed to her, the operation of the Holy Ghost in the first place, and the Hypostatic Union wrought by the power of the Father in the second place, the Child conceived and to be born of her shall be the Son of God. But each word has its own weight and importance, and must be considered singly. That which is to be born of Mary is in the first place Holy. This it might have been, even if it was not to be the Incarnate Son, because the operation of Holy Ghost, if it could have been employed for any other Conception than His, must necessarily sanctify both the mother herself and the Conception itself, so that whatever might be so born would be intrinsically holy. The Angel does not speak of the Child or the Son in the first instance, because this Child was to be both God and Man in one Person. He was to be One Person, in two natures, and this might not have been so well expressed if He had been spoken of in the first instance as a Person. Because of the operation of the Father, which the Angel has spoken of in the second place, the Holy that is born of Mary shall be called the Son of God, not therefore simply a holy birth, by reason of the preparation of the Holy Ghost, but a Divine Person, by reason of the operation of the Eternal Father bringing about the Hypostatic Union. Thus what was already holy, for the reason so often mentioned, was to be holy with the particular and ineffable holiness of the Son of God, by virtue of this union.

The Angel here uses the word born, or shall be born, in the same sense as on the occasion related by St. Matthew in his first chapter, when he speaks of the vision vouchsafed to St. Joseph at the time when he was in doubt as to his duty with regard to Mary and her Child. There he says to St. Joseph, that "which is born in her" is of the Holy Ghost. In the common acceptation of the word, our Lord was not as yet born. But He is said by the Angel to be born, because He was already perfect Man in the womb of His Blessed Mother, nothing could be added to the perfection of His Manhood, even as to the use and full development of His faculties of intelligence and of will. In that sense it was true to say of Him that He was already fully born in the womb of His Mother, and what the Angel had in charge to announce to St. Joseph was that He had been conceived by the operation of the Holy Ghost. In this place St. Gabriel seems to mean to imply that our Lord was to be perfectly and completely the Son of His Mother, and her Son alone, and not the Son of any earthly father, and that His substance was to be from her and of her, not a phantasm, or a substance taken from some other being, but really and truly hers. This was the effect of the operation of the Holy Ghost, while as the effect of the Hypostatic Union, which is attributed to God the Father for the reason already given, He was really and truly the Son of God even in His Human Nature. Thus, even apart from the Hypostatic Union, the Conception of our Lord differed from every other Conception, however holy. Let us explain this a little further.

St. John Baptist was to be born holy from his mother's womb, but he had been conceived in sin, and his sanctification came after his conception. In the case of the Immaculate Conception of our Blessed Lady, she was conceived holy and Immaculate, entirely free from all taint of sin. But the act of her Conception on the part of her parents was in the ordinary way, however highly sanctified by right intention and freedom from lust on their part, and thus an act not in itself holy. She might have been conceived in original sin, but for the intervention of the privilege of exemption accorded to her as the future Mother of our Lord, and for His merits. In this sense it is that she was conceived Immaculate. But our Lord could not have been conceived in any sense in sin, for the reasons already given, and thus the Angel speaks of Him in these words as the Holy, or the Holy One, Who is to be born in Mary. He was holy, with the infinite holiness of His Divine nature from all eternity, and, by virtue of the Union, His Humanity also received the "anointing" of which Scripture speaks in more than one place, that is the holiness of God. And again His Humanity was enriched with the plenitude of grace, of which we have already spoken, with all wisdom and grace of the Holy Ghost. Both these sanctities the Humanity of Christ had from the first instant of His Conception, and thus He was in the strictest and fullest sense of the words, the Holy One.

Again, with regard to the title of the Son of God. This belonged to our Lord both as God and as Man. He was of the same substance with the Father and possessed with Him the fulness of the Divinity. His power and might were the same with those of His Father, and as He did not become the Son of God at His Human Conception, the Angel says that He shall be so called, rather than that He should become. And He is said to be called the Son of the most High on another ground also, because He is to be manifested as such to the world, and to be honoured and worshipped as such by the faithful. As Man He is the Son of God, not by derivation of the human nature, but by virtue of the Hypostatic Union. His Humanity received thereby the natural filiation to God, because it pleased God to communicate to it the eternal hypostasis of His Son, and in that His Own Divinity. Thus the filiation or Sonship of our Lord to His Father is one, both as God and as Man, but He is the Son of God from all eternity as God, and as Man He is the Son of God by virtue of the Union which took place in time.

Lastly, the particle 'therefore,' the first word of the sentence of the Angel must be insisted on for the full intelligence of the whole passage. It connects the Divine Sonship of our Lord directly with the action of the Holy Ghost in sanctifying Mary, and the Conception in her, and with the action of the Eternal Father in overshadowing her. That is, it excludes the possibility of any collation or bestowal of the Divine Sonship at any subsequent period or point of time. It has been thought, for instance, by some heretics, that our Lord was born a simple man from His mother's womb, and that afterwards He merited or received the grace of the Divine Sonship. Other heretics, without supposing that He obtained this Divine Sonship by any merits of His own, still taught that He received it at a much later period, when He was baptized by St. John, and the Voice from heaven was heard, declaring Him to be the well-beloved Son, and the like. These falsehoods are confuted by the single word, 'therefore.' The graces and merits of the Sacred Humanity did not win from God the Divine Union. They were themselves the effects and fruits of the Divine Union.

It has already been said that our Blessed Lady had not questioned the truth or the possibility of the mystery which had been announced to her, on the part of God, by the Angel. She had only enquired what it was natural that she should enquire, how the mystery was to be carried out, especially as she was bound to remain for ever a Virgin. But though she had not asked, as Zachary had asked, how she should know that what was announced to her was true, though she had not asked for a sign of the certainty of the words of the messenger of God, it was due in the counsels of Providence that she should have a sign given her, by way of confirmation of the truth which had been revealed to her, and also for another purpose, namely, that of giving her an intimation of the line of conduct which it was the will of God that she should pursue, immediately after the accomplishment in her of the Incarnation of our Lord. For, as it is a part of the method of God in dealing with man, to predict beforehand everything great and wonderful that He intends to do for the benefit of man, so also it is a part of His method, to confirm any very wonderful revelation by some sign which may be a kind of evidence of it, even though the person to whom the particular revelation may be made does not need further evidence than the words of the messenger to whom the manifestation is entrusted. Thus it was natural and regular that some confirmation of the words of the Angel should be given to Mary, though she neither asked nor required such confirmation for her own sublime and perfect faith.

Again, the Conception of our Lord in the womb of His Mother had long been a subject of anticipation in the particular manner in which such anticipation was possible, that is, in the constant repetition in the Sacred history of the incident of the marvellous conceptions of children by aged parents, when, in the course of nature such conception was either impossible or extremely improbable. If God had condescended to prepare the marvel of the Incarnation by such anticipations, it seems only right and orderly that, when the Incarnation was to take place, it should be heralded by a fresh marvel of the same kind as before, and that this marvel should be adduced by the messenger of God as furnishing the crown and putting the finish to the long series of such providential anticipations. This would have been enough to prepare us for the announcement now added by St. Gabriel to all that he had already declared to our Blessed Lady on the part of God, especially as the announcement is concluded by words actually quoted from the Old Testament Scriptures where they occur on the first occasion of the anticipations of this order. And as has been said, another reason existed for the communication to our Lady of the state of pregnancy of her cousin Elisabeth, namely, that it was the design of God to bring about the visit of our Lady to St. Elisabeth without delay, and the intimation of the fact as it was, was the proper method for conveying to our Lady the desire of God in this respect.

"And behold thy cousin Elisabeth, she also hath conceived a son in her old age, and this is the sixth month with her that is called barren, because no word shall be impossible with God." Every word of this short sentence is full of meaning, and tends to confirm the truth of the announcement on which it followed, as well as to imply the opportuneness of the visit to St. Elisabeth which Mary was to make. The truth of the message is confirmed by the fact itself of the marvellous conception of St. Elisabeth in her old age, and of the approaching time of her deliverance, within three months more. She must have been well known to Mary, and so her sterility and advanced age could not be a secret to her. She is spoken of as "her that is called barren," as if to imply that her sterility was well known and a matter of common reproach to her on the part of enemies, and of sorrow on the part of friends. These things may be considered as describing the particulars of her case in such a way as to confirm the message to Mary, by the attestation of a marvellous conception on the part of one of her own kinsfolk.

On the other hand, the mention by the blessed Angel of the state in which St. Elisabeth was, so near to her by family ties, would naturally suggest to our Lady, even on the simple grounds of charity and kindness, that she should go to be of service to her under such circumstances. But there were higher grounds for her visit than those. It was implied by the Angel that there was something marvellous, not only in the conception of the child of Elisabeth, but also in his destination and in the office he might have to discharge in the kingdom of God. Such conceptions were not vouchsafed by God for nothing, and it would have been easy for Mary to see that the child might have some task to perform in connection with that great deliverance of the people and the world which was the purpose of the Incarnation itself.

And still further, these words of the Angel may have implied a kind of answer to any thoughts which might have arisen in the mind of Mary as to the immediate future, if she was indeed to conceive in her own womb the Son of God. Her first thought might naturally be whether she was to reveal to her holy husband the mystery which was to take place, or at least this thought might arise ere long after the Incarnation itself. For what could she desire more than to make St. Joseph the partner of her great joy! And then the words of the Angel might come back as a direction to her, rather to go to the home of St. Elisabeth, in the first instance, and there await further guidance from God.

The last words, "no word shall be impossible with God," are, as has been said, taken from the passage in Genesis in which the conception of Isaac is foretold to Abraham and Sara, when Sara is reproved for laughing at the prediction.[2] This was the first in the line of similar anticipations of the supreme miracle of the Conception of our Lord, as the conception of St. John Baptist by Elisabeth was the last. Thus the words may be considered as summing up, for our Blessed Lady at the moment of the Annunciation, the whole of this kind of evidence as prepared by God. The words also occur in a passage in the prophecy of Jeremias, where the prophet makes his prayer to God, "O Lord God, behold Thou hast made heaven and earth, by Thy great power and Thy stretched-out arm, no word shall be too hard to Thee."[3] And thus the full Scriptural evidence on which our Lady might build up her act of faith in the mystery now proposed to her acceptance was furnished and completed by the addition of the new marvel lately worked in the womb of her cousin.

It cannot be doubted that the words of Gabriel conveyed their full and due meaning to the mind of the Blessed Virgin. She was illuminated in the ways and promises of God beyond all others, whether of the Angels themselves or the saints of God on earth. The words of the Angel are simple and short, like the words of one who is sent to speak to a person of the most consummate intelligence, and

Gen. xviii. 14.   [3] Jer. xxxii. 17.

they must have set before our Lady's mind the full height and stupendous wonderfulness of the Incarnation. It was no longer the simple unexplained truth of the Conception of the promised Messias in her Virginal womb. It was the direct action of the Holy Ghost Himself that was to form and prepare the human part of the marvel, and the Eternal Father was to take His part in the Union of the Person of His Only-Begotten Son with the Humanity formed by the operation of the Holy Ghost. Mary was thus asked to believe that she was to become the Mother of God Himself by the operation of each Person of the Blessed Trinity. It might have been comparatively easy for her to understand that the prophecies and predictions and anticipations, with which she was so familiar, all pointed to the Divine character of the Messias Who was expected. It might not be so difficult to believe that His Mother was to be a pure and unsullied Virgin. But it was something more difficult to nature to grasp, at once and without hesitation, that she was herself to be the chosen Mother, the Virgin who was to conceive and bear a Son. It is one thing to believe such a mystery at a distance and as a matter of prophecy, and another to rise in a moment to the truth that it was to take place in herself, in her own person, in her own womb, then and there. But far beyond this difficulty rose the other, which was contained in the latest revelation made by the words of Gabriel, as to the Divine part in the great work of which we are speaking. Mary could understand in this nothing short of the full truth, that the Divine Person of the Son of God was to take flesh of her.

In all these ineffable wonders, as Mary knew, "no thing was impossible to God." It was within His power that the Incarnation should take place in the way described in the words of the Angel. It was within His power that a maiden of earthly strain should thus become a Mother by the direct action of the Holy Ghost and of the Eternal Father, that the Only-Begotten Son of God should make Himself her child in her womb in the manner implied by these words. But then again, that she was to be the Mother of God herself, she and no other, she the humblest of the humble, the lowliest of the lowly! Surely there was need here for a faith more ready, more sublime, more perfect than that of Abraham himself, the father of the faithful, when he was called on to believe that he was to be made the father of many nations, or again that his seed should be as the stars of heaven, or the sand by the seashore, and yet was told to offer the son in whom these promises were enshrined in sacrifice on the mountain. St. Paul justly indeed celebrates this faith of Abraham as the pattern and model of all faith, whether in Jews or Christians. "He was not weak in faith," he says, "neither did he consider his own body now dead, whereas he was almost a hundred years old, nor the dead womb of Sara. In the promise also of God he staggered not by distrust, but was strengthened by faith, giving glory to God, most fully knowing that whatsoever He has promised He is able also to perform." And of the other great trial of Abraham, the Apostle says, "By faith Abraham, when he was tried, offered Isaac and he that had received the promises, offered up his only begotten son, to whom it was said, in Isaac shall thy seed be called, accounting that God is able to raise up even from the dead."[4]

The Incarnation towers so far above all the other great works of God, as that nothing is really great in comparison therewith. Thus it stands to reason that all predictions and anticipations of it must necessarily fall infinitely short of it, in the power which they require for their accomplishment. But it is a part of the same truth, that the faith required to grasp at once and assent firmly to the revelation of the Incarnation, in all its wonderful details, as they had now been set before Mary, must be a faith far greater than any faith that had ever been exercised by any creature up to that time, or that could ever be exercised again. Yet this was what constituted, if of this also we may use the words of the Apostle, the trial of Mary. She was asked to assent in her mind to the truth as it was now set before her, and also to consent with her free will to be made the deliberate and conscious instrument of this awful mystery. Another truth follows inevitably from those already mentioned. If faith is the condition of pleasing God, and if God is pleased more and more according to the greatness of the faith which is given to His Word, it must surely be a self-evident truth that the act of faith now required of Mary was absolutely unique in its greatness, and therefore such as to make her pleasing and acceptable to God in a degree to which there can possibly be no parallel. Thus if we had no more knowledge of our Blessed Lady than that which is contained for us in

[4] Rom. iv. 18—21. Heb. xi. 17—19.

this simple narrative of the Annunciation, we should have enough to justify all the most glowing language concerning her greatness in dignity and in grace that has ever been used by those among the saints and writers of the Church who have been most distinguished in their praises of her. Her greatness in dignity is sufficiently contained in the statements which bring home to us the truth of the manner in which she is made the Mother of God. The immensity of her grace and of her merit before God is shown by the fact that she was asked to give to the words of the Angel a faith so stupendous as that of which we are now speaking, and that she did not fail in the trial to which she was thus subjected. But now the Divine part of this great mystery has been set forth, and it remains to see how the chosen instrument of this, the greatest of the designs of God, corresponded to the strain put upon her, and to the demand made on her faith and obedience.

CHAPTER VI.

THE FIAT OF MARY.

St. Luke i. 38. *Vita Vitæ Nostræ*, § 4.

THE blessed Angel had done his part. He had delivered his message in a few words, but in its full greatness and magnificence, and now heaven and earth, God and man, and the whole creation which was to be ennobled and elevated and purified and renovated by the Incarnation, waited for the answer of the humble Virgin of Nazareth. There was no delay, no hesitation, no half consent, no objection, no interposition of difficulty. God had said at the beginning, " Let light be, and light was." So now the word which was to bring about the accomplishment of the greatest of the designs and works of God followed instantaneously on the invitation on the part of God that it should be spoken. There can be no doubt as to the full intelligence on the part of our Blessed Lady of the meaning of the words of St. Gabriel. They involved the highest mysteries of the Divine Nature, which were not generally understood, even as far as human intelligence can grasp them, by the holy people of that time. They involved the full and clear doctrine of the Blessed Trinity, which, as we have seen in the explanation of the opening passage of the Gospel of St. John, was in great measure a hidden mystery as yet, not fully manifested to the Jews or recognised by them. They involved the marvel of the Incarnation and the manner of its execution by the operation of the Holy Ghost. They also involved the doctrine of the redemption of the world by means of the Passion of the Incarnate God, of the new Kingdom of Christ in the Church, and of the life everlasting in heaven opened to the children of men. And all the mysteries which were contained in the words of Gabriel were brought home to the faith of the Blessed Virgin in the most difficult way, inasmuch as they were connected with her own personal part in the carrying out of the designs of God. This added new difficulties to faith, beyond the great mysteries themselves which were contained in the revelation. Thus it falls under any due estimate that we may attempt to form of the grace now displayed by our Blessed Lady, that we should recognise the perfect intelligence of the mysteries which she manifests, as well as her perfect readiness to be made the instrument of the accomplishment of the decrees of God. Her ready answer, without any further questioning as to the manner in which the great work was to be wrought in her, shows sufficiently that there was nothing in the announcement of the Angel which was a difficulty to her faith.

Gabriel had spoken three times. First he had saluted our Lady with words of the most magnificent import, words of which she had penetrated the meaning, and at which, in her deep humility, she had been voluntarily and deliberately troubled, and there was perhaps in her mind this further thought, that they might not be entirely compatible with the execution of her virginal purpose, already offered to God by vow. She had said nothing, revolving first in her own most prudent mind what might be the meaning of so great a salutation. Her humility, as it were, looked up plaintively to God for help through His Angel. Then Gabriel had spoken again. His second words had conveyed an assurance that her humility would be aided by all the might of God, that she need not fear on the score of her virginal purpose, while they had also made it most clear that she was invited to be the Mother of the promised Messias. These words were mainly taken from the prophecies of His coming and His kingdom, and thus all that was startling and appalling to Mary's humility was made lighter by the witness of prophecy and the certainty that what was now to be done had been the revealed purpose of God from the very beginning. Our Lady answered this great announcement by a calm and simple question as to the manner of the execution of the mystery, a question naturally to be asked in any case, and which it was necessary for her to ask on account of her vow. Then Gabriel had spoken the third time, and his words this time had risen above the loftiest flights even of the prophetic choir, for he spoke as to one to whom the great doctrine of the Ever Blessed Trinity was familiar, and he proposed to her faith the whole wonderful design of the Conception in her Virginal womb of the Eternal Son of the Father by the operation of the Holy Ghost.

We have already spoken of the answers or of the silence of Mary in regard to these three sentences of the Angel. The first caused her that trouble of which the Evangelist speaks, the second elicited from her her question as to the manner of the execution of the design of God, while to the third she answered in a few words of which we have now to speak. It may be said that her words now, short as they are, furnish a complete and most characteristic answer to all three speeches of the Angel. He hailed her as full of grace, as having the Lord with her in a special manner, and as the Blessed one among women. These words, to one so enlightened as Mary, could not have conveyed less than the intimation that she was the chosen mother of the Messias, the Woman spoken of in the first revelation in Paradise, the Virgin who was to conceive and bear a Son in the prophecy of Isaias. She now answers this first part of the message of the Angel in her own perfect way. She does not speak as the chosen among women, as the royal Virgin of the house of David, as the Blessed one, between whom and Satan enmities have been placed by God. She speaks of herself in the way in which she delighted to think of herself, as the handmaid, the servant, the slave, of the Lord. The words imply her perfect submission, her delight in doing whatever her Lord might require of her, for the reason that He did require it. In those words she at once expresses her faith, her intelligence of the meaning of the mystery in which she was called to bear her part, and the principle of her conduct, that of obedience to God as her Lord and Master. When she adds, "be it done to me," she gives her assent and obedience to the particulars of the command conveyed in the second part of the message of the Angel, that in which she had been told that she was to conceive in her womb and bear a Son Who was to be called Jesus, Who was to be the Son of the Highest, and to have given to Him the throne of His father David, to reign over the house of Jacob for ever and to have a kingdom that should know no end. And when she adds the words, "according to thy word," she implies the most perfect faith in the great wonders of which the Angel had spoken in his announcement of the manner of her Conception, while at the same time she speaks with the most refined humility, not mentioning or dwelling upon these magnificent works of God which were to raise herself so high.

Thus every word in this last answer of our Blessed Lady, is the manifestation of some high virtue. Her readiness and joyousness in making herself the instrument of the designs of God are shown by the first word, "Behold!" Her profound humility reveals itself in the term by which she speaks of herself as the handmaid of the Lord. This word conveys also her reason for consenting. Great as was the honour, wonderful the grace, glorious the station on earth and in heaven to which she was invited, she did not clutch at them, or seize them, or accept them, for any other reason than because such was the will of God her Lord and Master, her Creator and her Preserver. The words "be it done to me," show her marvellous faith. For the Angel had not said she was to do this or that, but that the Holy Ghost should come upon her and the power of the Most High should overshadow her. She was to be in a manner passive, though willingly so, in the execution of the great mystery. Her consent was asked, but the work was to be the work of God in her. And the last words "according to thy word" show her faith and humility, as has been said, as also her joy that the accomplishment of the work was to be brought about in the manner which increased instead of diminishing or impairing the glory of her chastity. "Be it done to me according to thy word," as if no other way could be so perfectly beautiful, so entirely pleasing to her.

The same words must also be understood as gathering up in themselves all the intense desires with which this Blessed Mother had looked forward to and longed and prayed for, the accomplishment of the Incarnation for which she had yearned and longed more ardently than all the old prophets and saints from the beginning of time. Indeed she seems to speak, not in her own name only, but in the name of the whole race of which she was the representative in the Incarnation, because God and man were to be united in her womb and by means of her. She speaks in the name of the whole creation, for the whole creation was to be raised to union with its Creator by the mystery to which she now gave her consent. Her *fiat* is the prayer of all the world, rising up with the final and ineffable efficacy which was to prevail and win the greatest mercy of which even God is capable towards His creatures. St. Paul tells us that the whole creation groans and is in labour for the revelation of the

Sons of God in the resurrection of the last day, because then even the visible and material universe will be delivered by virtue of our Lord from the bondage and vanity to which it has been subjected by the sin of man. And now Mary seems to stand between God and His creatures, the highest of all as yet existing, because the One Who is infinitely higher than Mary was not yet conceived. And she raises her humble voice to the throne of God, and says, " Let it be as Thine Angel has said ! "

" And the Angel departed from her." His work was done with the conclusion of his embassy and the consent of the Blessed Virgin, and it was fitting that she should be left alone with her God that the work of the Incarnation might be wrought in her by Him. Much might be said about the execution of the Divine design, but it will be enough to give the few paragraphs in which the devout Alvarez de Paz draws up his contemplation in this great truth. " Having heard the answer of the Sacred Virgin " he says, " the Angel departed from her with joy, because he had received so happy an issue of his embassage, and wondering that he had heard from the tender girl before him words of so much humility and prudence. He departed at once, that he might set me a pattern of my conversation even with holy men. For as soon as my duty is discharged, I should at once return to my heaven in my cell, and appear before Thee, O my God, by Whom I had been sent forth. He indeed departed, but Thou didst not depart, O Thou God and Lord of Angels. At the same moment Thou didst form, of the most pure blood of the Virgin, a human body perfect with all the distinctness of its organs, and Thou didst then create and join to that body a most perfect soul. And Thy Word assumed this body and soul, this humanity, to be His own, and raised it to His own personal subsistence, so that there was One Person alone in the Divine and in the Human nature. Thy Holy Spirit then endowed this Human nature with all graces and gifts, espoused it to Thy Word, and thus left accomplished this mystery, the work of consummate goodness, perfect and complete in all details.

"O Most Loving Father, Thou didst rejoice now because Thou hadst given to us the greatest gift Thou couldest give, Thine own Son. Thou didst love Him, the Infant just conceived, infinitely more than all created things. Thou didst rejoice, O Son of God most Wise, because Thou hadst made us partakers of such great benefits, and Thou didst love that humanity which Thou hadst taken to Thyself, never to lay it down again throughout all eternity. And Thou didst rejoice, most Holy Spirit, because Thou hadst found the way for the remission of our sins and our justification, Thou hadst found Him Who was to redeem us. And Thou also, most pure Virgin, for thou didst understand in an ineffable manner the mysteries which had taken place in thee, thou didst see thyself the Queen of Angels and the sovereign of all the world. And I rejoice for all these joys thus combined, and because I find myself the son of the Father, and the brother of the Son, the dwelling place of the Holy Ghost, the poor client of the Virgin, and the companion of the Angels.

"And now I will speak with Thee, O Word of the Father, Son of God clothed with my flesh, the Messias and the Christ promised in the Law. I will speak with Thee, but before I congratulate Thee on Thy greatness, tell me, I beseech Thee, art Thou He that was to come, or do we look for another? "I indeed am He that is to renew Jerusalem, I that speak justice and am thy protector to save thee." Tell me again, I beseech thee, what did Thy blessed Soul see in Thee in that first moment of its creation, that I also may know Thee, and deal with Thee according to Thy worth? "I saw that I was taken up into the Deity in unity of Person, and was so the true and natural Son of God. I saw that I was made the head of men and of Angels, appointed the King and prince of all creation, free from any, even the slightest sin, which I could not possibly commit, surrounded by infinite grace and holiness and by all virtues and gifts connected with this mighty grace, endowed with knowledge of all things past, present and to come, with immense glory, the clear vision of God, with power to work all miracles, and for the remission of all sins." But why, O tender Child, is Thy robe red, why hast Thou a Body that can suffer, when according to the rights of Thy glorious Soul it ought to have been itself glorious, impassible and immortal? "That I might give thee, O Man, an example of humility and patience, that I might suffer for thee, that I might make My Body a sacrifice and victim to be immolated for thee." I adore Thee then, my God and my Saviour, I bless Thee, I congratulate Thee, for all Thy gifts which I desire from my heart to be Thine, and offer myself to be Thy slave.

"And now show me, O Only Begotten Son of God, what didst Thou do when first Thou didst see Thyself to be so highly exalted? " When I saw Myself in the womb of My Virgin Mother to be assumed to the Divinity, and adorned with gifts so ineffable, I loved My Father with a most ardent love, from Whom I had received benefits so great without any previous merits, I gave Him thanks with most burning affection. I humbled Myself most lowlily before Him, as one Who of Myself was nothing and had nothing. And then with the greatest readiness I offered Myself to serve Him." And what then O Infant Word of God, did Thy Eternal Father do? " He showed me the race of man altogether lost to the devil and subject to sin, He showed Me Himself injured and outraged by so many sins of men, and moved to indignation. He showed Me also the manifold afflictions, injuries, the stripes and wounds, and the death itself, which I was to undergo, and He commanded Me, as a mark of My gratitude, and as a service of obedience, to love men, to bear all these evils for them, and redeem them from the slavery of the devil. And then I looked upon you My brethren, and I embraced you with most ardent love. I was immensely grieved at the injuries done to My Father, I had compassion for you, and I made Myself subject to all those pains for the sake of redeeming your race, I took on Me the burthen of your redemption, and I said, O My God, I will it, and Thy law in the midst of My Heart." Therefore my most loving Redeemer, I give Thee immense thanks for taking on Thee this burthen, and I acknowledge that I have received from Thee all the good gifts which I have hitherto enjoyed, all that I now have, and all that I am to have hereafter. May I look to Thee not only as my deliverer, but also as my Teacher, and may I endeavour to learn from all Thy deeds and sufferings true virtue and purity of heart."[1]

The theological writers, who have treated of the subject of the great graces bestowed upon our Blessed Lady, usually consider that at the moment of the Conception of her Divine Son she was adorned by God with a new and immense dowry of graces. We cannot doubt that during the short scene of which the historian of the Annunciation speaks, she must have merited immensely, by her most faithful and perfect practice of the highest virtues under the most difficult circumstances and conditions. The whole history of created sanctity can contain no instance in which the human soul manifested higher and more perfectly beautiful perfection. Thus, for this reason if for no other, we should naturally be inclined to adopt the opinion of the theologians just referred to. But there is some greater reason for the wonderful advance in sanctification of which they speak, than the simple correspondence of this Blessed Mother to the occasion of meriting and multiplying graces in the Annunciation. For the act of the Incarnation was the greatest act of the Divine mercy and condescension possible. It was the fulfilment of the loftiest and most far reaching of the counsels of God. It

---

[1] Alv. de Paz, Vol. v. *De materis Orationis mentalis*, liii. p. 2, med. 3.

was the elevation of the whole creation by its union with the Creator. The dignity to which Mary was then raised was unparalleled and can never be paralleled. It was an occasion on which the consent of the chosen instrument of the Divine counsels was most reverentially asked, and for which she had been prepared by special graces from the beginning of her existence. It is not possible to think of God that He did not make it the occasion, not simply of rewarding the incomparable perfection of Mary by gifts of grace corresponding to the immensity of her merit, but also of adding, out of His own exhaustless stores of grace, a fresh treasure and abundance of gifts far beyond and above her merits.

St. Thomas and others think that this singular increase of grace from the free bounty of God is signified in the words, "The Holy Ghost shall come upon thee." They say that at that moment the source or *fomes peccati* was altogether taken away in her, having before that time been simply bound up and rendered powerless. Again they say that at the Conception of her Son her grace was finally consummated. Some have gone so far as to say that she was now made so perfect that she could no longer advance in perfection. Others, as Albertus Magnus, speak of three plenitudes of grace in Mary, the first of which they call the plenitude of sufficiency, which she had from the beginning, the second of which they call the plenitude of abundance, which she received at this point of her life, when she conceived her Son by the operation of the Holy Ghost, and the last, the plenitude of singular excellence, which she gained in the remainder of her earthly course. Suarez adds that we may form a reasonable conjecture, in support of this doctrine of her wonderful increase in sanctity at this time, from the facts of the Visitation which took place so soon afterwards. For then the presence of our Lord sanctified the blessed Precursor in the womb of his mother, and St. Elisabeth herself was filled with the Holy Ghost. If these saints were to profit so much by the mere visit of our Lord in His Mother's womb, how much more must she have profited by His continual abiding in that most pure womb? And if He could bestow such abundant graces on those who were so comparatively distant from Him and loved by Him so far less, how much more must He not have done in the way of sanctification, for her who was so close to Him, His own Mother, so far dearer to Him than all creation beside herself?

Before we pass on to the sequel of this mystery in the visit of our Blessed Lady to St. Elisabeth, it will be well to dwell for a moment on the comparison, or rather the contrast, which the history has so often suggested to the Fathers between the first and the second Eve. The simple fact of the contrast being so often drawn, and drawn by some of the very earliest of the Christian writers, shows that it is not independent of a tradition, which those Fathers probably inherited from the Jewish Church, of the great position of our Blessed Lady in the counsels of God and also in the records of prophecy. It is not likely that these early Fathers would have made the comparisons which they do make, unless there had been some such traditional interpretation not only of the history but also of the prophecy.

Something has been said on this subject in the former volume, to which the present is a sequel, and the present place is the natural place for the fuller drawing out of the parallel suggested by these most ancient Fathers.

In the first place, then, the very name given to Eve by her husband, which was not given till after the Fall, is a kind of anticipation of our Blessed Lady, as if Adam had called his wife "the mother of all living,"—whereas she was in truth the mother of all doomed to die, who had introduced death into the world, and entailed the heritage of misery on all her descendants,—on account of the prophecy by which the sorrows of the Fall had been so mercifully assuaged. This point in the comparison is brought out by St. Epiphanius and others.[2] "If you consider only external things and things obvious to sense," he says, "the origin of the whole human race on earth is derived from this same Eve. But in truth it was from the Virgin Mary that the Life itself was introduced into the world, so that Mary should bring forth the Living One and be the Mother of the living. . . . "Another thing also may be considered in each, that is, in Eve and Mary, and indeed a thing worthy of wonder, since Eve brought to the human race the cause of death, by which death was imported into the world, Mary furnished the cause of life by which Life itself was produced for us. For that cause the Son of God came into this world, that "where the offence abounded, there also grace might abound more."[3] Whence death had come, thence life drew nigh, that in the place of death

[2] Epiph. Hær. lxxviii. n. 18.   [3] Rom. v. 20.

life might succeed, that He our Life Who was born of woman that He might be our Life, might shut out from us the death which had been brought in by a woman. But because while, being yet a virgin, Eve dwelt in the garden, she had there offended God by disobedience, so from the Virgin came the obedience to which grace belongs, when the advent of the Incarnate Word made flesh, and of the Eternal life from heaven, was announced to her."

We shall speak presently of the contrast between the obedience of Mary and the disobedience of Eve, which forms the great feature in these comparisons of the Fathers, and which is connected so closely with the antithesis between the disobedience of Adam and the obedience of our Lord on which St. Paul often insists. But another point in the contrast, which is prior in the order of time, is that which relates to the two messengers of evil and of good by whom the two Virgins were addressed at the time of their trial. The one is Satan, and his object is to bring about the ruin of the whole human race by the disobedience of its first parents, and the other is Gabriel, the Angel of the Incarnation, whose object is to bring about the redemption of the whole world by the obedience of our Lord, to which the obedience of His chosen Mother to the Divine decree concerning herself was the necessary preliminary. Each of these Angels, the evil and the good, approaches the object of his message when she is alone. But Mary is praying and Eve is idle. Satan begins by a rude and insolent question, for it called into doubt the wisdom or the goodness of God. Gabriel begins by the salutation of our Lady in holy words which led her mind back to the prophecies and the great promises and works of God. Gabriel says "the Lord is with thee." Satan says "why hath God commanded you that you should not eat of every tree of Paradise?"

Again, the manner in which the temptation on the one hand and the salutation on the other is received is also full of contrast. Mary does not answer. She is alarmed, in the deliberate manner which we have explained, and thinks over in her heart what manner of salutation this may be. That is, she takes refuge in her deep humility, and prepares herself by thoughtful prudence for the best manner of meeting the message which God had sent her. Eve, on the other hand, answers thoughtlessly at once, without guard or precaution, as if there could be no danger in parleying with one who spoke disrespectfully of God. The very words were an invitation to disobedience, for they suggested that God should be taken to task by His creatures, that His motives, and the reasons for His commands, might be examined by those to whom these were given. Eve tells the tempter the whole of the case without reserve. He had said nothing about the tree of life as yet, but she names it as distinct from all the other trees, and she even softens the strength of the prohibition, for she says, "that we should not touch it, lest perhaps we die." Thus she lays herself open to the temptation which was to follow, she almost courts it, she gives every handle to the cunning foe to insinuate it, to induce her to disbelieve and then to disobey God. Satan first suggests disbelief, then he lies concerning God, then he leaves the temptation to work its way with his victim, by telling her that she will gain instead of losing by her disobedience. The miserable apostate suggests the very motive which had been the cause of his own fall, for he says, "you shall be as gods," and he had fallen for daring to be ambitious of rising to an equality with God.

On the other hand St. Gabriel sets before our Blessed Lady the most magnificent acts in her favour on the part of God Himself, and he uses the prophetic words with which she was familiar in conveying his message. Mary must have understood from the first, not indeed the manner in which the great counsels of God were to be executed in her, but the character of the work for the sake of which her consent was asked, both that it was a work decreed by God from the beginning, and that it was the work by which He was to be most highly glorified and the human race redeemed. Eve considered only the satisfaction that she might derive from the eating of the fruit. " The woman saw that the tree was good to eat, and fair to the eyes and pleasant to behold, and she took of the fruit thereof and did eat and gave to her husband and he did eat." Mary, on the other hand, hung back from the honour out of humility, and out of her love for chastity, and when she gave her consent after the last words of St. Gabriel, it was given simply on the ground of obedience, not of the glory and dignity to which she was herself to be raised.

With Eve the question of obedience or disobedience counted for nothing, with Mary nothing counted but the motive of obedience. Obedience was the one virtue by which it pleased God to test His children in the Garden of Paradise. Obedience was the appointed virtue by which the world was to be redeemed by the Son of Mary. The obedience of Mary was not the cause of our redemption, but it was the forerunner of the obedience of our Lord, and it made the Incarnation possible in the manner in which God had decreed it. The disobedience of Eve was not the cause of the ruin of the human race, because we fell in Adam, not in his wife. But the disobedience of Eve led to the disobedience of Adam, by means of which we all fell, only to be redeemed by the Son of her who said, " behold the handmaid of the Lord, be it done to me according to thy word." Eve was persuaded to doubt the word of God, daring to hope that it should not be with her and Adam according to His word. Mary believed the word of God sent to her by St. Gabriel, and obeyed at once and with the most perfect faithfulness.

Thus it is not wonderful that we find these early Fathers, St. Justin Martyr, St. Irenæus and Tertullian, attributing such marvellous efficacy to the obedience of Mary. St. Justin[4] says that by the same way by which the disobedience was brought about by the serpent, by the same way it was to be put an end to. " Eve, while a virgin, and incorrupt, took in the discourse of the serpent and brought forth disobedience and death : but the Virgin Mary, who had received faith and joy, answered the Angel Gabriel, announcing to her good tidings, namely, that the Holy Ghost should

[4] St. Justin, *Dial. a Tryph.* n. 100.

come upon her and the power of the Most High overshadow her, and that therefore the Holy One to be born of her was to be the Son of God, saying, 'behold the handmaid of the Lord, be it done to me according to thy word.'" St. Justin is followed by St. Irenæus his contemporary, who dwells in the same way on the contrast between the obedience of Mary and the disobedience of Eve, and goes still further on in attributing to the obedience of the one the reparation of the disobedience of the other. "So the knot of the disobedience of Eve receives its solution by the obedience of Mary, for that which the virgin Eve bound by incredulity, that the Virgin Mary loosened by faith."[5] This same thought St. Irenæus repeats in the famous passage in which he says that our Blessed Lady became the advocate[6] of Eve, a passage of which we have not the original Greek. And there is the same doctrine contained in the passage from Tertullian usually quoted in this connection, in which he says, that "Eve gave credence to the serpent, and Mary gave credence to Gabriel, and the sin committed by the credulity of Eve was blotted out by the faith of Mary."

It does not seem as if these ancient Fathers, representing, as has been pointed out by Cardinal Newman, Syria and the Holy Land, the East, Africa, Rome, as well as Gaul, could be fairly understood as meaning less than this in their estimate of the position of our Blessed Lady in the work of our redemption—that she has as much to do with our Redemption as Eve had to do with

[5] St. Iren. liii. 22, (33) n. 4. See also lib. v. 19.
[6] Tertull. de Carne Christi, c. 17.

our Fall. It is untheological to say that we fell in Eve, as has been just now remarked, and it may be equally untheological to say that we are redeemed by Mary. But it is the simple truth to say that our Fall was through Eve and it is equally true to say that our Redemption comes through Mary. No other way of speaking can be said to satisfy the circumstances of the case. Eve was a willing, an active, a deliberate, a responsible agent in the work of our ruin. Mary is the same in every respect in the work of our Redemption. Neither of them was simply an involuntary unconscious instrument, whether of our Fall, or of our restoration. And yet this truth, when considered in all that it involves and implies in the counsels of God, and in His ways of dealing with us, contains all that has ever been said of the greatness of our debt to our Blessed Lady in respect of the Incarnation, all that her most devout children have said concerning her marvellous dignity or her mighty power with God for us. Thus we may place this account of the Annunciation by the side of the opening words of St. John's Gospel in its theological importance. The opening words of St. John, "In the beginning was the Word" and the rest, correspond to the account of the Creation in the first verses of Genesis. They are the relation of the beginning of the new Creation. These verses of St. Luke about the Annunciation correspond to the passage in Genesis in which the history of his Fall is given. They contain the history of the reparation of the Fall, and of the fulfilment of the promise immediately made to Adam and Eve, by the gift to mankind of Jesus and Mary.

CHAPTER VII.

OUR LORD'S LIFE IN THE WOMB.

ONE great Divine reason for the immense addition of graces and spiritual gifts which we believe to have been bestowed upon our Blessed Lady immediately after the Incarnation, must be found in the new position in which she was placed to our Lord as His Mother. This relation included a great variety of duties and opportunities, and on these we do not propose to linger in the present chapter. There is one most important element in this new position which should not be left unmentioned from the very first. The change which had taken place in the world was infinite in its intrinsic wonderfulness, and also in the duties which it imposed on the whole of Creation. God had become a creature. The material universe had now in its midst its Lord and Sovereign, not as He had always been in every part of the world which He had made, but in a new mode of existence, and that a human mode. He had made Himself an Infant. He was still and could never fail to be the Lord and God of all, but He was now present among His creatures as one of them. He had thrown Himself upon them, leaving the throne and the glory and the majesty and the endless worship of

Heaven behind Him, and He made Himself dependent on them for the homage and honour due to Him.

It sometimes happens in a land like our own, that a lonely priest begins a humble mission in some upper room, or in the kitchen of a cottage which he has hired. He is sent in the hope that he may gather around him some few poor peasants, the workmen on a railway, or the toilers in a factory. He has no home but that which he is obliged to use also for the time as his temporary chapel, and in the safest and loneliest spot in the little dwelling he raises a poor altar. He does his best for its decoration. Some poor servants help him with their savings, he is able to set apart altogether the small but decent room in which the altar is raised, and there, some morning, he has the happiness, not only of celebrating the Adorable Sacrifice, but of consecrating a few hosts, and enshrining the ciborium which contains them in a modest tabernacle. There for the first time since the change of religion, the Blessed Sacrament is reserved in that village or suburb. God has come to make His dwelling among men. The world around knows nothing of its Neighbour. No one suspects that in that little upstair sanctuary is dwelling the God of gods, and Lord of lords. The house is the same as before, the village is the same as before, men come and go, and pass and chat, it may be they offend the Divine Majesty within a few yards of His abode, it may be they lift up their hearts to Him, or resist some temptation, or practise some simple act of charity, or refrain their tongue from evil words and their eyes from licentious looks, close by Him. But all the time the good and the bad alike know nothing of His nearness, they think nothing of the choirs of Angels hovering around, giving to their King and Lord their homage all the more devotedly for the very reason that earth seems to know nothing of Him.

That priest and the few followers of the Faith who are in the secret, feel in their hearts an immense light and happiness indeed, but also an immense weight of responsiblity. They are in trust for the whole neigbourhood around, to show honour to the hidden King. If they fail Him they do so advisedly and knowingly, and they feel that on their faithfulness may depend the issue, whether the boon of His presence is to be continued to their homes and their neighbours, or whether it is to be taken away again, never to return. Such in kind, though far greater in degree and intensity, must have been the feelings of the Blessed Mother of God at once, after the Incarnation. Mary understood what had taken place, as no one else could understand the condescension of God. She knew His worth and rights, as no one among the highest seraphs knew them. She knew what was the blessing of His presence, and what the dues to His Majesty. But He was her own. No ordinary presence, even as of the Blessed Sacrament in the tabernacle was that in which He dwelt in her. He had taken His Flesh and His Blood from her substance. He lived by her life. He was sustained in His human existence by her. She was nearer to Him than the priest who offers Him on the Altar, nearer to him than the Angels who kneel in adoration wherever He is to be found; Flesh of her flesh, Bone of her bone. And He was her own in the other sense, which involves so infinite a trust, so limitless a responsibility. She alone knew of Him. She alone was to discharge the duties of the whole visible creation in honour of Him, thanking Him, adoring Him, praising Him, loving Him for His condescension. If we can suppose heaven emptied of its citizens, and one Angel alone left to adore the Divine Presence of the Ever-Blessed Trinity, we might compare that Angel's thoughts with those of Mary.

It will certainly help us to understand the immense grace required for a position of this kind, to consider a little what that life was of our Lord which began at the moment of the Incarnation, and continued uninterruptedly for the nine months which had to pass before the first Christmas Day. It is a part of what we term in general the Holy Infancy which has a kingdom of its own in Christian devotion, like the devotion to the Babe of Bethlehem, or to the many years of the Hidden Life at Nazareth. It contains both these, for it is the Babe of Bethlehem Who is dwelling in the womb of Mary. And never was He nearly so much hidden, even in the quietest years of His life at Nazareth, as during these nine months. It is clear that each part of this great devotion has its own features and characteristics. It is also clear that this phase of it can have been practised by no one from the beginning but our Blessed Lady herself, though at a point of time which is not directly discernible, it must have spread to St. Joseph, St. Elisabeth, St. John Baptist, St. Zachary. Moreover, it may have become known before the time came for the journey to Bethlehem to others of the immediate relatives of our Lady or her holy Spouse. We shall attempt in the few following paragraphs to give a short sketch of the considerations on which this great devotion has to feed itself.

God might have become man without going through all the ordinary stages of human existence, including the first stage of all, the nine months in the womb of a Mother. But He did not choose to be different from us in this respect, and the consequence of His condescension is that we have to contemplate the theological truths which are involved therein. We cannot imagine that this chain of wonderful and beautiful truths was unknown to our Blessed Lady and to St. Joseph, and to the other Saints mentioned above, in the order of time in which it pleased God that it should become known. It is natural to think that the homage due to God Who had made Himself a creature was entrusted to them, and that it was not to be delayed until the humble birth at Bethlehem. We must suppose that God did not leave His own greatest work unrecognized and unhonoured, even though all the homage of Angels and saints may be as nothing before Him. A very short survey of this great field of contemplation, as we may suppose it to have been laid open to Mary and to others after her, must be enough for us here.

The history begins with the Fiat of Mary. At that moment, as has been already said, our theology teaches us that, by the action of the Holy Ghost, a part of her most pure blood was formed into the perfect Body which was to be that of our Lord, and that at the same time, God created the Human Soul which was to dwell in that Body. Mary received, at the same time, a marvellous increase of grace and knowledge, corresponding, as it were, to her elevation at that moment to be the Mother of God. The Body was made small, as that of other infants, it was made, as the saints tell us, not only most beautiful, but also most delicate, and capable of the utmost suffering, while the glory, impassibility, and other gifts which were connatural to a body which was to be the body of a Divine Person, were suspended, in order that the decrees of God might be carried out in it. The Soul which was created for it had all the natural excellencies which became it, and it was enriched also by immense gifts of grace. We are forced to put all these things in some succession, but the act of God in them all was simultaneous and in a moment. So also was the essential and substantial act of the Incarnation itself, by which the soul and the body which were created and united, became the Soul and the Body of the Eternal Son, made Man. Here is enough for Angels and saints to feed on in endless contemplation. But the knowledge of these marvels implies praise, wonder, adoration, thanksgiving, oblation, and other affections, and it is natural to suppose that these were paid duly at the time, as the knowledge concerning them was communicated to them, both by Mary and by Joseph. It is unreasonable, with the Scriptural account of the Visitation before us, to exclude from this reverent worship either St. John, or his parents, St. Elisabeth and St. Zachary. Beyond these, it must be left to devout conjecture alone to extend the range of the human worshippers of the Infant God. But at the time of which we speak, Mary alone possessed the secret.

The next great field of contemplation under this head, is that which contains the consideration of the excellencies of the Sacred Humanity. It became at once the highest of all God's creatures, present, past, and future, for all that God Himself can create and elevate must be lower than that Humanity which is His own. The union with the Divine Word implied the communication of all the Divine Perfections, and the right to the adoration and homage of Angels, men, and all creatures. It implied the sanctification of that Soul by the substantial sanctity of God, and its being made, not only essentially holy in itself, but the source and origin of the sanctification of others. To say that it was absolutely and necessarily impeccable, and free from the faintest shadow of the sin which other infants contract in their conception, is superfluous. It was the Soul of the Incarnate God. It was full of all grace, and the source and fountain of grace for others. It was adorned with every possible virtue in the highest perfection, so that it could not, in the strictest sense of the words, advance and increase in grace or in virtue. It was full of all knowledge and all wisdom, knowledge of God, of itself, of all things. It knew the past, the present, the future perfectly. Angels and men, and all other creatures, lay open before it, to the very inmost thoughts and movements of their affections and intelligences, the good, and the evil, and the imperfect, in all, as clearly as all will lie open before Him when He sits at the last day to judge the world. And all the treasures of wisdom and knowledge thus communicated to His Soul, our Lord directed from the first in the most perfect manner to the love and service of His Father.

The seven gifts, as we call them, of the Holy Ghost were in their consummate perfection in the Soul of our Lord at the first. The gift of wisdom was in Him a most lofty contemplation and a most loving enjoyment of all the mysteries and secrets of God, a gaze full of intense love and joy on His infinite perfections, attributes, designs, judgments, and ways. The gift of intelligence or understanding showed Him among other things, all that had been arranged and decreed and foretold concerning Himself; the plan of His life and the measure of His work from His birth to the end, with all the circumstances of His wonderful actions and ineffable sufferings. The gift of counsel in the same way, showed Him exactly what to do in every occasion, what was the best in every conjuncture, how every moment of His life was to be most perfectly spent and employed, for the glory of the Father. The gift of fortitude secured the most ready and punctual and complete execution of whatever the gift of counsel showed Him to be done. So it was with the other gifts. His gift of knowledge opened to His soul the full and penetrating insight into all created things, what was their real value according to the designs of their Creator, their end, their use, their relative worth or worthlessness. His piety filled Him with the tenderest and most just affections of reverence and love towards His Father, His Blessed Mother, St. Joseph, and all those with whom He was immediately concerned, and also to all men, all Angels, and all creatures which have been created by God, all in their due rank and proportion; all loved and honoured with the true and most faithful and most appreciative affection and dutifulness of His Heart. And lastly the gift of fear was in Him in perfection in that way in which it could be in Him, that is, a perfect awe and respect for the greatness of God and all that is His and comes from Him, a deep sense of loving dependence on Him as His creature the work of His Hands, in Whom all things live and are and subsist.

It is needless to say that this beautiful Soul in itself, and apart from the life which it was to lead, and which it began at once to lead, in the full exercise of all its faculties in the womb of Mary, was the object of the most tender joy and complacency and delight to God. The Eternal Father rejoiced to see His Son clothed with that human nature in which He was to do so much for the glory of His Father and for the benefit of mankind, out of love for His Father and for our salvation. It was a part of this joy and complacency that He had made Mary His Mother so full of grace and every perfection, and raised her to a dignity so high in heaven and on earth. And He rejoiced also in all the treasures of grace which the Sacred Humanity had received for us, and for the use which His Son was to make of them in distributing them so largely and bountifully among men, thus producing a glory and a beatitude which are to last for endless ages in the next world. It was a joy to the Eternal Son that He was now at last become Man and able to carry out the designs of His Eternal love for the Father and for us, that He could now unite to the Human Nature which He had chosen all His Divine perfections and powers, and He rejoiced especially in the humiliation which this union implied for Himself, because it was the Will of His Father. It was a joy to the Holy Spirit to see His work accomplished, and that Human Nature perfected by the union with the Divine Person of the Word, into which He was to pour all His gifts and graces in order that they might be communicated to us.

We must next pass on to the Life of our Lord in the womb of His Mother. It was a Life that began at once in full vigour of mind and heart, a vigour which was to last on throughout all eternity. It was a Divine Life, wholly directed to the glory of God, a Life of merit in His sight so great as to suffice for the redemption and glorification of a thousand worlds. It was a Life which was not His own, inasmuch as it was from the first devoted to God and to us. The Soul of Jesus was perfectly conscious of, and took immense delight in, its own elevation, its union with the Divine Person, its immense gifts and privileges, its prerogative as the source of all spiritual blessings to our Lady, St. Joseph, all the saints and all the faithful, the possible source of infinite blessings to infinite numbers of souls that would never actually enjoy them. All the blessings, actual and possible, and all the souls to whom they were to be given or might have been given, were perfectly present to it from the first moment. It began at once its life of interior work for God, with the utmost fervour, with unrelenting perseverance, with the utmost purity of intention, and with the full, tranquil, and deliberate purpose to gain all the holiest ends for which such actions could be offered. The Soul of our Lord at once saw God perfectly with the plenitude of beatific vision, and here again it had this not only for Itself, but also for others. To see God was to understand His infinite greatness, to adore Him with the most perfect worship as a creature, to love Him most intensely, and all creatures in Him and for Him, and especially men who had been made our Lord's brethren by the Incarnation. Then followed gratitude, thanksgiving in His own Heart, and in the heart of His Mother. For the *Magnificat* reveals to us, as we shall see, what it was that our Lord inspired in her at that time. And, as far as was consistent with God's decree, and in due time, in the hearts of the other Saints of the Incarnation, Joseph, Elisabeth, Zachary, John, the same holy exercise was kindled into life by the presence and grace of our Lord.

This blessed Soul also saw and understood the human world into which He had come, Mary, His own Mother, Joseph, whose office was to be His Father, St. John His Precursor, and the whole race of man, past, present, future. Then came the vision of the miserable state of the race of which He was now one, its need of redemption and restoration, and the will of the Father that this should be His work. This led to His oblation of Himself for this purpose, of which St. Paul speaks in the Epistle to the Hebrews, to His renouncement of the rights of His Body, in order that He might suffer, and the rest. The whole of His own future on earth and in Heaven, as well as that of all souls, was clearly manifested to Him.

There is another head of consideration on this subject which is found in the virtues which were especially practised by our Lord in this life of His in the womb. He was of course, at this, as at all times of His Life, the pattern of all virtues, but there are some which seem more particularly to belong to this period, on account of the conditions under which His marvellous existence was carried on, as there are other similar circumstances in His Life in the Blessed Sacrament, to which this life in the womb of Mary bears so much resemblance. Thus it may be said that our Lord was Incarnate at the bidding of obedience, inasmuch as it was an act of obedience on the part of His Mother that made the Incarnation possible in the counsels of God and actual when it took place. Our Lady's words, "be it done to me according to thy word," were the signal for the Incarnation. He remained in the womb, notwithstanding the perfection of His Manhood both in soul and body, for the full natural space of the nine months, out of obedience to the usual laws in such cases. And one of His occupations in the womb was to offer Himself continually to be obedient, not only to His Eternal Father for Whose love He became Incarnate, but also to all who in any way or measure represented Him, as our Lady His Mother, St. Joseph who was to be in the place of His Father, and even to all authorities lay or ecclesiastical who had derived their power from Him.

In the same way, when we consider the perfection of our Lord from the moment of His Conception in intelligence and the use of His faculties, we cannot but be astounded at the extreme lengths to which He went in His humiliations during this interval before His birth. The Church sings of Him, " Thou didst not abhor the Virgin's womb," and although those words of hers may have more than one meaning, they seem to express her sense of the depths of His humiliation. It was in a manner fitting in the ways of God and to the character of our Lord, that when He had received in His Human Nature the very highest possible exaltation by the union with the Divine Person of the Word, He should at once seek to humble Himself to the very utmost, by His imprisonment in the womb of His Mother. And yet this does not adequately express the humiliation of our Lord, on account of His perfect consciousness and possession of all His faculties. For these enabled Him to surpass the actual humiliation of His sojourn in the womb by the affections of humiliation which His Sacred Heart conceived while there, in which He desired and decreed to humble Himself not only before God His Father and Lord, but beneath the feet of the lowest and vilest of His creatures.

Another special virtue of this period of our Lord's life is His marvellous meekness. God has become

Man, but He has laid aside the majesty and the mightiness in which He appeared of old, as when He gave the Law on Mount Sinai. He is especially, as He delights to call Himself, for our sake, meek and humble of Heart, and He begins the practice of this virtue in the womb of His meek and humble Mother. He begins at once to appease the anger of His Father towards men, by this extreme meekness, and He prepares Himself, as it might seem, by the practice of this most beautiful virtue from the beginning, for that exercise of it towards men in His later life which made it His most characteristic virtue. The same may be said of His practice of the love of poverty. For He is here entirely dependent on His Mother for sustenance, and He has, as the Apostle says, being rich, made Himself poor for our sakes, that He might communicate to us the true riches of heaven. And this poverty which He began to practice now He continued throughout His whole Life.

Patience, the suffering of all inconveniences and incommodities, is another of these virtues of this stage of the Infancy. This again was more to Him than to others, on account of the perfection of the use of all His faculties which was from the very beginning, and even this suffering of confinement and straitness and darkness and the like He increased, by the interior acts of His patience. For in the womb itself He was continually looking forward to the torments which He was to undergo, far greater and more painful than those sufferings which He then actually experienced, and His Heart stretched itself also to that tender sympathy which made Him make His own all the sufferings of others in the world, especially those which were to be undergone in any way for His sake, or by those who specially belonged to Him. There remain a few other virtues more particularly practised in the womb by our Lord. Such was in a special manner the exercise of prayer and contemplation, which formed the most direct occupation of the Sacred Heart during these months, in which our Lord engaged Himself in the contemplation of His Father's greatness, and also in the prayerful compassion for our miseries. Such was also the practice of silence, the inseparable companion and guardian of prayer and the spirit of prayer, in which it is needless to say, the time of our Lord's existence was entirely spent. Such was the love of perfect retirement for the sake of being alone with God, a virtue of which we have many examples of our Lord recorded even in His most active Life, but which belongs in a special manner and degree to the Holy Infancy all through, but particularly to the Infancy before the Nativity.

In all these points it is natural to suppose that our Lord's Life in the womb was understood by His Blessed Mother, at least, from the very beginning. It was her special duty and delight to adore Him in this stage of His infinite condescension, all the more because she was either entirely or nearly alone among mankind in having any cognisance of these humiliations and virtues. This would be occupation enough to feed her soul and heart. But there are other ranges of truth connected with the Infantine existence of our Lord, of which we have not yet spoken. For we have said nothing as yet of the titles and prerogatives of our Lord, which were His by right from the first moment of the Incarnation, and which called for the homage and acknowledgment of His creatures, all the more because they were His for their sakes. Such was His Royal Majesty, His headship of the human race and of all creation, His Power as Lawgiver, as Redeemer, as the Light and Sanctification of the world, as the Prince of Peace, our Spouse, our Pastor, our Example. He is not more truly King of Heaven and of earth, now that He reigns at the Right Hand of the Father, than He was when Mary carried Him in her womb. But now His Throne is honoured by the incense of the continual adoration of millions of Saints and Angels, and the homage of all earth and heaven. Then He was unknown on earth, and the multitudes of His Saints had not been admitted to heaven, which He was to open to them as the fruit of His humiliations. All the particulars of His condition were manifested to His Mother.

It was Mary's office to honour Him in the name of all, to sympathise with His humiliation and His sufferings, to join her heart with His in the continual stream of loving acts of thankfulness and adoration and self-oblation which rose from Him before the throne of His Father. We see some of the breathings of the Sacred Heart in the *Magnificat* of which we shall presently have to speak, and we cannot doubt that the presence of our Lord with her in this most marvellous way was a grace which raised her daily higher and higher in her most consummate perfection. We are nowhere told of the secret intercourse and converse, which united the Hearts of Jesus and Mary in a continual exchange of the most fervent affections at this time. This is a secret of heaven, though we cannot doubt that every movement and thought of our Blessed Lady must have been divinely influenced thereby. No heart was like hers for perfect docility to interior movements and the inspirations of God, and it is natural to think that no heart was more likely to receive them in so great abundance and magnificence. Her position with regard to our Blessed Lord was altogether unique, in heaven and on earth.

If our Lord can be so lavish of His interior converse, as we see Him to have been in the case of some of the saints of whose interior history we know the most, revealing Himself especially to them with the utmost familiarity at times such as that of Holy Communion, it is only rational to think that His communications of His secrets and His intercourse, Heart to heart, with His Blessed Mother, must have been far surpassing anything of which record remains to us. The ecstasies and raptures of the saints who have been most favoured in this respect, in which their existence seems to have been altogether absorbed and their ordinary life superseded, need not be looked for in her who was so much nearer to Divine things than anyone else could be. Thus she could bear the most wonderful communications of a supernatural kind without having the calm tenour of her life disturbed thereby. It is not surprising that nothing of this kind should be recorded of our Blessed Lady, that the very scanty accounts which have reached us of her, represent her as walking on from day to day, without anything about her to attract notice from men. But the thoughts on which we have been dwelling may show how unlikely it would be that she should have been left without the perfect intelligence of the mystery that had taken place in her, in all its bearings. And if this is supposed to have been the case, we can understand how sublime and interior a life she must now have led until the time when our Lord came forth from her sacred womb in the stable of Bethlehem.

CHAPTER VIII.

THE VISITATION.

St. Luke i. 39—56.   *Vita Vitæ Nostræ*, § 5.

THERE can be little doubt that the Annunciation and the Incarnation were immediately followed by the Visitation, as we call it, of our Blessed Lady. The manner in which this mystery is related by St. Luke, who seems to speak of our Lady as if she were altogether alone in her journey, both to the house of her cousin, and when she returned thence to Nazareth, suggests the opportunity of some remarks on the relation of these Gospel narratives to the actual history which it is well to make at the outset of the part of our work on which we are now engaged. It is well also to remind ourselves of certain truths concerning the manner of the dealings of God with souls, as well as concerning the formation of the Gospel history as we have to form it, which may help us the better to understand the narrative on which we shall now for some time be occupied. We shall speak first of these ways of God in general.

No thoughtful person can doubt that one of the most beautiful parts of God's dealings with His creatures is the manner of His conduct of single souls, one by one, along the path which His Providence has chosen for them. His wisdom, His love,

His patience, His foresight, His indulgence, and other wonderful attributes, shine out more and more conspicuously, in proportion as we come to be able to understand these methods. But in our present state of imperfect knowledge and feeble intelligence, the whole of this great range of the works of God can hardly be said to be within our reach. His thoughts are not as our thoughts, and His ways are not as our ways. He reserves to Himself the knowledge of the human heart, and we are consequently without even the preliminary and elementary knowledge of His own action thereon. All that we can say is that the little which we know shows us how wonderful and beautiful the whole must be.

But it must be remembered that God has not only a special treatment for each one of His children, but that He deals with us all, not singly, as if there were no other soul in the world but our own, but by using us for the instruction, edification, enlightenment or crucifixion one of another, in such a way that the threads of each life which He guides so unerringly are intertwined with the threads of all the lives of all those we come across, those with whom we live, those above us or under us, our friends and our enemies, our family, and strangers with whom we are thrown into contact, and that no eye but His own can trace out the innumerable influences under which our character is formed and our trial carried out, the services we render one another, the mischiefs we do one to another. A man's character is affected by his home, and by his companions outside his home, and he works in his turn on all around. A family is tinged, or stained, or elevated, by every single member of all of whom it is made up. An accident, as it seems, takes away the mother, or the father, or chains some one of the children to a sick bed, deprives the brothers of the softening influence of their sisters, or leavens the whole by the introduction of some single stranger, a teacher, or a servant. Nothing of this kind is without its influence, and, if this be so, how multitudinous are the influences under which we live! Who can think out all the effects that he has experienced, from what seem chance events, meetings, separations, bereavements, connections? Yet all these things and a thousand others are managed for us by the forethought and decree of God. We can only repeat that His ways are not as our ways, and His thoughts are not as our thoughts. Each soul is the subject of a separate discipline and treatment by Him, and He arranges the thousand lives which are continually interlacing, in such a way as to make the discipline He allots to each one have on all the others, in the degree in which He so wills it, the effect He intends for each.

Let us apply this to the case of our Blessed Lady and St. Joseph. It has been said that in the case of the frequent miraculous or marvellous Conceptions, of which mention is to be found in the annals of Sacred Scripture, it had usually been the case for the husband of the mother of the saint or hero who was to be born to be told beforehand of the promised Conception of the child. Every thought in our Blessed Lady was perfectly well ordered and calm. Her mind was not so overpowered, even by the greatness of the message of the Angel or of the mystery which followed on that message, that she could forget her natural ties and relationships, and especially those which connected her with St. Joseph. It is true that he could have nothing to do with the mystery which was to be carried out by the operation of the Holy Ghost. But she was still his wife, still bound to him by the closest affection, an affection only deepened and intensified by the union of hearts between them on that very point of the preservation of the most perfect purity. The great elevation which had come to her, and which had made her the Mother of God, did not destroy the duties, the relations, the dependence on him to which her marriage vow bound her. But she had received no commission or hint to inform him of what had passed. Nor was she told how or when the communication would be made to him.

It is impossible that our Lady could fail to notice this omission, and to understand that it must have a meaning and a purpose. Here, amid all the joy and the responsibility which had come to her was a question which she might ask herself, and await the solution in the Providence of God. It cannot be doubtful that she must have longed, in the calm and perfectly submissive manner in which she could long for any thing not yet declared as the will of God, for the moment when he whom she loved so tenderly could share her happiness and give her his sympathy and assistance in the great work laid upon her of honouring the Incarnate King of heaven and earth. But the "times or moments," as our Lord said to His Apostles just before his Ascension, are kept by God in His own power, and it is not for us to know them. One of the delicate methods which He often adopts for the eliciting some very beautiful exercises of virtue, is the delay of something desired, the selection by Himself of the proper moment, sooner or later, when something is to be done or to be made known. He is as wonderful in His choice of moments as in His choice of instruments and of means. He makes perfect and ripens souls like flowers, one by one, and His beautiful working on each must take its own time. We cannot doubt that this, too, was well understood by our Blessed Lady. It was one of the things she would keep and ponder in her heart, that God must have some beautiful design of His own with regard to her Spouse. She would not indulge her natural affection so far as to ask, as St. Peter asked about St. John, "Lord, and this man, what?" when our Lord answered him almost severely, "what is it to thee?"[1]

It appears to have been the plan of God that St. Joseph, whatever he might think or surmise, or even know, in a human and ordinary way, concerning the mystery which had taken place, was to be left without any Divine direction concerning it until the time came when his own action was requisite for the carrying on of the sacred mystery. In this God only proceeded in the way which He so often follows, of leaving His saints in the dark about His future decrees concerning themselves, until the necessary moment comes. For the delay which is thus secured for the silent working of His graces in the hearts which are so dear to Him, is often the

[1] St. John xxi. 23.

most precious opportunity which is afforded them in a whole life, for the exercise of the most sublime virtues. It may be a period of exquisite trial, but of trial exquisitely corresponded to, by a patience, a humility, a charity, a prudence, and an exercise of confidence in God under difficulties, which may win for the person who is thus tried the very highest of crowns. It was characteristic of Eve that she should go at once to Adam with her miserable discovery of the sweetness of the forbidden fruit. Mary kept her secret to herself and to her God, leaving it to Him to reveal it in His own time and way to St. Joseph, confident that the time and the way which He would choose would be the best for her and the best for her Spouse. We can hardly imagine her speaking before she had the command to speak. She might hope, but she could not know, what was to be the counsel of God as to her husband's future position to her or her Child. But in so mighty and lofty a mystery every detail was in the hand of God alone. That the Holy Family was to have a divinely appointed head, and that that head was to be St. Joseph, was a decision not yet manifested, and which could not be taken for granted.

Never, in truth, have the servants of God been otherwise than silent and secret as to the favours He has bestowed upon them or the great commissions which He has confided to them. To speak of such things without necessity would be altogether inconsistent with the saintly character. On the other hand, God was to give to St. Joseph the opportunity of that peculiar and unique trial to which his faithfulness was exposed, and which we shall have presently to endeavour to explain. There would have been no room for this, which was the condition, in a certain sense, of that incomparable eminence which he was to attain in the kingdom of God, if the common ways of human action had been followed, and the husband of Mary immediately informed, on the authority of God, of the mystery which had been carried out in her womb by the operation of the Holy Ghost, and of the position which he was himself to occupy in relation to the mystery. Thus we see in this, as in all the delays of God, that He holds back from what seems to us so natural and so much an object of desire, for the wisest reasons, in order to make the boon when granted more precious, the grace when won more deep and lasting, the joy more intense, the blessing in itself greater, because conferred on a soul more fitted by expectation, trial, and desire for the reception of the highest graces. While we are tempted to chafe in impatience, God is ripening the soul in which we are interested for gifts more excellent, and the glory so long delayed is all the more splendid, when it comes as the conquest of prayer and the crown of the patient exercise of virtue.

It will be well also in the present place, to make a few remarks on the narratives of the two Evangelists, St. Matthew and St. Luke, on whom we are dependent for our information concerning these early mysteries of the Gospel history. It is necessary to repeat over and over again, that we must always bear in mind the scope and aim of each single Evangelist, in considering the relation of what he has written for us to the statements of any other, and also to the general course of the history independently of its particular annalists. We have no single continuous narrative of these events. We have two independent statements, not covering the same ground, nor professing, even together, to make up a continuous account of all that happened. Each Evangelist leaves out much. We implied just now that there is an instinct of silence about holy persons, especially about those who are the chief personages in the Gospel history. There is also a rule of silence in the Evangelical historians themselves, as to those circumstances of the story which do not directly refer to the object which each one of the several writers has in view. That St. Matthew omits much and that St. Luke omits much which might have been said, is obvious at first sight. We have to make up one complete account, not only by joining the two narratives together, but also by reminding ourselves of much which is not directly mentioned by either, but which must have taken place, and which is implied in what they say, or in what we know from other sources.

We have an instance of this last class of facts in what has been said of the vow by which Mary, and, as it seems certain, St. Joseph also were bound. This vow is nowhere mentioned, but we are as certain of it as if it had been mentioned, from the words of our Blessed Lady to the Angel at the Annunciation. If we continue our examination of the narrative of St. Luke, on which we shall now have to comment in reference to the mystery of the Visitation, we shall see at once that it has to do with nothing which did not take place in and with regard to our Blessed Lady herself. St. Joseph is not mentioned, from the time at which his name occurs as the husband to whom our Lady was espoused when St. Gabriel was sent to her, till the time when he is mentioned as going up to Bethlehem to be enrolled with Mary his wife. Whatever part he may have had in the Visitation is not mentioned, nor is there any mention of his hesitation about taking to him his wife, after she had been found with child by the Holy Ghost, nor does St. Luke tell us how that hesitation was set at rest, by the vision of the Angel enjoining him to take the part of the father of the Child. As far as St. Luke is concerned, there is no word about any of these things.

On the other hand it is equally true that St. Matthew leaves out altogether the mysteries of the Annunciation, the Visitation, and the Nativity itself. He says nothing at all about the reason which took the Holy Family to Bethlehem before the Nativity. Of course it would be most unreasonable to suppose that the first Evangelist was ignorant of these things. What is essential for us to imprint on our minds is that it would be equally unreasonable to expect him to mention them, unless they fell in with the direct object which he had before him as he wrote, and which he served by mentioning the hesitation of St. Joseph, which proved the Divine and Virginal Conception of our Lord, and the Epiphany, which proved that He ought to have been born as He was born, at Bethlehem, by the witness of the prophecies, interpreted

K

by the Jewish authorities themselves. The two narratives must be understood as each perfectly true and authentic. But no argument can be admitted which rests simply on the silence of either, with regard to some point which it would have been inconsistent for either to have mentioned, considering the direct and only object which that particular Evangelist had before him.

Let us now apply these truths to the narrative before us of the Visitation. It is, as has been said, entirely confined to the briefest possible account of the doings of our Blessed Lady. "And Mary rising up in those days, went into the hill country in haste, into a city of Juda, and she entered into the house of Zachary, and saluted Elisabeth." Such is this simple statement, and, if we were to suppose that it tells us all that passed, we might imagine that our Lady, a young and most modest bride, left her home without any communication with her husband, and travelled a distance of two or three days' journey at least, alone and unguarded. If this had been the case, it is probable we should have been told how it was that so extraordinary a course was taken by her, without any direct guidance from God. It is impossible to suppose, in the first place, that she took this journey without the cognizance and permission of St. Joseph. He had over her movements the rights of a husband, and she is not likely to have been guided to disregard them. The truth is that the Evangelist does not mention what is obvious and what ought to be taken for granted.

In the second place, there is no reason at all for supposing that she took this journey unaccompanied by St. Joseph. The Annunciation took place at the time of the year when it was the custom of the Jews to resort to Jerusalem for the great feast of the Pasch. We know from St. Luke that it was, a few years later than this, the custom of St. Joseph and our Blessed Lady to go up from Nazareth at this time. It is most likely that this devotion had been practised by them from the very beginning. Thus the opportunity for the journey of Mary may well have been furnished by the incidence of the great feast almost immediately after the Annunciation. She might go to Judæa with her husband and on the way to the feast. The town in which St. Zachary and St. Elisabeth lived was some distance beyond Jerusalem, and thus it seems certain that St. Joseph would accompany our Lady, after they had paid their devotions in the Holy City, to the home of her kinswoman. If this was so, we may pause for a moment to reflect on the presence of the Incarnate God, in the womb of His Mother, at this great feast, the same at which He was afterwards to offer Himself as the true Paschal Lamb, and on the affections and thoughts of that Blessed Mother, who had, so few weeks before, perhaps, left those sacred precincts as the Virgin bride of Joseph, thinking only of the holy resolution she had offered to God of perfect purity in the marriage state, and of her great desire to live to see the Incarnation, and be herself the humblest among the handmaidens of the chosen Mother of God. And now she found herself that chosen Mother, and she had already in her womb the promised Saviour of mankind!

The sacred text does not linger on this visit to the Temple which our Blessed Lady may have paid in her passage through Jerusalem, for it dwells on nothing that does not belong strictly to the subject before us. The haste which our Lady used in her journey is directly mentioned, probably because it was desirable to show the quick obedience of the Blessed Virgin to the suggestion of the Angel, a haste perhaps urged on her also by some special impulse of the Holy Ghost. For this language is usual with Sacred Scripture, when the special impulse of the gifts of the Holy Ghost is signified, as when it is said that the Spirit drove our Lord into the desert to be tempted by the devil, and on other such occasions. It would be natural for our Lady, if she once left her home, to hasten on her journey, because it was for her an unusual thing to find herself in public, exposed to the gaze and company of men. "She entered into the house of Zachary," and this shows that she knew it, and that she knew she would be welcome, as among old and dear friends, if on no other grounds connected with the mystery which had made her the Mother of God. Her salutation of St. Elisabeth shows her familiarity with her, and also her humility, for it seems to have been the custom for the lower in rank to salute the higher. She was the Mother of the unborn King, but she would make herself humble in all things, and her motive in this journey, after obedience, may have been principally one of charity, hoping that, as St. Elisabeth was old and infirm, she might be of use in waiting upon her. Nor could she find any occupation more congenial to her own humility than thus to make herself the handmaid of the mother of the Precursor. She had longed, as has been often said, that she might be the servant of the Mother of God and now that she has received herself that unapproachable dignity, she at once lowers herself where she can, and makes herself the servant of Elisabeth.

But though this had been the chief motive of Mary in her journey, God had other and higher aims in bringing it about. For it was His design to use her presence, and that of our Lord in her womb, for the sanctification of St. John in the womb of his mother, and for the filling St. Elisabeth herself with the Holy Ghost and the spirit of prophecy. These great blessings were to be conferred through the presence of our Lady at once, and as she was to remain for nearly three months in the house of her cousin, it must be supposed that the benefit of her abiding presence and continual conversation was not less great than that of her first salutation. God may have had other designs also, with regard to the trial of St. Joseph, but the motive which was present to the mind of the Blessed Mother herself was probably that which has been mentioned, of charity and humility.

The salutation of our Blessed Lady to her cousin was probably the ordinary greeting of love and affection, without more than might show that she was aware of the great blessing which had been vouchsafed to St. Elisabeth. At least we have no mention in the Gospel account of anything more. But the words of Mary, who had within her womb the Incarnate God, were words of power as well as simply significative of the thoughts or goodwill of the speaker. Thus, the moment that they sounded in the ears of St. Elisabeth, two wonderful outpourings of grace followed. The one of them affected the infant Baptist in his mother's womb, while the other wrought wonderful effects in his mother herself. St. Elisabeth was the first to hear the blessed words of the salutation of Mary, but the effect of grace appears to have followed first in her infant son. The words struck on the ears of the mother, but their power first reached the soul of St. John. Their effect was his sanctification in the womb, that gift which had been predicted for him by St. Gabriel, when he was commissioned to announce to his father Zachary the conception of the Precursor. Gabriel had said that he was to be filled with the Holy Ghost even from his mother's womb. The effect which now followed is dwelt on by many of the holy writers of the Church. Up to that moment the soul and body of the Baptist had shared the common lot of the souls and bodies of all infants born of the race of Adam. The soul had been joined to the body at the instant of conception, but the life which they had shared together had been the usual life of obscurity, slow advance in natural growth, the intellectual faculties in germ rather than in activity, with only that kind of animal consciousness which is usual in such cases. They lay under the ban of original sin. The prayers of his holy parents had risen continually for St. John, ever since his conception, but the moment of his delivery from the common state of distance from God had not yet come. He was a holy child, if his parents' merits could have made him holy, but no merits of theirs could roll away for him the cloud which hung over his existence on account of his descent from Adam.

The voice of our Blessed Lady, which conveyed the power of the Divine Infant Who lived in her womb, altered the whole state of the blessed child of Elisabeth. When St. Peter lay in his prison in Jerusalem, the holy text tells us that "an Angel of the Lord stood by him, a light shined in the room, and striking Peter on the side, he raised him up, saying, Arise quickly, and the chains fell off from his hands."[1] This may be taken as a kind of image of what took place in the womb of St. Elisabeth. The voice of the Mother of God was as the Angel who stood by St. Peter. The room was filled with light. That is, the whole existence of the child, dark and sad and sombre before with the overhanging cloud of the displeasure of God, or at least of the absence of His grace, was full of light and joy and life. The chains fell off, the bonds of original sin, the imperfections and penalities of the state of estrangement from his Creator, the miseries of an intelligence merged in torpidity and a will fettered by impotence, a mind clouded with ignorance and a heart in which there had been as yet no spark of love. The Angel said to Peter, "Arise quickly," and the arising of the soul of the child of Elisabeth was rapid indeed. He was at once awakened by Divine grace to the full use of his faculties, and the streams of grace, bearing on their bosom the virtues, theological moral and infused, and the gifts of the Holy

[1] Acts xii. 7.

Ghost, poured themselves into and over his soul. He understood his God, he knew his own relations to Him, the end for which he was made, the office he was to discharge. He broke out at once into the full exercise of faith and hope and charity. He knew the presence of our Lord, he knew Who He was, and what was His work in the world for his salvation and the salvation of all mankind. The change which in others is gradual and progressive, from one point of intelligence to another, was made in him in a moment. He at once became perfect man in the use of his intelligence and will, and in the knowledge of Divine things and of his own duties. The sun rose on him in a moment, without any preceding twilight. And at the presence of his Lord and Saviour, he, the first of all as far as we know, except the Blessed Mother, manifested by outward sign his joy and love and reverence, and homage. He leapt in the womb for joy.

At the same time another great operation of grace was going on in the soul of the blessed Elisabeth herself. It is commonly said by the Fathers who have spoken on this mystery, that the Child was first illuminated and then the mother, and that the Divine illumination passed from the soul of the Child to the soul of the mother, as the power of grace which was exerted in their favour passed first from the Child in the womb of Mary, and then by means of her voice reached the soul of St. John and then the soul of Elisabeth. The Scripture does not tell us the order of these sanctifications, though the opinion of the Fathers is enough for the authority of the account just given. Elisabeth was filled with the Holy Ghost. She received the full illumination needed for her comprehension of the mystery and for her own witness thereto. She may have seen in her cousin, when she first embraced her, nothing more than the marvellously gracious and unearthly maiden whom she may have seen not long before in the precincts of the Temple. She may have known something of her wonderful gifts from her birth. She may have been present at her presentation in the Temple. She may have conversed about her with the holy Joachim and Anna. She may have marvelled what was to be the destiny of one so singularly marked out for great things by the circumstances of her birth and childhood. She may have known of her marriage to the blessed Joseph, but she could have had no thought of the dignity to which she had now been raised. She might have welcomed her with joy and love, but without veneration. But as soon as the voice of her salutation sounded in her ears the infant leaped in her womb for joy.

These simple words contain the whole of what we have been saying about the sanctification of the Baptist, and they also signify the cause of the further grace now bestowed on his mother. Elisabeth understood by a Divine light, what had taken place. She understood the mystery of the Incarnation, the fulfilment of the prophecies, the beginning of the accomplishment of the salvation of the world. She knew that our Lord was there present in the womb of His mother. She understood the leaping of her babe in her own womb as his greeting and joyous homage to the Incarnate King, and that it was no simply natural or involuntary movement, but the deliberate expression of joy, which signified that he had so much at which to rejoice, in the accomplishment in himself, at that moment, and by virtue of the salutation of our Lady, of the promise of spiritual deliverance and elevation which had been made to his father concerning him at the time of the announcement of his future conception. More than this, the words of St. Elisabeth show also that she had then revealed to her the details of the Annunciation itself as made by the Angel to Mary. Her words take up the very words of the salutation of Gabriel, and complete them. The Angel had stopped short at the declaration of the blessedness of Mary, before the Incarnation had taken effect. Elisabeth continues, in the words which the Church has ever since used, to declare the blessedness of the fruit of the womb of Mary, after the Incarnation had taken effect. All these evidences of the wonderful effect which followed on the salutation of our Lady are contained in the few words in which the Evangelist relates what now passed. " Elisabeth was filled with the Holy Ghost and she cried out with a loud voice and said, 'Blessed art thou among women, and blessed is the fruit of thy womb! And whence is this to me, that the mother of my Lord should come to me? For behold, as soon as the voice of thy salutation sounded in my ears, the infant in my womb leaped for joy. And blessed art thou that hast believed, because those things shall be accomplished that were spoken to thee by the Lord.'"

The loud cry of this venerable saint must be understood as the effect of the great fervour of spirit in which she spoke. She spoke under the immediate impulse of the Holy Ghost, and the revelation to her of the wonderful mysteries of the Incarnation could not have preceded her words by many seconds of time. Mary's salutation had probably been gentle and modest, in a low tone of voice, and St. Elisabeth is moved so strongly by the Holy Ghost that she cannot contain herself. "Blessed art thou among women!" These words are, as has been said, the last words of Gabriel's salutation and the first of hers. They contain in her mouth all that they contained in his. She adds the other words, "blessed is the fruit of thy womb," showing that she knew of the accomplishment of the mystery which the Angel had spoken of as future. Both Mary and the fruit of her womb are blessed in the highest degree and measure. But He is the source of all blessing, He cannot be otherwise than most blessed, because He is the Incarnate God. Mary, in all her blessedness, receives from His fulness in this as in all other respects. In this sense it is that the Fathers say that the latter blessedness is the cause of the former, though the blessedness of Mary is truly and perfectly such. The next words of St. Elisabeth seem the natural acknowledgment on her part of the great favour and honour done to her by the visit of her cousin. "Whence is this to me?" What merit is there in me, that, when I ought to be waiting on her and paying my homage to her, the Mother of my Lord should instead come to me? Then she goes on to declare, not exactly how it is that she has known what has passed, but the wonderful effect, in herself and in her Child which have followed from the salutation of Mary.

The reason and cause of the knowledge of St. Elisabeth concerning the Incarnation could not be the leaping in her womb of the unborn child. The reason for her knowledge was that she was filled with the Holy Ghost, and especially for the purpose of her being a witness to, and so far in some sort a companion of, Mary, in the accomplishment of the designs of God. The leaping of her Child in the womb was an evidence to her of the change that had been wrought in him and in his favour, by the presence of the Unborn God and the voice of His Blessed Mother. In this sense we may understand the connection between the words of St. Elisabeth. She knew that the fruit of the womb of Mary was most blessed, because He was at that moment manifesting His spiritual power, as present in Mary, by the sanctification of His Precursor. Thus the exultation of the Child in her womb was an evidence of the presence of the Incarnate God in the womb of Mary, and not only of His presence, but of the active exercise by Him of that power of sanctification which belonged, and could belong, to Him alone. For she understood by the enlightenment of the Holy Ghost, as we have said, that the leaping of her Child was nothing less than a manifestation of his full intelligence of the mystery of the Incarnation, and of his joy and gratitude at the wonderful share which he himself had then and there received of the spiritual blessings with which that mystery of Divine condescension was fraught.

This may supply the reason why St. Elisabeth first speaks of the leaping of her child in her womb.

It was an evidence of the marvellous effects on his soul of the presence of his Lord. He came to be the prophet of the Highest, as his father sang afterwards in the *Benedictus*, and now, as some of the Fathers are fond of saying, he anticipated his office and declared preternaturally the presence of his Lord. St. Elisabeth goes on at once to speak of the blessedness of Mary. She is not only the blessed among women, as having been chosen from all eternity to be the Mother of God, as having been, after her Divine Son, the great subject of prophecy and of type, as having been brought into the world in the wonderful way and with the wonderful privileges which belong to her great vocation, but also as having corresponded most faithfully and most perfectly in the time of her trial to the designs of God, and so having secured the execution of the Divine promises conveyed to her at the time of that probation by the mouth of the Angel. This is the meaning of the last clause of the greeting of St. Elisabeth, "Blessed thou that didst believe, because those things shall be accomplished that were spoken to thee by the Lord." This shows us that St. Elisabeth, as has been said, was at this time divinely enlightened as to what had passed between the Angel and our Blessed Lady, and that she now is commissioned to give on the part of God a further assurance to her that thoe great promises shall be accomplished. Her Son is to be the Son of the Highest. He is to have given Him by God the throne of His father David. "He is to reign in the house of Jacob for ever and of His kingdom there shall be no end." These are the things that were then spoken to our Lady by the Lord. For the still more wonderful things which formed the last portion of the message of Gabriel, that the Holy Ghost should come upon her and the power of the Most High should overshadow her, and that the Holy One to be born of her should be the Son of God, had already had their fulfilment and were no longer future, nor could the blessing which they conveyed to her ever be recalled.

This prophecy of St. Elisabeth shows us the very close connection between the two mysteries of the Incarnation and Visitation. It may be said, in a certain sense, that the former mystery is incomplete without the latter. Not that anything could be added to the truth and completeness of the Incarnation by any number of subsequent mysteries, but that the Divine counsels required that the relation between these two mysteries should be established through the confirmation of the former by the circumstances of the latter. We have seen that the last words of St. Gabriel at the Annunciation referred to the conception of the Precursor in the womb of St. Elisabeth, and they implied, though not by way of direct command, that it was the will of God that Mary should immediately undertake the journey which ended in the Visitation. For it was the rule in the revelation of any most sublime mystery that something should be added by way of confirmation or sign of the truth which had been revealed, even though there was not exactly any need, in the soul of the saint to whom the revelation was made, of such confirmation for the purpose of securing his faith in the revelation itself. In the same way, the fulfilment of the sign given by way of this confirmation is a part of the Divine counsel in such cases, and it is this completeness which is added by the Visitation.

It is needless to insist how clear it is, that the faith of Mary would have been the same if she had never gone to visit her cousin, and if, when with her, she had not received this magnificent testimony to the truth of the message of the Angel. Her faith would have been the same, in its essential perfection, but it cannot be supposed that the circumstances of the Visitation did not send a glow of joy through the heart of Mary, making her faith itself full of its own radiance. Nothing can be added to the essential happiness of the Saints, and yet they can receive an accession of joy when they are specially honoured in the Church on earth. In this sense Mary herself might be confirmed by these new prodigies. Their natural effect was that all who knew them should be so confirmed. And in the unfolding of the Divine mysteries to the gaze of Angels and of men, it is easy to see how much is added to the splendour of the Incarnation by the Visitation. The Visitation gave God the opportunity of declaring, by a series of marvels of the highest kind, that what He had promised to Mary by the mouth of Gabriel had already been performed as far as the Incarnation of His Son, and that it would be still further carried out, in due time, by the exaltation of the Child of Mary. There may have been other designs of God in this arrangement of His Providence. It may have been a part of the preparation of St. Joseph, and of the full consummation of the faith of St. Zachary, that all this should take place, even though the faith of our Lady herself was beyond and above all such confirmations. And the close connection between the two mysteries may be further seen in the fact, that it is not till the Visitation is completed that our Lady breaks forth into her great canticle of thanksgiving, of which we shall begin to speak in the following chapter.

CHAPTER IX.

THE CANTICLE OF MARY.

St. Luke i. 46—56. *Vita Vitæ Nostræ,* § 5.

THE praises of St. Elisabeth had forced the Blessed Virgin to speak. Up to this time she had said nothing about herself, or the great blessing which had been bestowed on her. She left all this to God. The Holy Ghost inspired the exultation of the infant in the womb of her cousin and the exclamation of St. Elisabeth, so full of knowledge of the Divine mystery, and of honour to Mary. Thus it was now necessary for her to speak, that she might turn the praise away from herself to Him to Whom all praise, all honour, all glory, all gratitude, are due, and in doing this she pours herself out to an extent altogether without parallel in the Gospel history. All the remaining words of our Blessed Lady do not amount to nearly as many as are here contained in her praise of God. Thus the simple fact that she now speaks, and for the purpose and to the effect for which she speaks, is a fresh revelation to us of the character of Mary.

But the Canticle of which we are now to speak is not only important to us as the revelation of the thoughts of our Blessed Lady herself. If it were no more than that, it would still be infinitely precious to us. For the thoughts of Mary are the thoughts suggested to her by her Divine Son, as her most proper and natural thoughts under the circumstances of the time. Thus they breathe to us the first inspirations of His Sacred Heart, as well as the affections of His Blessed Mother. The Canticle of Mary stands first among the Canticles of the New Testament. It gives them their character and dominant note. Mary is now speaking in her own person, indeed, but, more than this, she speaks as the representative of the Church, of the whole human race redeemed by the great mercy of the Incarnation. She is uttering the first hymn of thanksgiving of the whole creation which has been renovated and elevated by that mighty mystery. Her *Magnificat* sounds on and on in all ages of the Church, the accompaniment, as it may be called, to the great sacrifice of thanksgiving which is perpetually offered all over the world in the Blessed Eucharist. The meaning of these few and simple words can never be so fathomed as to exhaust it. There is no affection of thanksgiving, and homage, and loving gratitude, which cannot find here its fitting expression, just as no petition, or desire, or need, or prayer, but can find itself adequately expressed in the Prayer taught us by our Lord. All prayers are summed up in the Lord's Prayer, and all thanksgivings are summed up in the *Magnificat*. The other great Canticles of the Church take their key from this. We shall see how the *Benedictus* and the *Nunc Dimittis* carry on the strain of which this is the beginning. There is a perfect continuity between them, which shows how entirely they are inspired by the same Divine author, though the parts which they have to take in the chorus of praise are not identical.

The *Magnificat* begins by the note of thanksgiving. This is in some measure suggested by the praises of St. Elisabeth which immediately occasioned it. But it is also the natural and peculiar note of the New Testament. The whole of the Old Testament was a looking forward with desire to the blessing of which Mary was now the living and conscious instrument and home. The promises on which the saints of the Old Testament lived were now fulfilled in her. She had in her womb the Son of the Woman promised in Eden, the seed promised to Abraham and a long line of chosen saints after him. She had the Son of David, the King of Israel, the Redeemer of Whom Job had spoken, the Child predicted by Isaias and Jeremias and Micheas, the desire of all nations, the expectation of the whole world. The whole of the Old Testament had been the breathing in various strains of the intense longing of the world for its deliverer. The New Testament has another duty to fulfil, that of thanking God for the accomplishment of His promises. Thus the characteristic of the New Testament is joyous thanksgiving, and the first word of the thousand strains of this affection to God which were to rise to His throne from the race of man, is spoken by the Mother of God in the house of St. Elisabeth. We see the spirit of the *Magnificat* all through the New Testament. It meets us over and over again in the Epistles of St. Paul. If thankfulness and rejoicing are the characteristic graces of the Christian Church, every note of hers in which they are breathed is an echo of the *Magnificat* of Mary. The *Gloria in Excelsis*, the Angelical hymn of the holy sacrifice, is an expansion of this canticle.

Mary is thus our first Christian teacher, as well as the Mother of our God in His Human Nature. Our Lord teaches us how to honour His Father, and His Mother teaches us how to honour Him, how to thank Him for His infinite mercy in becoming one of us. This office of hers to us flows from her office towards Him. For the nine months between the Incarnation and the Nativity she was His one great worshipper, and she discharged to Him the duty of adoration and thanksgiving for the whole race of man, and for the whole creation which He had elevated. And now that she has to speak and to leave behind her a record, in which the affections of her heart are enshrined for our use, we may well take her utterances as given to us by God as our lesson in this respect. The subject of her song is our Lord, the Incarnate God. She speaks of herself only in reference to Him and her position with Him, which involves our own relations to herself, as we shall see. She takes one after another the great attributes which are manifested in His condescension in the Incarnation, and she makes each one a separate subject of praise and thanksgiving. This is the shortest possible description of the *Magnificat*. One thing more must be added by way of preface. Our Blessed Lady takes as her pattern, and as the foundation of her Canticle, one of the canticles of the Old Testament, the canticle of Anna the mother of Samuel, a song of thanksgiving which we cannot doubt had been taught her by her own mother St. Anne. She uses it much in the same way as St. Gabriel had used the language of the prophets in his Annunciation to herself, not repeating exactly any single passage, but using their words, so that almost every word of his could be found somewhere in their prophecies. This should be kept in mind in our consideration of this canticle of our Blessed Lady. She uses also language taken from other parts of Sacred Scripture, as we shall see as we go on. Her mind ranges over the whole of the dealings of God with man in the way of mercy, and over the whole of the records of those dealings as contained in the inspired books.

It may be well, at the beginning of our comment on this Canticle, to set before ourselves the old song of thanksgiving from which it is taken in the manner which has been said. The occasion of the canticle of Anna, which has been adopted by the Church in her Breviary, is well known. But it will be seen how far beyond the present blessing of the birth of her long desired Child the holy mother rises in the course of her thanksgiving. It is impossible to doubt that the sequence of thought in the *Magnificat* is to a large extent in direct correspondence with the sequence of thought in the canticle of Anna. This is enough to show us the importance of the consideration of the older song of thanksgiving. "My heart hath rejoiced in the Lord, and my horn is exalted in my God. My mouth is enlarged over my enemies, because I have joyed in Thy salvation. There is none holy as the Lord is, for there is no other beside Thee, and there is none strong like our God. Do not multiply to speak lofty things, boasting, let old matters depart from your mouth! For the Lord is a God of knowledge, and to Him are all thoughts prepared. The bow of the mighty is overcome, and the weak are girt with strength. They that were full before have hired themselves out for bread, and the hungry are filled, so that the barren hath borne many, and she that had many children is weakened. The Lord killeth and maketh alive, He bringeth down to Hell and bringeth back again. The Lord maketh poor and maketh rich, He humbleth and He exalteth. He raiseth up the needy from the dust, and lifteth up the poor from the dunghill, that he may sit with princes, and hold the throne of glory. For the poles of the earth are the Lord's, and on them He hath set the world. He will keep the feet of His saints, and the wicked shall be silent in darkness, because no man shall prevail by his own strength. The adversaries of the Lord shall fear Him, and upon them shall He thunder in the heavens. The Lord shall judge the ends of the earth, and He shall give empire to His King, and shall exalt the horn of His Christ."

It is plain at first sight that the plan and order of the Canticle of our Blessed Lady are both very mainly suggested by the canticle of this holy mother of Samuel, who had, no doubt, spent the time which intervened between the birth and weaning of her child in very close communion with God. Her hymn is a hymn of thanksgiving, but also a hymn which is full of prophetical inspiration, while it takes in, as has been said, ranges of the great works of God which reach far beyond the immediate occasion of the thanksgiving which gave rise to it. The first strain of exultation and rejoicing is very like that of our Blessed Lady, when she says, "My soul doth magnify the Lord, and my spirit hath rejoiced in God my Saviour." The words in the two Canticles seem almost identical. Then Anna goes on to speak of the great attributes of God, and she mentions especially the two attributes of holiness and strength. These are the two attributes on which our Lady dwells when she says, " He that is mighty hath done great things to me, and His Name is holy." Then there follows, in the canticle of Anna, a passage in which the saint rejoices, as it seems, over the victory she had gained over her rival. But she generalizes the subject considerably. She speaks against pride of language, about the humiliation of the strong and the exaltation of the weak, how the hungry have been filled and they that were full before have hired themselves out for bread. Here we have the foundation of the second part of the Canticle of Mary, in which she celebrates the might which God hath showed in His Arm, how He has scattered the proud in the conceit of their hearts, how He hath put down the mighty from their seat, and hath exalted the humble, how He hath filled the hungry with good things and sent away empty the rich. The second parts of each Canticle are therefore identical in subject and in tone.

Anna goes to a third strophe, as it may be called, in which she seems to prophecy of the future glories of the Kingdom of God. "The poles of the earth are the Lord's and upon them He hath set the world. He will keep the feet of His saints, and the wicked shall be silent in darkness, because no man shall prevail by his own strength. The adversaries of the Lord shall fear Him, and upon them shall He thunder in the heavens. The Lord shall judge the ends of the earth, and He shall give empire to His King, and shall exalt the horn of His Christ." These verses contain many prophecies, which were fulfilled, in the first instance, in the life of the holy Child of whom Anna was the mother. It was under Samuel that the Israelites were delivered from the bondage of the Philistines, and one of his remarkable miracles was that he caused thunder to be heard from heaven at the time of the year when it was unusual. Moreover, he was the prophet and judge of the Land of Israel, and it was his office to choose, or point out, the first kings of the holy people, one of whom, that is David, was the direct ancestor of our Lord, Who was to inherit his throne according to a long line of prophecies. And lastly it seems that this is the first place in the Old Testament in which the word 'Anointed,' or Christ, is used in a prediction of our Lord.

The passage in the *Magnificat* which corresponds to this last passage in the earlier canticle of which we are speaking, is that with which the Blessed Virgin concludes, saying, that God has been mindful of His mercy, and has fulfilled the promise made to the fathers. " He hath received Israel His servant, being mindful of His mercy, as He spake to our fathers, to Abraham and his seed for ever." The language is not so glowing and full as that of the prediction in the earlier canticle, for our Lady speaks of the accomplishment of the promises rather than of the promises themselves. The strain of this last part of the *Magnificat* is taken up immediately by the second Evangelical canticle, which we know as the *Benedictus*, in which the glowing passage in the canticle of Anna is more than surpassed. Thus it is easy to trace throughout the whole of the *Magnificat* the influence of the earlier song of thanksgiving, inasmuch as the parts of each are the same in character and in number, and it cannot be doubted that our Blessed Lady must have had the song of Anna in her mind. We shall presently find the differences which underlie these resemblances, but yet it is well to begin our explanation of the *Magnificat* by this reference to the type, so to say, on which it was moulded. The fact that the canticle of Anna was thus the ground of the Canticle of our Lady, does not, of course, exclude the constant reference throughout to other passages of Scripture also.

One more remark may be made in general, before proceeding to the consideration of single passages. We find in the two canticles, though more in that of Anna than in that of our Blessed Lady, continual reference to enemies who have been overcome by the might of God, to the humiliation of the strong and the exaltation of the lowly. This is a characteristic of most of the Scriptural canticles, and we shall meet it again presently when we come to speak of the canticle of St. Zachary, the *Benedictus*. The song of thanksgiving to God is not without its strain of rejoicing over defeated foes or rivals, as may be considered to be the case in the canticle of Anna. Yet, on the other hand, it seems almost impossible to suppose that so holy a person could be really guided to indulge in a mere strain of triumph over the downfall of a rival. The truth seems to be, and it is a truth which will help us very much in the interpretation of the *Magnificat* itself, that all through the canticles of the Old Testament, and through those also of the New in their degree, there runs the reference to that defeat of the enemies of God which was first predicted in Paradise, when enmities were placed between Satan and the Woman, and the seed of the Woman and the seed of the serpent, enmities which were to issue in the defeat and destruction of the power of Satan by means of the seed of the Woman.

It is not too much to think that when Moses sang his song of triumph over the defeat of Pharao, when Debbora and Barak sang their song over the defeat of the host of Sisera, when Judith sang her song over the destruction of the army of Holofernes, and in all similar cases, the prime contemplation in the inspired strain was not simply the deliverance which then had been achieved for the people of God. It was the great victory of which all such deliverances were types and anticipations, the victory to be achieved by the Son of Mary on the Cross for the redemption and deliverance of the human race, and the exaltation of the glory of God, by their admittance to heaven as heirs of a greater inheritance than that of which the fraud of Satan had seemed to deprive them. Thus it is that we always find in such strains certain more sublime thoughts and subjects, which rise so far beyond the immediate occasion of the victory which has been won. In the same way we find the great promises made to Solomon, as the Son of David, blended almost inseparably with the glories which can belong only to our Lord. Thus, once more, we shall find that the Canticle of our Lady takes us back in thought to the scene in Paradise when the first great promise was made to man. It is the song of thanksgiving of the second Eve for the immense privileges bestowed upon her, and it is also her song of triumph over the enemies allotted to her by the decree of God Himself in the first promise and prophecy. We may now go on to the first strophe of the *Magnificat*.

" And Mary said, My soul doth magnify the Lord, and my spirit hath rejoiced in God my Saviour, because He hath regarded the humility of His handmaiden, for behold, from henceforth, all generations shall call me Blessed." There may be in these first words something of an answer to the lofty praises which had been uttered concerning her by cousin St. Elisabeth, but the answer is couched in the words of Scripture, and rises beyond the immediate occasion. This is Mary's version of the beginning of the canticle of Anna, " My heart hath rejoiced in the Lord and my horn is exalted in my God, my mouth is enlarged over my enemies, because I have joyed in Thy salvation." There is also an echo here of the beautiful prayer of the prophet Habacuc. " For the fig tree shall not blossom, and there shall be no spring in the vines. The labour of the olive tree shall fail, and the fields shall yield no food, the flock shall be cut off from the fold, and there shall be no herd in the stalls, but I will rejoice in the Lord, and I will joy in God my Jesus."[1] Our Lady not only uses the antithetical form of language in which the Hebrew poetry is usually cast, but she must be understood as intensifying and deepening her meaning in the latter clause beyond the degree of its force in the former clause. This is the natural effect, indeed, of her words, for it is in the nature of things that to rejoice in her Saviour is something beyond magnifying her Lord. Her rejoicing in her Jesus, for we may render the words so if we please, is something founded on her magnifying of her God, and at the same time something greater, in that it is more to have God as her Saviour, than to have Him simply as her Lord. In the subjection to God all creation shares, in the salvation wrought by our Lord not all creatures share. The second blessing is the extension of the first, the second affection is the fruit of the first, and yet something more than the first.

It has been said that the words of the Blessed Virgin are here almost identical with those of the elder saint whose canticle she is following. But they are not quite the same. The most important difference lies in the variation of the words used by our Lady, when she says that her soul magnifies the Lord, and that her spirit rejoices, or hath rejoiced, in God her Saviour. We here seem to touch on that distinction between the soul and the spirit which meets us also in other passages of the New Testament, as when St. Paul says of the power of the word of God, that it reaches "to the

[1] Hab. iii. 17, 18

division of the soul and spirit,"[2] or when the same Apostle says to the Thessalonians that he prays "that their spirit and soul and body may be preserved,"[3] and the like. St. Thomas teaches that the soul and the spirit signify the same thing as to its essence, which, as the soul, animates the body, and is the principle of life and of the energies of all the bodily powers, while it has also higher functions than this, inasmuch as it is the principle of intelligence, which we have in common with the higher orders of the creation of God, who are incorporeal, and, as we say, spiritual only. Thus the spirit, though not essentially distinct from the soul, is something higher in its functions than the soul which is required for the animation of the body. The spirit can soar to immaterial things, and can grasp the truths of the invisible world, it can rise to God Himself and the truths which belong to Him. When it is said by our Lady that her soul magnifies the Lord, it may be meant that her whole being is occupied in praising, glorifying, honouring, and adoring God, and when it is said that her spirit rejoices in God her Saviour, it appears to be meant that all the higher faculties of the intelligent being which God has given her are flooded with the light and intense joy which naturally belong to the loftiest contemplations of which a created intelligence is capable, her spiritual ken being turned upon the magnificent range of the manifestations of Himself by God in the mystery of the Incarnation and Redemption.

The words which our Blessed Lady uses in each

[2] Heb. iv. 12.   [3] 1 Thess. v. 23.

of these clauses are perfectly appropriate and in harmony with the exercise of the several functions of the soul and spirit of which she is speaking. For her whole mind and heart and being are engaged in magnifying God, in giving Him all the homage and worship and thanks which His infinite goodness and greatness deserve at her hands, while her spiritual faculties especially are filled with the highest of all affections, the affection of joy, which, in spirits less strong, less balanced, and less under command of the will than hers, would have rapt her into ecstacy and taken away from her the use of her ordinary faculties, with an intensity and overwhelming power under the effects of which she might have seemed as one dead, as has been often the case with the saints who have been visited the most forcibly by spiritual delights. Our Lady was so great, so full of Divine strength, and peace, and calm, that she could bear what others could not have borne in the way of these delights, which, in her, corresponded perfectly with all her full intelligence and appreciation of the great things which God had done in her and for her. Yet they left her mistress of herself, and she speaks of them so calmly and with so much composure because they were the ordinary contemplations of her mind.

The words of our Lady, therefore, set before us an immense range of benefits which she has received from God, benefits which are displays of His magnificence and of His wonderful attributes, as well as boons and gifts to her. When she speaks in the first clause of magnifying the Lord, we may consider that she is dwelling in thought on the great displays of God's goodness to her in all that is embraced by His dealings with her as her God. And when she speaks in the second clause of rejoicing in God her Jesus, we may consider that she has before her mind and heart, as the object of thanksgiving and the most intense joy, all that God has done for her, as we say, in the way and order of redemption. God would still have been her God and Lord, as He is the Lord of all creatures, even if He had not become also her Saviour and Redeemer, and her Saviour and Redeemer in that particular and unexampled way, as regards the extent of the benefit, in which He did become both to her. We all receive from Him this twofold treasure of blessings and gifts, what He gives us as our Creator, our Father, our Provider, our Governor, our Guide, our Defender, in the first place, and what He gives to us in the second place, as our Incarnate Saviour, the Redeemer of our souls and bodies, the Victim of our sins, the source of all pardon and grace to us, the Giver of eternal life.

We may consider that the words of which we are speaking show us that our Blessed Lady habitually fed her thoughts and contemplations on the greatness and goodness of God in each of these orders, and that she constantly raised her heart in thanksgiving to the footstool of His throne for each. No one but herself could count out so faithfully and so distinctly the immense series of those wonderful benefits. No one but herself could so well understand their value, the love with which they were given, their effects on her, in time and in eternity. The long list of blessings began in that eternal love of

God for her which had no beginning and was to have no end, and which was the original fountain, the perennial source, of all the gifts bestowed upon her, whether in the order of nature or in the order of grace. It was from this love that had proceeded her election and predestination to the position she was to occupy in the Kingdom of her Son. It had shown itself in all the predictions concerning her, which were so many renewals of the Divine purpose, as well as of the Divine declaration of that purpose, in all the Providential preparation for her coming into being, in the long line of favours and providences which had watched over and preserved her ancestors for her sake, and the wonderful arrangements and counsels by means of which she had been brought into the world at the time and in the way foreknown and chosen by God. Then it had poured itself out in the creation of her most perfect body and soul, in the grace of her Immaculate Conception, and in the immense dowry of gifts which accompanied that unique privilege.

It must be remembered that all the measureless graces bestowed upon Mary, even those which were given her to make her fit to be the Mother of God, might have been given to her, even without respect to the decree, or the Divine intention, by which she was to be made the Mother of our Redeemer. Thus we sing of her, in her Litanies, *Mater Creatoris* first, and *Mater Salvatoris* next. It is not likely that in the mind and heart of Mary these two ranges of graces and favours were not distinctly recognised, or that the most tender gratitude was not rendered by her to God for each. If it had been the decree of Providence, as so many theologians have thought that it might have been, that our Lord should become Incarnate, and the Head of the new Creation, without having to take on Himself the work of the Redemption of the world, then Mary would still have been His Mother, and her love and joy and gratitude to Him would have been endless and measureless. She would have counted over, in her matchless intelligence of Divine things and of the counsels and acts of God, every single gift which she would then have received. But as yet there would have been no place, in that large and deep gratitude of hers, for other favours, transcending the former, in mercifulness and in magnificence. We do not often think of the attempt to give to ourselves an account of the wonderful gifts which we have received from God in either of these great orders, and the gratitude of Mary may well be made an example and an incentive to us in the holy habit of careful and particular thanksgiving. And again, this thought brings to our mind the large range of God's mercies to so many of His creatures, whom He is not to redeem. For many of His creatures belong to orders of beings which are incapable of redemption, in the strictest sense, because they are incapable of free will or of sin, and have no future life awaiting them. Others again, by their own ingratitude and abuse of the opportunities afforded them by God of profiting by the dispensation of redemption, though it is offered to them, are not to have Him actually as their Redeemer, and these are still His debtors in the order of Creation and Preservation and Providence.

There is also an immense and most glorious part of the Creation of God to which these first words of our Lady apply, and in whose name we may almost imagine her as singing the song of thanksgiving to Him. For being the Mother of God she is raised above the Angels, and is indeed, as we call her, their Queen. The Angels have not been redeemed in the strictest sense of the word, for the Precious Blood was not shed for them, but for the race of man alone, though they also have received immense gifts and graces and benefits from Him as the Redeemer of mankind. And as the graces of Mary were higher than those bestowed upon the Angels, though their nature is higher than hers, she can sing to God, as the Creator, the hymn of thanksgiving in a loftier strain, and with more full intelligence of the magnificence of the gift of their and her own creation, than can be found in them. And so no hymn of the Angelic choirs can have risen, since their first creation, and since their confirmation in grace after their trial and victory, more perfect in kind and more entirely worthy of acceptation before the throne of God than this her *Magnificat*. "My soul doth magnify the Lord!" To magnify the Lord is to form the highest and largest conceptions of His greatness and goodness, to form those conceptions into the shape of mental and most heartfelt praise and estimation, and then to pour this praise out in whatever way is open to the heart or soul in which they spring up.

We cannot really magnify God. That is, we cannot make Him greater than He is, but we can most truly enlarge and deepen our conceptions concerning Him, we can extend our appreciation and knowledge of Him by the consideration of His works as they are more and more manifested to us. For all increase of our appreciation of Him is an increase of our power of praising Him for what we more and more appreciate. This is in truth the occupation of the Angels in Heaven, who are ever learning more and more to understand God, and this will be the blissful occupation of the Saints and Blessed in Heaven, throughout all eternity. Our Lady's words include all that is here suggested. They show us her characteristic grace of contemplation and study of the Divine attributes and works. They illustrate what is said of her, more than once, in this part of the Gospel of St. Luke, that she kept all that passed and pondered it in her heart, as the mysteries of the Incarnation were, one after another, unfolded before her and in her. The Church's hymn, or rather the hymn which the Church has caught from the Angels, the *Gloria in excelsis*, is but an expansion of the first words of the *Magnificat*. It contains the glorification of God, not simply for His works as Creator, but especially for His work as Redeemer and Saviour of the human race. All the affections of the *Gloria* may be said to be contained in the first words of our Lady The several affections which succeed one another in the *Gloria* are all more or less contained in the few words before us. The praise of God, the blessing of God, the adoration and worship of God, the giving Him glory, the giving Him thanks for His great glory, that is, the affections of admiration, of praise, of benediction, of ardent desire for His greater glory, and that glory should be given to none but to Him to Whom it all belongs, all these things may be found in the meaning of this verse of the *Magnificat*. The words open to us the heart of the Blessed Mother, the first of pure creatures, and they reveal to us also the affections of the Sacred Heart itself, then beating and glowing with love in the womb of Mary. Thus it is not wonderful that this Canticle should be, beyond all others, the song of the Church, for where can her children learn a more perfect expression of the affections which they ought to conceive towards God than from the hearts of Jesus and Mary?

But we must pass on to the second clause of this opening strophe of this great Canticle. It has been already said that we may consider this second clause as especially commemorating the benefits of Redemption, in distinction from the benefits of Creation and Providence. It refers, therefore, to that second great ocean of graces and gifts poured into her soul, as the fruit of the Redemption wrought for her by her Son, as well as for all the rest of the world, indeed, in a most true sense, for her, more than all the rest of the world. She received more abundantly than all the saints together, the fruits of the Sacrifice of the Cross and of the Precious Blood. Others were redeemed after they had been touched by sin. She was redeemed that she might not be touched by sin. In others sin is pardoned and atoned for, in her it was shut out by a plenitude of graces, all of which were paid for by the Passion of her Son. As for the abundance of her graces and the perfection of her virtues, it can only be repeated, that as has already been said, she began where the highest Angels reach, and she continually multiplied her gifts through the whole of her long life with a rapidity and multiplicity which are hers own alone. Moreover, she was continually receiving fresh dowries of grace as the great mysteries succeeded one another in the life of our Lord and in her own. And yet all this immeasurable accumulation of grace was the fruit of the merits of her Son. Most truly therefore is He to her a Jesus, more than to all others, by the ransom He has paid for her, the share He has given her of His merits, the dignity to which He has raised her, and the glory which corresponds to that dignity and to the love with which He regards her.

The holy affection of joy of which our Lady here speaks, as answering to the blessings which she had received in the order of redemption, is the very highest and most tender of all spiritual affections, the most utterly incomprehensible to the worldly and sensual. Joy is the very life of God Himself. Thus when our Lord speaks of the very highest consummation of the blessedness which awaits the saints in heaven as their reward, He says that it will be said to them, " Enter into the joy of thy Lord." When then our Blessed Lady speaks of her spirit rejoicing in God her Saviour, she speaks of something even beyond the contemplation and intelligence, and magnification and glorification of God, of His greatness and of His goodness, whether in the order of creation or the order of redemption. She speaks of the enjoyment of His sweetness and ineffable beauty and loveliness, as her own. Joy is the crown and flower and essence of the life of the holy Angels in Heaven, it is imparted in a measure to the saints and servants of God even upon earth, and of course, it was imparted in a pre-eminent and singular measure, in a way unique and incommunicable to others, to the one heart which was the heart of the chosen Mother.

Our Blessed Lady changes the words of the prophet who has been quoted, for he had said that he would rejoice, and she says that her spirit has rejoiced. He was looking forward in hope and desire to the promised Incarnation of the Son of God, and to all the boons which were to come to the world therewith. But Mary has already received our Lord, the expectation and hope of the prophets came into her sacred womb, and that moment of ineffable bliss and delight remains with her for ever, not as a memory, but as a joy ever fresh, a joy which palls not nor grows old, because it is in a most true sense ever renewed and intensified. She can never be other than the Mother of God, and she can never lose the joy of becoming the Mother of God. She was full of grace before, and yet as St. Gabriel said, at that time the Holy Ghost was to come upon her and the power of the Most High to overshadow her, and she received a fresh plenitude of all the graces and fruits of the Holy Ghost, the love, the joy, the peace and the rest, of which St. Paul gives the long catalogue in one of his epistles. This great treasure of holiest affections our Lady sums up in the few words in which she declares that her spirit hath rejoiced in God her Saviour.

The second part of this first strophe of the Canticle passes to another head of the benefits of God to Mary. For what she has hitherto spoken of are benefits which are in their measure common to her with all mankind. We do not all receive in equal abundance these great gifts and blessings of which she has spoken hitherto, the blessings of Creation and Providence and preservation. That is to say, some are more highly gifted in natural boons than others, some have a larger share in the actual benefits of redemption than others, as we see at once when we contrast the state of a happy Catholic population with that of a population which has either forfeited by the sins of its rulers or ancestors, the blessings of Catholic communion, or has to live altogether outside the pale of Christianity, under the miserable bondage of heathenism, or of some form of false religion. When we compare the blessed inmates of the cloister with those who have to battle their way to heaven amid all the dangers of the world, although we know that God takes care of all His children, and will shield them from all the dangers to which their worldly condition may expose them, if they are faithful to His grace, we can see even in these universal gifts of His that there is some inequality of distribution. In any case, every one has a share of the common blessings which God lavishes upon all, but besides these, every one also has a long list of personal and particular favours for which to magnify God and for which to rejoice in God his Saviour. Thus, then, our Blessed Lady after having glorified God for the blessings which are common to her with all those on whom He has bestowed them in any measure, being the Father and the Provider and the Redeemer of all, goes on to commemorate the particular favours for which she is debtor to His exceeding peculiar and personal love.

There is the same onward progress from general blessings to personal blessings in the Canticle of Anna, as when the Saint speaks of her horn being exalted over her enemies, and the like. Our Lady's words are, that she magnifies the Lord and rejoices in God her Saviour, " Because He hath regarded the humility of His handmaiden, for behold from henceforth all generations shall call me blessed." The Latin word which is rendered in our version by the word humility, is of ambiguous meaning. For it is used to denote lowliness, misery, an abject and externally afflicted condition, as well as the interior virtue of the soul which is commonly meant by our word humility. But the original word in the Greek text denotes the former rather than the latter, and thus it is most probable that the humility of our Lady, which God is here said to have regarded, means her poverty, her insignficance, her obscurity, her low and poor estate, her worthlessness as it appeared in her own eyes, and not the virtue of her humility. Indeed it might hardly become a truly humble person to speak of herself as so humble, especially in a way which implied that her humility had attracted the gracious regard of God, and brought down on her the greatest favours from Him. But even if this were not so—for our Lord speaks of Himself as meek and humble of heart, and what our Lord might say of Himself that also our Lady might say of herself—it would still be an argument against this interpretation of the word here, that her humility was a grace which she had received from God originally, like all other graces, and that He had regarded her to give it to her, and not found it in her as the ground and cause of His great gifts to her.

It is probable also that the words of which we are speaking are cast in the form in which they are cast, and are what they are, by way of an antithesis between the qualities which our Blessed Lady has been contemplating in her God, and those which she finds in herself. The greatness of God which she magnifies, is contrasted with the littleness, the nothingness, of one who is nothing more, and claims to be nothing more, than His servant and handmaiden. The title of Lord answers to the title of handmaiden, and the greatness of God answers to the humility, in this sense, which our Lady sees in herself. Finally the meaning of these words seems to be fixed by the simple and interesting fact that, as they stand before us in the Greek text of St. Luke, they are a quotation from the words of Anna herself, to whose canticle, as has been already said, there is a continual reference all through the *Magnificat*. The identical words occur in the prayer of Anna to God, when she was in great affliction on account of her sterility, "And she made a vow and saying, O Lord of Hosts, if Thou wilt look down on the affliction of Thy servant,"[4] and the rest. The word

[4] 1 Kings i. 11.

which is here rendered affliction is the same word which is rendered in our version of St. Luke by the word humility.

God is said in the Sacred Scriptures to look on, or regard, in more ways than one. He is said to look down upon everything in the way of knowledge, or in the way of favour and blessing, or in the way of chastisement. Thus He is said in the Psalms " to dwell on high and to look down on the low things in heaven, and on earth."[5] He is said in the Book of Genesis to have had respect to Abel and his offerings but not to Cain and his offerings.[6] And again in the Psalms, " He looketh upon the earth and maketh it tremble."[7] It is needless to say that here the word is used in the second signification. He has regarded the low estate of His handmaiden with favour and exceeding mercy and love, raising her to the very highest position that can be occupied by a creature such as she is. In more than one of the passages in the Old Testament in which the words used here by our Blessed Lady are found, in which God is said to have regarded or looked upon the low estate of one of His servants, the reference is, as here, to the favour which He has bestowed on the person in question by making her a mother in some marvellous way, or after a long time of expectation and disappointment.

The same remark may be made as to the following words, " For behold from henceforth all generations shall call me blessed." St. Elisabeth had

---

[5] Psalm cxii. 5. [6] Genesis iv. 4, 5.
[7] Psalm ciii. 32.

called our Lady blessed among women on the score of her great faith, and it is undoubted that her great faith was rewarded by the confirmation to her of the Divine decree, whereby she had been chosen to be the Mother of God. But the blessing itself which was granted to her, after she had shown her wonderful faith, was something most lofty and unique in itself, and it is this that our Lady seems to imply when she says, "Behold from henceforth all generations shall call me blessed." The blessing lay in the incommunicable gift of being made the Mother of the Incarnate Word. It is this, therefore, and not the faith which her cousin had spoken of, that is the cause why all generations shall call her blessed. All her privileges and gifts are based on this one great act of Divine condescension, that which St. Gabriel had spoken of when he said, "The Holy Ghost shall come upon thee and the power of the Most High shall overshadow thee, and therefore the Holy that shall be born of thee shall be called the Son of God." The words themselves, "all generations shall call me blessed," are, as has been said, an apparent reference to ths words of the ancestress of our Lady, Lia the eldest wife of Jacob, at the birth of Aser.[8] Thus the words refer to the same kind of blessing in each case. They are a comparatively humble and summary form of expressing our Lady's wonderful elevation, but at the same time they represent its source and principle, with the most perfect accuracy. For the Incarnation is a work of God which can never pass away or be undone, and

[8] Genesis xxi. 13.

therefore the blessing which it brings with it to the chosen Mother can never pass away or change. The act of God in making her His Mother is the fertile source of all the blessings which she is to inherit, a spring of life, so to say, for ever welling up in fresh glories and honours, as its fruits manifest themselves and multiply themselves more and more generation after generation. As the fruitfulness of the Incarnation is ever fresh and ever increasing in its applications and manifestations, so in the same way does the glory and blessedness of Mary increase and spread itself more and more widely, and higher and higher, with that fruitfulness of the Incarnation in which she has borne her part and in which she has a share. She can never be other than the Mother of God, and every effect of the Incarnation is an effect of her consent, in the sense in which we have already explained her part in the great work of God.

These words also contain the prophecy of the carrying out of the decrees of God, by which He has arranged that Mary's position in the Kingdom of His Son shall not be hidden and unrecognised, but known, honoured, and proclaimed in a thousand ways through all time, and in every place. Our Lord said afterwards of the blessed Magdalene, that wherever the Gospel should be preached in the whole world, there also should be known what that woman had done, for a memorial of her. There is the same decree with regard to Mary, and its accomplishment, which is here predicted, is founded both on the direct Will of God and also on the essential nature of the blessing which has been bestowed upon her. For it is not possible to think rightly and adequately of the Incarnation, without recognising the elevation of the Mother of God. When St. Peter declared to our Lord, " Thou art the Christ the Son of the living God," his words contain by an inherent necessity, as a part of the truth which they set forth, the proposition of the blessedness of the Mother of the Incarnate Son. All heresies against the Person of our Lord contain the denial of her blessedness, and as the Church sings of her, she has destroyed all heresies in all the world, because the true doctrine concerning her refutes all of them. All the faithful, everywhere and at all times, re-echo the words of the woman who lifted up her voice out of the crowd to our Lord saying, " Blessed the womb that bare Thee and the breasts which gave Thee suck." These words contain the whole Christian theology concerning her.

Our Lady's words thus imply the foreknowledge of all this glory, as if she had before the eyes of her mind the whole of that immense honour which was to show itself in the countless devotions of the whole Church all over the world for her glorification, the churches and chapels and shrines, the pilgrimages, and confraternities and religious orders which were to spring up, age after age, till the very end of time, the labours of theologians to vindicate and explain her privileges, the homage of the chief saints, who have always led the way in celebrating her and having recourse to her power and merciful compassion, the true and heartfelt devotion of the millions of the Church's children who would in very truth, reverence and love her as their Mother. She sees the endless glory on earth and in heaven which was to be hers, and she humbly lays it all at the feet of God from Whom it comes, and traces it all up to the one single source of the merciful regard which He has had for the lowliness and nothingness of His creature and His slave. All was to be His gift, and all was to be given back to Him.

It is natural that we should find the Christian writers giving the widest possible meaning to the expression of our Blessed Lady about the generations who are to call her blessed. All mankind, Jews and Gentiles, men and women, the saints and the ordinary faithful, the laity, and the priesthood, the rulers of the Church, and their subjects, kings and queens, the noble and humble, rich and poor, virgins and married, parents and children, widows and orphans, free and slaves, Angels and men, the dwellers in heaven, and on earth and in Purgatory, all and everywhere and at every time, in every stage of the world's history, all who acknowledge our Lord as their Redeemer are to acknowledge also the singular beatitude and grace of her who is made His Mother. And their acknowledgment is not to be called forth by the simple fact alone that at a certain moment of history, when the fulness of time had come, she became the Mother of her Divine Child. It is founded on the universal belief of the glory which is now and for ever hers, and also on the truth that men have had personal experience of her power and her compassion, and that the perpetual harvest of the homage of all this world is called forth by the unceasing showers of her beneficence, generation after generation.

We may now pass on to what we may call the second strophe or part in this great Canticle, though it must not be supposed that there is any real break in the close connection between each successive sentence and that which follows or precedes it in order. The canticle of Anna had gone on, after celebrating and rejoicing in the mercies of God in general, to speak of Him as most holy and most powerful, and as the Lord of all knowledge. This strain is repeated in the Canticle of Our Lady, who speaks of God as having manifested Himself mainly in the exercise of three of His great attributes in His dealing with herself, and as having thereby regarded the low estate of His handmaiden, and brought out her glorification and benediction by all generations. These three attributes are His power, His holiness, and His mercy. " Because He that is mighty hath done great things to me, and His name is Holy, and His mercy is from generation unto generation to them that fear Him." These words may be considered, according to the genius of the Hebrew language, as rehearsing the three great attributes of which mention has been made, as if our Lady had said, " He hath done great things to me, Who is mighty, and Whose name is Holy, and Whose mercy is from generation to generation unto those who fear Him." For the Incarnation is at once the greatest possible exertion of the power of God, the greatest possible manifestation of His Holiness and sanctifying grace, and also the greatest possible exertion and effort of His Divine Mercy.

The thoughts here suggested are inexhaustible in their range and extent, but a few words must suffice to sketch out the immense field thus opened out to us. Reference has already been made to the teaching of St. Thomas,[9] who says that God can go beyond what He has done in goodness and perfection in all things except three, and that these three are the Incarnation of the Word, the Divine Maternity, and the beatification of man by means of the vision of Himself. For in these three things God has given Himself, to the Human Nature which He has united to Himself in unity of Person, to Mary as His Mother, to be her Child, and to man to be his eternal felicity and the consummation of his bliss. The whole of the great act of power which was required for the Incarnation is contained in the gift of Himself to Mary as His Mother, and therefore He that is mighty hath done great things to her. Besides the great exertion of power contained in the mystery of the Incarnation, He has exerted His power in the most wonderful manner in causing her to conceive by the operation of the Holy Ghost, in giving her at once the glory of the most perfect Virginity united to the most fruitful maternity, and raising her to all the other privileges which have been spoken of in a former chapter, when we were treating of the salutation of the Angel.

In the second place, our Blessed Lady speaks of the other great attribute of the Holiness of God, as manifested in His dealings with her. For there

[9] Summa i. 25, 6.

is reference to the manifestation of an attribute, when His Name is spoken of in connection with that attribute. Here, again, we have no difficulty in understanding what it is to which our Lady refers, although it is impossible for us to trace out all the magnificent details of the Divine counsel of the Holiness of God. The Incarnation was, in the first place, the one special work of the Holiness of God, whether that attribute be considered in reference to the Person Who became Incarnate, to the manner of the Incarnation, to the object in view in the Incarnation, or to the results of the Incarnation, in the work which it accomplished, and in the fruits it has produced on earth and in heaven. But especially we may suppose that our Blessed Lady means to pour out her heart in thanksgiving for the personal graces bestowed upon herself as the chosen instrument of this most Divine work, beginning with the wonderful grace of her Immaculate Conception, and the immense dowry of graces which she then received. Among these especial and wonderful measures of sanctification would come the grace of her accelerated use of reason, with the power of acting interiorly according to the most perfect rule of holiness, and the wonderful history of her increase in sanctity day by day, and hour by hour, on which we have more than once said something. She knew, in the language of St. Paul, the gifts that had been given her by God, and she raised her voice in thankfulness for them. She was the greatest recipient of the plenitude of grace with which the Sacred Humanity of our Lord was stored, not for Himself but for us, and the source of all her sanctification was to be found in her election to be the Mother of God.

And, in the third place, our Lady celebrates the mercy of God, as the other attribute of which the great things done to her are the result. The counsel of the Incarnation was a work of infinite power, and a work of infinite holiness. But the power and the holiness were, so to say, the means for the accomplishment of a great design of mercy. Mercy indeed the Incarnation would have been in itself, as the Creation of the world was an act of mercy, even if there had been no fallen race to be redeemed, no debt of infinite justice to be paid thereby. But in truth it was a work of mercy, of restoration, and reconciliation, and atonement, and satisfaction, besides being a work of infinite condescension, and compassion, such as might have been manifested by the elevation of a created race to union with its Lord and Creator, though the created race had never offended His justice, or made itself liable to His wrath. As it was, the Incarnation was an act of mercy in this last and extremest sense, and its length and heighth and depth and breadth, as the Apostle speaks, can only be measured by an intelligence like that of the Blessed Mother of God herself, and by that only inadequately.

In order fully to understand the dimensions of this great mercy we should be able to comprehend the majesty, the rights, the holiness of God Himself, and then, and in contrast to these, we must fully understand the unworthiness of the offenders and their entire dependence on Him, the ingratitude, the full light with which they sinned, the utter impossibility of any due compensation on their part to the justice which they had outraged, the hopelessness of any fitting reconciliation by any efforts on their own part. And then must be added the magnificence of the atoning sacrifice, the dignity of the Victim, the plenteousness of the redemption wrought out by Him, the immense height to which the fallen race were to be raised, and the depth of the humiliation by which this was to be bought. And all this must be supplemented by an intelligence of that compassion of God, of which St. Paul speaks, when he dwells on the truth that God wrought it all while we were yet His enemies, and with the full fore-knowledge that so many would, by their own fault, neglect or refuse to profit by the immense condescension and mercy with which God provided for their redemption. In all these respects there is no work of God in which He has so wonderfully manifested His mercy as in the Incarnation.

Our Blessed Lady does not simply speak of the mercy of God as especially shown in the mystery of which she had been made the instrument. She speaks moreover of the mercy of God which is from generation unto generations on them that fear Him. In this she seems to refer to the special characteristic of the Divine counsel of mercy which was now finally accomplished in the Incarnation. The special characteristic of which we speak is this, that the fruits of the Incarnation were always available from the beginning of the world, and were not kept back from mankind, if certain conditions on their part were fulfilled, even though the actual atonement for sin and the reconciliation of man with God were not brought about till the fulness of time, as the Apostle speaks. Our Lord as St. John calls Him in the Apocalypse, was the Lamb slain from the foundation of the world. Thus from the very first the fruit of the Precious Blood which was to be shed on Calvary could be applied to the souls of all those who did their part to secure the effects of that great future sacrifice. Thus our Blessed Lady's words carry us back to the first promise made before the expulsion of the fallen pair from Paradise, and she brings out, as a special cause for her thanksgiving, this most tender and careful provision of God Who, while He determined, for reasons of His own Divine wisdom, not to grant the favour of the Incarnation immediately on the Fall, still provided that its benefits should not be delayed and held back until the full debt had been paid to His justice, according to His decree.

This seems to be one of the reasons for this mention of the ever enduring ever ready mercy of God from generation to generations, as if it had been natural to our Blessed Lady to go back to the very beginning of the great work of mercy of which she speaks, and to pour out her heart in thankfulness for this special provision of compassion, as well as for the great mercy of the Incarnation in general. Her heart and mind seem to stretch themselves to the whole breadth and length of God's mercifulness, so as to leave no part of it unacknowledged and uncelebrated. And, indeed, the mercy of which she thus speaks, if it is this that she has in her mind, is one of the most marvellous of the many mighty marvels of His goodness. Never till the great day of account shall we know what multitudes of souls, in all ages, in all parts of the world, under all dispensations, have had the grace granted them to profit by this wonderful arrangement of infinite compassion. Men had only to fear God, under whatever dispensation they lived, and this holy fear would lead them, in some way or other, to reconcile themselves to Him, so as to plead practically, though unconsciously as to any full knowledge, the atonement to be made by our Lord before the Divine justice. And then the grace of reconciliation through the Precious Blood would descend on them as efficaciously as if they had lived in the fullest light as to the conditions of that reconciliation. And, we may surely believe, indeed, we are, in a certain sense, bound to believe, that this arrangement of God's mercy has been fruitful at all times and in all places to an extent in some measure corresponding to the infinite love and wisdom which gave it birth. So it is right to think of all the inventions of God's goodness, that they are never made for naught, that His Providence secures their practical efficacy, because they spring from His love for souls.

If we may thus suppose that the words of Mary were divinely guided so as to contain the acknowledgment of this immense remedy, we may also look on the same words as in another sense prophetical, not only as explaining the counsel of God in the past, but also as anticipating its loving provisions in the future, as long as the world shall last. For now that the great counsel has been executed, now that the promised Seed has come and the predicted atonement carried out, the mercy of God dwells in the indefectible and world wide Church, and the means of grace are laid open in full abundance to all nations and to all generations, and this is to last on, by the decree of God, until the end of time. The one condition is practically that which our Lady mentions, that of the fear of God. For no one who has the true holy fear of God will ever be disobedient to His arrangements in the Church. The true fear of God will lead to her those that are outside without any fault of their own. And those who resist her authority and rebel against her unity will do so because they have not the fear of God.

Such are some of the truths contained in this part of the *Magnificat*. Our Lady lifts up her voice to commemorate and make known the exercise in the Incarnation of these three great attributes of which we have been speaking, the power, the holiness and the mercy of God. She does this in her own name, and in the name of the Church and the whole race of Adam, but in her own name in a peculiar manner, because she is herself the greatest recipient of the benefits of the Incarnation, being made thereby the Mother of God, and thus raised to a height in His creation which has no parallel. She is herself the greatest instance of the working of God's power, she has received more than all others together of the communication of His holiness, and she is herself the greatest object of His compassionate mercy. She has received far more than all, as her elevation is so far above that of all others, and she is made also, by a special provision of His love, the vessel of mercy, in the sense that she not only receives grace for herself, but has also the privilege of being the channel of graces to others, not as we all receive of the fulness of grace which is in our Lord, but because it is her special office to have a part in the shedding on all others, by the patronage and intercession which belong to her as the Mother of the Redeemer, the streams of His grace.

It is very remarkable how these simple words of our Blessed Lady, the humblest of the daughters of Eve, speaking of the personal favours and graces which she has received from the bounty of God, are yet such as to contain and set forth the whole doctrine of her unexampled elevation in the kingdom of her Son. In no other of the Scriptural canticles, however glowing may be their language as to the benefits bestowed on mankind or on the chosen people, in connection with the personal blessings or privileges of those who lift up their hearts and voices in thanksgiving, can words be found in which the great scheme of redemption by means of the Incarnation is thus bound up with their own personal elevation and instrumentality. Our Blessed Lady begins by speaking of the great things which God has done for her and in her. These great things are no less than the whole counsel of redemption and glorification of which we speak. The power of God, the holiness and sanctifying grace of God, the special and ineffable mercy of God, are the springs of the great things which God has done for her, and it is His work in her that is the one channel to mankind of the great benefits which flow to them from the exercise of these great attributes. Holy Anna speaks in general of the wonderful way in which God shows His power, of His care for His people and for His anointed. Zachary speaks of the God of Israel visiting and working the redemption of His people. But he is not himself the channel or the instrument of these mercies, and when he comes to address his blessed son, he only says that he shall be called, and therefore be, the prophet of the Highest, and the like. But in the words of Mary there is something more. She is as it were taken up into the counsels of God, she is made the depository of the treasures of the graces of the Incarnation. The great work is wrought in her in the first instance, and because of this it is that all generations are to call her Blessed.

Having thus celebrated the great attributes of God as manifested in the mystery carried out in her sacred womb, our Blessed Lady proceeds to describe, in the words of sacred Scripture, the particulars of the great work of mercy and power which has been wrought. Here again we must remind ourselves of the canticle of the ancient saint, whom she is so closely following in her own song of thanksgiving. We find in the canticle of Anna the foundation of the next strophe in this *Magnificat*. Anna had said, " The bow of the mighty is overcome, and the weak are girt with strength. They that were full before have hired themselves out for bread, and the hungry are filled, so that the barren hath borne many, and she that had many children is weakened. The Lord killeth and maketh alive, He bringeth down to hell and bringeth back again. The Lord maketh poor and maketh rich, He humbleth, and He exalteth. He raiseth up the needy from the dust, and lifteth up the poor from the dunghill, that He may sit with princes and hold the throne of glory." Our Blessed Lady's words are fewer, but it is evident that they are chosen with reference to the model which she had in her mind. "He hath showed might in His arm, He hath scattered the proud in the conceit of their hearts. He hath put down the mighty from their seat and hath exalted the humble. He hath filled the hungry with good things, and the rich He hath sent empty away." We have now to consider the meaning of these words in the mouth of our Lady, and to see what precisely is the action of God which she thus celebrates.

It has been said that many expressions in the canticle of Anna seem to refer to the rivalry between herself, and the other wife of Elkanah, a rivalry which had cost her many bitter tears and which was now at an end, because she was herself the joyful mother of children, and the reproach of her barrenness had been wiped away, by the birth of one who was to be a great prophet and servant of God. At the same time we have also seen that the language of the Old Testament canticle itself rises far higher than anything that can belong merely to the personal history of Anna. The truth seems to be that, to all the saints of the Old Testament, the personal or historical events of this character, events which consisted in great providential deliverances or chastisements, whether of the enemies of the chosen people or of the chosen people itself, and so also of private persons within it, were naturally and instinctively looked on as typical, and as having a reference to the action of God in humbling His enemies and in exalting His servants, time after time. All these things as St. Paul says, "happened to them in a figure," and the figurative character of the history was easily recognised. Thus it would come naturally about that a great personal favour, such as that which had been granted to the holy mother of Samuel, would pass in her mind into a figure of the deliverances which God might be expected to work for His people. And these historical deliverances, again, would be interpreted as having a spiritual aspect, as being prophetic or representative of the great spiritual deliverance from the bondage of sin, and Satan, and death, which was the great subject, both of prophecy, and of the yearning expectation of the people of God. This strain of spiritual hope and forecast runs through all the great canticles of the Old Testament, and explains to us, in the way now intimated, much of the language of those beautiful hymns of thanksgiving.

Many commentators on the *Magnificat* have understood the words which are now before us in an historical sense, as if they referred primarily to the great deliverances wrought by God for His people. The principle of God's Providential action whereby He is continually humbling and bringing down the proud, and exalting the lowly, does indeed run throughout the whole of the Jewish history, as it runs equally through the whole of His dealings with single souls. As it belongs to His infinite goodness and greatness to show His power His holiness and His mercy continually, so also is it a part of His character to show His might especially in scattering the proud in the conceit of their hearts, and in exalting the humble. This characteristic of God is a part of His infinite justice and goodness, and it is witnessed to in a thousand places of Sacred Scripture. Something more than this, indeed may be said. For this is a part of God's method of action which seems especially to call for honour and gratitude from those saints and servants of His who can understand it. It was in reference to an instance in which this law had been put in execution by His Father, that our Lord broke out into His beautiful strain of thanksgiving, " I thank Thee and confess to Thee, Father, Lord of heaven and earth, that Thou hast hidden these things from the wise and prudent, and hast revealed them unto little ones. Yea Father, for so it hath seemed good in Thy sight."[10] Now these words of our Blessed Lady are a kind of echo, or rather an anticipation, of that thanksgiving of our Lord. It is a matter of the purest joy and thanksgiving to her, for which she magnifies the Lord and rejoices in God her Saviour, not only that He has looked on the humble and lowly condition of His handmaiden, and showed forth in her the magnificence of His power, and holiness, and mercy, but also that He hath showed might in His arm, and hath scattered the proud in the conceit of their hearts, that He has set down the mighty from their seat, and hath exalted the humble.

God therefore is always acting in this way, always confounding the proud, always exalting the humble. The principle is found over and over again in the sacred history. He that exalteth himself shall be

[10] Matt. xi. 25, 26.

abased, and He that humbleth himself shall be abased, and He that humbleth himself shall be exalted. This was the case when the proud Egyptians were overthrown in the Red Sea, when David was put in the place of Saul, when he overcame Goliath, and so on throughout the history. The words are used by our Lord in His account of the Publican and the Pharisee, as conveying a general principle. God alone is great, God alone has any true excellence or beauty of His own, and He will not bear that the poor worms of earth, or any other of His creatures, should dare to take to themselves as their own any glory or honour or credit which does not belong to them. For to do this is to lie. It is in a manner incumbent on God in His providence to put down the proud. He loves humility because it is truth, because it gives all glory to Him. Humility is thus so dear and precious in His eyes that He cannot forbear from raising it up and doing it honour, because, the more it is honoured and reverenced, the more glory redounds to Him. And we know that some of the saints have said that it was the love of humility that drew Him down from Heaven to become Man, that He might Himself have as Man this most precious gift which He could not have as God. It has a beauty to Him which He cannot, as it were, resist. It is like the sweet grateful trustful dependent smile of love with which the child looks up to the parent, to whom it owes everything, and which the parent can only return by pressing the child closer to his heart.

But we must suppose that these words of our Blessed Lady refer, particularly and especially, to some one great or greatest instance of this wonderful law of the dealings of God with His creatures. What then, we must ask, was the particular exertion of the power of God of which she speaks, when she says, "He hath showed might in His arm?" Of whom in particular was she thinking, when she rejoiced because He hath scattered the proud in the conceit of their hearts? Who are the mighty ones whom she means, when she says that "He hath put down the mighty from their seat," and who are those whom He has raised on high when she gives thanks because "He hath exalted the humble?" And in the same way, who are "the hungry who are filled with good things," and who are "the rich who are sent away empty?" The principle of interpretation which we are following throughout must be our guide to the answer which we give to this question. The subject of the whole of this Canticle is the great power and goodness of God as displayed in the Incarnation, and this being laid down as a general principle, we must find the special meaning of these words in something which was brought about in and by the Incarnation. The Incarnation itself is the great work of might which our Lady says God hath showed in His arm. The arm of God is the scriptural expression for His power or might, but it seems to be sometimes used distinctly for the Incarnate Son, Who as St. Paul says "is the power of God."[11] The famous chapter of Isaias on the Passion of our Lord begins in that way, "to whom is the arm of the Lord revealed?" In any case, it is in that mystery that we must find

[11] 1 Cor. i. 24.

the explanation of the words of our Lady. The expression of scattering the proud is taken from one of the great historical psalms, "for Ethan the Ezrahite,"—where we find the words, "Thou hast humbled the proud one as one that is slain, with the arm of Thy strength Thou hast scattered Thy enemies."[12]

This leads us to the conclusion which seems the safest and most natural as to the question now before us. The proud who are scattered in the conceit of their hearts, must be these proud beings who have been humbled and defeated and brought to naught by the Incarnation of the Son of God. The mighty who are put down from their seat are those whose empire and principality have been annihilated by the Incarnation. The humble who are exalted and set on high are those who have been so exalted by the Incarnation. Thus it seems plain that our Lady's words refer primarily to the rebel Angels, who have been scattered in more than one way in the conceit of their hearts. We are told by some of the Fathers, that Satan and his associates turned away in scorn from the idea of worshipping their God in the inferior nature of a man which He was to take upon Him. They thought themselves worthy, and able and strong enough, to seize the highest thrones in heaven, to make themselves equal with God. They thought they would owe allegiance and obedience to no one. And this very thought of their hearts was like a poison working in their whole being, taking from them all true power and strength, all wisdom and

---

[12] Psalm lxxxviii. 11.

happiness, turning them into devils, much as if the lifeblood of a man had been turned into fire, and remained for ever to course through his veins as the cause of unutterable torment. This was the conceit of their heart, to turn away from God in their pride and rebellion. And the thought itself separated them for ever from the one only object of their love, the one only cause of their happiness, for the hope of regaining which now they would undergo most willingly the extremest tortures. And having been cast down from the most glorious and happy condition which was anywhere to be found among the creatures of God, they became at once the most miserable and the most hopeless. This was the first scattering of the proud in the conceit of their hearts in the history of creation. And then by virtue of the humiliation of the Son of God to an inferior nature, which had been their great stumbling block, the race of man was raised in their place to the inheritance of the thrones in Heaven which they had forfeited, so that God might be for ever glorified, not only in the casting down of the proud, but also in the exaltation of the humble in their place, which are wrought by the Incarnation. It is true, that among the Angels themselves there were the countless and most blessed spirits who stood firm and faithful to God in their time of trial. No doubt, the good Angels were exalted, as the proud were scattered, and their exaltation was the exaltation of the humble. In this sense these words apply to them. But our Blessed Lady is speaking of the direct effects of the Incarnation, and therefore her words seem to be most rightly understood in reference to men.

Again, the rebel Angels conceived the thought of dragging down to the misery of their own fall the race of Adam. They tempted our first parents, envious of their innocent happiness, and also hating them with a special hatred, because they were destined to succeed to those blessed homes with God, which they had themselves been once intended to fill, and which they had lost by their pride. And so in the conceit of their hearts, they devised, and even brought about, the fall of man. And then once more, the conceit of their own hearts became the cause of their more utter ruin and humiliation. For the fall of man was not left unpitied and unredeemed by the immense goodness and mercy of God. His enemies might seem to triumph, but their triumph was to be turned to their own destruction. They had counted on the justice of God, of which alone they had themselves any experience, and they reckoned that God would deal with man as He had dealt with them. They made no account of His mercy. They could not penetrate the secrets of His wisdom, nor imagine that He might find the way at once for the satisfaction of His justice and for carrying out at this same time the behests of His own mercy. The most enlightened intelligences in Heaven, of the Cherubim and Seraphim, could not have devised what God was about to do. No one but God could have thought of it and no one but God could have executed it. God Himself became man, and satisfied His own justice by becoming man. He raised the fallen race, not only to the height which it might have attained if it had never fallen, but far higher. This was to be the effect of the humiliation of Jesus Christ, Whom our Lady carried in her womb when she sang this song of triumph. The elevation of man corresponded to the humiliation of the Son of God, and what our Lady has in her mind is that wonderful exaltation founded on that still more wonderful humiliation. Here again, the Incarnation is the cause of all.

And thus once again, the conceit of the hearts of these enemies of God was the cause of their utter defeat and ruin. The malice which drove them to the cunning device of seducing man from his allegiance to God, issued in the immense display of goodness and mercy which is contained in the Incarnation. The commentary on these words of the *Magnificat* might perhaps be found in two pregnant passages of St. Paul, whose office it was to catch the truths almost hidden in the sayings and doings of our Lord,—and, in this respect, the words of His Mother may be considered as His own—and draw them out fully in theological language for the instruction of the Church in all ages. St. Paul has two famous passages which illustrate this text, and, it may be, were suggested by it. In the first he speaks of the humiliation of our Lord, both in the Incarnation, and in the Passion. Of this last it was not yet time for our Lady to speak. "Let this mind be in you which was also in Christ Jesus, Who being in the form of God thought it not robbery to be equal with God, but emptied Himself, taking the form of a servant, being made in the likeness of man and in habit found as a man. He humbled Himself, becoming obedient unto death, even to the death of the cross. For which cause God also hath highly exalted Him, and hath given Him a name which is above all names, that at the name of Jesus every knee should bow, of those that are in heaven, on earth, and under the earth, and that every tongue should confess that the Lord Jesus is in the glory of God the Father." [13] Here we have the last portion of the passage of the *Magnificat,* the exaltation of the humble, whether on earth or in Heaven, in time or in eternity. For in the exaltation of our Lord, as the reward of His humiliation, the whole principle and cause of the exaltation of all who follow Him in His humility are contained. In the other great passage, to the Colossians, the Apostle draws out the other part of the words of the Mother of God, those which relate to the scattering the proud. He speaks of our Lord as " blotting out the handwriting of the decree that was against us, which was contrary to us," the decree of the justice of God which was brought upon us by the sin which the evil Angel suggested to our first parents. "And He hath taken it out of the way fastening it to the cross, and spoiling the principalities and powers, He hath exposed them confidently in open show, triumphing over them in Himself." [14]

These two passages taken together may be considered as giving a complete picture of this great work of God, of which our Lady here speaks. The might God hath showed in His arm is the benefit of the Incarnation. The proud are the evil Angels whom St. Paul speaks of as the principalities and powers, who were so proud as to seek to be equal with God, and to these St. Paul alludes in his words

[13] Philip. ii. 5-11.   [14] Col. ii. 14, 15.

about our Lord not "thinking it robbery" to be equal with God. The conceit of their hearts, in which they have been scattered, is the evil design and counsel which they had conceived, and which in every case, and in all particulars, turned out to their greater confusion. For their design to rise to the highest throne of Heaven led to their being cast down into hell. Their plot to seduce man in which they seemed to succeed, led to the overwhelming mercy of the Incarnation, and the redemption thereby.

If we follow out the history of these proud enemies of God and man, we shall find other instances of the operation in their regard of this law of which our Blessed Lady speaks, instances which are also connected with the great work of the Incarnation. We know that our Lord in His life on earth was, from the first, the object of the especial hatred and suspicion of Satan and his evil Angels, and the history of that Life is almost the history of their devices and plots against Him. It is not exactly clear how far they divined Who He was, for, notwithstanding all their knowledge of history and of prophecy, the insane pride of their hearts made them blind in the midst of daylight, as to discerning His majesty hidden under the veil of humility. The great crime of the Passion was brought about by them, and it seemed to their malicious hearts the greatest of their triumphs. , Here again they were scattered in the conceit of their hearts. For, by the Passion they brought about their own entire overthrow, and if they had des:red to contribute to the glory of God, to the honour of our Lord, and to the good of the human race, they could not have done so more efficaciously than by what they did in their malice in bringing about the Passion.

These words are true also of their work all over the world, which had been going on almost since the Fall itself. They had laboured to draw to themselves the homage and adoration of mankind, putting themselves in the place of God, and usurping His rights, substituting, moreover, for His holy and pure law and worship, their own abominable inventions of falsehood and impurity. Here again, they contrived their own humiliation. It was the work of the Incarnation as the Apostle says, to destroy the works of the devil all over the world, and they had to undergo the mortification and humiliation of witnessing the destruction of the system of paganism which they had organised, which fell to pieces as of itself before the preaching of the Cross. All this is included in the words of St. Paul. Their wicked usurpation of the place of God, all over the heathen world, led to their greater destruction when the Church spread throughout nation after nation, just as their insane hatred for our Lord in His life time, when they did not know Who He was, and when they devised the treachery of His Apostle, and the whole wickedness of His murder by His enemies, led to the actual accomplishment of the design of God for the salvation of man by the sacrifice of the cross. Thus the Apostle, as we may say, draws out the thoughts of the *Magnificat*, and there is scarcely anything in his glowing language which is not founded on these simple words of Mary.

The other words of the passage on which we are

engaged put the same great act of God's mercy in another light. It is no longer the humiliation of the proud and the elevation of the humble, but it is the filling the hungry with good things, and sending away empty the rich. This language has its foundation in the canticle of holy Anna, of which we have already spoken. Our Lady must be thought to apply this image in the same way as the former, to the mystery of the Incarnation. Her words are so few and so pregnant in their meaning, that we must suppose that every one of them must be studied singly, and that no one can be passed over as if it could be merely a repetition of what had been before said. This passage in the *Magnificat*, which we have reason to understand primarily of the dealings of God in the government of His Kingdom, more especially with the rebel Angels in the great mystery of the Incarnation, contains, as it appears, at least three several principles of those dealings, each of which may be considered as something distinct from the rest. For our Lady tells us first that God shows might in His arm, and scatters the proud in the conceit of their hearts. Then she adds that He puts down the mighty from their thrones and exalts the lowly. In the third place, she says that He fills the hungry with good things, and sends away empty the rich. She seems to speak of the same classes of the creatures of God under the several names, first of the proud, the mighty and the rich, and then of the humble or lowly, (for that is the proper meaning of the word humble here also), and the hungry who are filled. She seems to refer in each of these clauses to the evil Angels on the one hand, and to the race of men elevated by the Incarnation on the other. But still her description of the enemies of God represents them under these several aspects, as proud, as mighty, or as it might be more closely rendered, princes or potentates, and thirdly, as rich, that is, as rich, satisfied, conscious of no needs, with no desire for more than they have. In the same way the objects of God's mercy are spoken of by her as humble or in low estate, and then again as hungry. Each of these parts of the description must be looked on as conveying a meaning of its own, which it is for us to endeavour to discover and to contemplate by itself.

It is also clear that there is a kind of progression in these several statements. It is as if our Lady went from one point to another in the Divine methods on which her mind is fixed. It is one thing to scatter the proud in the conceit of their hearts, another thing to put down princes from their thrones, another thing, again, to send away empty those who consider themselves rich. The proud might conceivably have been left on their thrones after the defeat of the conceits of their hearts, still more they might have been cast down from their thrones, and yet not sent away altogether empty. The successive stages in the manner in which God has dealt with them mark each an increase on the former in severity of chastisement. And in the same way there is an advance in bountifulness in the method adopted with the objects of God's favour when they are first said to be exalted, then filled with good things. The whole misery in which the rebels are plunged seems to require the full description as it is contained in all these statements, and the full measure of the goodness of God through the Incarnation seems to require the corresponding statements on the other hand. From the first series we get the whole view of the dealings of God with His enemies, and from the other the full view of His dealings with those on whom His love sheds itself forth in this great mystery.

We have already explained the chastisement of the pride of the enemies of God and man in His scattering them in the conceit of their hearts. Our Lady immediately adds the other feature, that they are set down from their thrones. Power, dignity, glorious state, rank in the Kingdom, were all theirs. Indeed these were the very gifts which became to their malicious and foolish hearts the sources of their pride, and so also of their fall. And after this sin of theirs, it could not be in harmony with the greatness and holiness of God to leave them on their thrones of power and dignity. Thus the second great act of His mightiness in punishment of their rebellion was to depose them therefrom. St. Jude speaks of them as the "Angels who kept not their principality, but forsook their own habitation."[15] Not that these privileges were their own irrespective of the gift of God, but that they were intended to be theirs for all eternity, if they had been faithful. This humiliation of the enemies of God is usually spoken of in Sacred Scripture as being accompanied by that other act of God's

[15] St. Jude, 6.

power, the elevation of the poor and weak and insignificant race of mankind in the place of the fallen Angels. The words of our Blessed Lady seem to refer not only to the canticle of Anna which has been already quoted, but also to the words of one of the Psalms which almost repeat the words of the mother of Samuel, where it is said of God that "He raises up the needy from the earth and lifts the poor from the dunghill, that He may place him with princes, with the princes of His people." [16] But it is not necessary that in these passages of Scripture, in which it refers to the casting down of the rebel Angels and the exaltation of men in their place, there should always be a distinct mention of the substitution of the latter in the place of the former. It is not a substitution of race for race, but of the faithful among men in the place of the unfaithful among the Angels, and this substitution is the great fruit of the Incarnation of which our Blessed Lady is here speaking.

The contrast which is suggested by the words before us is that between creatures of God, by nature full of power and knowledge very far surpassing those of mankind, creatures magnificently gifted in intelligence, in their power of using, applying, retaining their knowledge of things both divine and created, and the poor race to which we belong, so feeble in its capacities of mind and will, so dull in understanding and penetrating the truths within its natural reach or communicated to it, so slow in acquiring them and so quick in forgetting them, so laborious, so insecure, in its reasonings and conclu-

[16] Psalm cxii. 7, 8.

sions, so inconstant, so wanting in perseverance, in power of attention, or of soaring above the things of sense. Both naturally, and in reference to the gifts received in their supernatural elevation, the Angels are mighty, great, and wonderful in their magnificence and in their elevation above the comparatively poorly furnished race of mankind, in which the spirit is linked with the body, and the whole being thus joined on to the lower grades of creation.

Again, as has been said, the word used by our Blessed Lady concerning the Angels implies power, rank and rule, and in this also they are greatly elevated above mankind. Man is the lord, in a certain sense, under God, of the material creation in the midst of which he is placed, but the Angels are the princes of the heavenly kingdom and they are entrusted with the administration in a very large degree of the material universe. They were truly princes and the occupants of thrones of great dignity and power. The higher Angels also had a distinct office in the way of enlightening the lower classes of spirits. From all these they are cast down, in consequence of their pride and rebellion. Not that their natural powers are destroyed or taken away, but that they lose their seats in heaven, and their high estate as the ministers of God over His works is exchanged for the miserable service which they render, against their will and intention, in seeing the evil which they contrive, and the malice which they are allowed to exercise, turned by His good Providence to His glory and the good of those whom they tempt and assail. None of the blessed above, save those only who have passed out of this world before they became capable of the exercise of freewill, will wear crowns in the heavenly kingdom to which the hatred of these enemies of God has not contributed. And if in the case of the wilful sinners against light and grace their malignant efforts have met with success, it will be only for their own greater ignominy and chastisement in eternity, and God will be glorified for ever by the manifestation at the last day of all that He has done for those who thus throw themselves away, showing how entirely their destruction has been their own work.

The exaltation of the humble of which our Lady speaks must be understood of the effects of the Incarnation both in this world and in the next. In his natural state and condition man is lower than the Angels in a thousand ways, as has been said. But by the virtue of this great mystery, whereby God has become Man, those who share this inferior being and nature are already raised to dignities which surpass those given to the Angels themselves. One of mankind is One of the Three Divine Persons, and His Mother reigns over the whole realm of God as second only to Himself. The children of men become the sons of God by adoption, because God has become one of the children of Adam. Even in this world men can exercise powers in the new Kingdom which are not committed to Angels. They can absolve sin and retain sin, they can consecrate the blessed Body and Blood of Christ, they can administer the sacraments, they have power given them over the evil Angels, and, by the grace of God, they can lead the holy Angelic life, which is a greater wonder in them than in the Angels themselves, because the Angels have not the corruptible body linked to the spiritual soul. And the crowns and thrones which are to be won in the heavenly kingdom by the children of men are thought in many instances to be among the very highest rewards there, while the dominion of the saints reigning in heaven, as already exercised by them for the benefit of men, is a truth witnessed to by more than one of our Lord's sayings and parables, and one of which we have daily experience in the Catholic Church. We cannot set any limit to the number of the elect who are to share these glories, but it is commonly thought that it will at least equal that of the lost spirits who have forfeited their thrones by their rebellion.

These remarks may serve as some kind of commentary on the second portion of this description by our blessed Lady of the effects of the Incarnation, in reference to the rejection of the evil Angels and the elevation of man in their place. In the last member of her comparison our Lady inverts the order of her words, for she says first that God hath filled with good things the hungry, and then that He sent away empty the rich. Thus we have a third element in the dealings of God with the classes of which she is speaking. We may say that first He gives them their being and their gifts natural or supernatural, then He allots to them rank, dignity, power, and then He feeds them, according to the capacity of their condition and nature, with the good things which He has to bestow, which are all, in a certain sense, communications of Himself. There is no limit to these goods, because He is

Himself infinite in all goodness and excellence. The only limit can be in the capacity of the various beings whom He chooses to make partakers of Himself; and in His own free and personal choice in giving. This capacity may be limited in them in two ways. It may be limited by the powers of a created and finite nature, and it may be limited by the greater or less co-operation of the created will with His grace and light. But as far as the capacity reaches, there is no limit to the continual feeding with the good things of God of those who are here described as the hungry who are filled by His endless goodness. It is the characteristic of the good things of God, that they do not generate satiety in those to whom they are given. They that eat them hunger still, and they that drink them are still thirsty. Their hunger and thirst are not the painful cravings of want, but the ever fresh impulses of an infinite joy. In this sense it is that the blessed Angels in heaven are ever hungry and thirsty after the good things of God, the communications of Himself on which they live. They are filled, and yet there is always room for more in the capacity of their beatitude, as there are ever fresh supplies ready for them in the infinite resources of the Divinity. And thus perhaps it may be, that our Lady puts the filling of the hungry first in this part of her description, because the myriads of the good Angels came before her mind as being for ever more and more filled with those blessed streams of the Godhead, from all participation in which their miserable fellows are shut out for ever. The chief agony of their state of endless torment is the intense craving of their hunger after God and their thirst after God, which are never to have the slightest satisfaction, and, as they know, in consequence of their own free choice and deliberate malice. And it is most significant of our Lady's true appreciation of the lot of the enemies as well as of the friends of God, that she leaves the other torments of hell to be implied, speaking directly only of that which is in truth so preeminent in its misery as to make the rest comparatively nothing. To her the beatitude of heaven is the possession of God, the utter misery of hell is the loss of God.

But here again we must not forget that the main and direct subject of the portion of the Canticle of our Lady on which we are now occupied, is the contrast between the treatment of God by the fallen Angels and His treatment of the race which He has united to Himself in the Incarnation. And, certainly, never was there so great an instance of the mercy which consists in the feeding of the hungry with good things, as when the race of man, famished and fainting unto death for the lack of the grace of God, for the want of truth, the food of the intelligence, of light, of spiritual strength, of the hope of peace and reconciliation, and of all other most necessary means for the maintenance of moral and spiritual life, was admitted to the great banquet which is spread for it in the kingdom of the Incarnation. The land flowing with milk and honey, fertile and teeming with all good things that could refresh the long wandering tribes of the desert, and fill their hearts with joy and gladness and thankfulness, all the imagery of the most glowing descriptions of the prophets, would be as nothing by the side of the truth in this case of the filling with good things of the hungry. For nothing material can adequately describe the hunger of the soul, nor can any material abundance of provision and refreshment equal the truth of the magnificence and prodigality of the spiritual goods which the Incarnation has brought home to the very doors of every one in the Catholic Church.

It is here that we seem to touch on the effects of that particular counsel of God, whereby it was ordained that the benefits of the Gospel kingdom should not be imparted to the world in their fulness, until mankind had had long experience of the miseries of a state of destitution, in which they had learned their own utter helplessness and want. For by nature we are made such as to want our God with an infinite need, and even if we had never fallen we should still yearn for Him with unutterable hunger. But the cravings of the mind and heart of man were enormously enhanced by the terrible condition in which our Fall placed us, and by the effects of the long night of ignorance and degradation into which the actual history of the race shows it to have been plunged. We see some traces of this thought in the canticle of Zachary, which carries on so many of the suggestions of this Canticle of Mary. Zachary speaks first of the blessedness of the effects of the Divine Visitation, delivering men, already perhaps in the grace of God and with some amount of knowledge concerning Him, from their spiritual enemies, and enabling them to serve Him without fear in holiness and justice before Him all the days of their life. And then, at the close of his canticle, the Saint goes on to speak of the enlightenment of those who were sitting in darkness and in the shadow of death, perhaps intending to signify the further benefits of the Incarnation to those who were more or less outside the sphere, even of that partial knowledge of God which was the lot of the chosen people.

The saints of God, as far as we can know them in their perfection in this world, are what we might expect from the wealth of graces, the enlightenment and ennoblement, which are conveyed in the dispensation of the Incarnation. It is more true to say that the saints show us what all mankind might be made, if they faithfully corresponded to grace, than to say that they are exceptional instances of benefits of God, which are reserved only for a few favourites of the great King. And the lowest and most degraded of the heathen nations that are still to be found in parts of the world where the power of the Church has either never reached or been altogether driven away, are specimens to us of the depth of misery to which human nature can sink without the knowledge of God. If we wish to measure the abundance and magnificence of the good things of God, and to compare them with the hunger and want which His bounty has filled, we have but to put together these two extremes. And then we must remember that the most abundant imparting of the good things of which we are speaking which can be made in this world to the souls of the saints, is comparatively nothing to the overwhelming magnificence with which they are fed in the kingdom of heaven. Moreover, as in the next world the fulness of those who are filled is so much greater than that which can have place here, so also is it with the cravings of those who crave and are not satisfied. The holy souls of Purgatory long after their God with a calm tranquil longing, for their wills are perfectly united to His, and they would not see themselves in possession of Him before they are fitted for that measure of His possession which is to be their lot for ever. They know that the time will come when their detention from Him will end, and yet the intensity of their desire is strained to a measure which nothing on earth can equal. And if their longing for God is so beyond our imagining, what must be the hunger of those who are never to enjoy Him at all? The words of our Lady seem to pass lightly over their miseries, when it is only said they are sent away empty. These few words contain the whole of their misery, or at least they represent its chief and most utterly miserable feature. Empty, indeed, and with what an emptiness! No language can express their torments in the simple loss of God. No stroke of evil fortune, the loss of the favour of a sovereign, or any other temporal cause of utter ruin in the things of this world, reducing the richest and the most prosperous to a state of abject misery and destitution, can produce so wretched a poverty, craving, famine, starvation and despair, as when the rich dwellers in heaven were sent away, by their own fault empty, beggars, famished, writhing under the certainty that their case was hopeless for ever and for ever, to the dreadful eternity of Hell.

It will be remarked on a comparison of the

Canticle of our Lady with that of the canticle of the Old Testament which we have named as having furnished, in a certain sense, its outline and succession of topics, that there is much less in the words of our Lady than in those of Anna about any personal enmity or conflict between herself and the proud and mighty of whose humiliation she speaks in this part of her song of thanksgiving. We shall find something more about our enemies in the canticle which immediately follows this, that is, in the *Benedictus* of St. Zachary. Still, we trace here the presence of the thought of the enmities which God was to place from the beginning between the promised Mother and Satan, and between his seed and hers, although her mind is too calm to admit of any personal triumph, and she dwells exclusively on the Divine action in her own exaltation. Some of the writers who have left long works of the history of our Lady, and notably the famous Maria de Agreda, have much to tell us of the continued assaults of Satan and his emissaries on our Lady herself, as if each step in the onward march of the mystery of the Incarnation had been fiercely contested by these enemies of God and Man, especially in the way of attempts to lead astray or to frighten the Blessed Mother herself. It may not be at all unlikely that she was exposed in the providence of God to many interior trials and attacks. It must always be remembered that with her the temptation could not be as with ourselves, who have as it were traitors in the camp who will, if they may, co-operate with our enemies, in consequence of the imperfection introduced into our nature by original

P

sin. The path along which our Blessed Lady was led is not revealed to us, but it may have been one of suffering in this respect also, which would make her more entirely like her Blessed Son.

We come now to the last portion of this Canticle. In this our Lady speaks of one more of the great attributes of God as manifested in the work of the Incarnation. This is the attribute of His wonderful and most patient faithfulness. "He hath received Israel His servant, being mindful of His mercy, (as He spoke to our fathers,) to Abraham and his seed for ever." In the original, the clause about speaking to the fathers is parenthetical, as if it had been said, " He hath received His servant Israel so as to remember His mercy to Abraham and his seed for ever, as He spoke to our fathers." Thus there are three stages, so to speak, of this faithfulness of God. He executes His design, by laying hold on His servant Israel. This is done so as to make the act an act of the remembrance of the mercy, which He had before resolved upon. And lastly, it is not only the remembrance of a mercy, but the fulfilment of a promise of mercy. The act is one thing, the remembrance of mercy is another thing, and the accomplishment of the promise is another thing. All these are commemorated singly and specially by our Lady in these words, as if it were her characteristic not to let fall in her hymn of thanksgiving any one particular of the gracious mercies of God.

The word which is used for what is "received" in our version, is a word kindred to, though not identical with, that used by St. Paul, when he speaks of the Incarnation in the Epistle to the Hebrews. There he says, " Nowhere doth He take hold of the Angels, but of the seed of Abraham He taketh hold.[17] The actual words of our Lady are taken from a passage in the prophecies of Isaias, where God is introduced as saying, " But thou Israel art My servant, Jacob whom I have chosen, the seed of Abraham My friend,"[18] the word translated " chosen " being the same with that here used for the word received. It implies, no doubt, in the thought of our Lady, no common kind of helping, or receiving, or choosing, but that taking hold of which the Apostle speaks, when He dwells on the truth that God has taken on Him human nature, and made Himself Man of the seed of Abraham.[19] This then must be thought to be the meaning of our Lady in this place, to mention once again the supreme grace and condescension of God in the Incarnation, and then to go on to point out, in her strain of thanksgiving, that the Incarnation was, in the manner in which it had been carried out, an instance not only of the power, and the holiness, and the mercifulness of God, but also of His faithfulness.

God might have become man by a new creation, as Adam, without father or mother. But it pleased Him to become Man in the way in which He did, by making one of His own creatures His Mother. And it pleased Him to do this by choosing this blessed Mother from a particular race and family, which He had pointed out from the earliest times as the object of His choice. He chose to promise what He was to perform, and to perform what He had promised, to show Himself not only merciful, but

[17] Heb. ii. 16.   [18] Isaias xli. 8.   [19] Heb. ii. 16.

mindful, faithful, careful to keep His own word, and not to be driven from redeeming His pledge and crowning the hopes which He had raised by giving it. Our Lady speaks only of the faithfulness of God as to His promise to His servant Israel, and Abraham, but she might have gone on further in the catalogue, as St. Zachary immediately carries on the strain, in speaking of the house of His servant David. The privilege of belonging to the royal line, to which the promise had been finally confined, was a privilege which was not shared by St. Elisabeth and St. Zachary, and their blessed son St. John, and so perhaps our Lady stops short in her song, that she may leave to the mouths of others to celebrate the faithfulness of God to her own favoured family.

Our Lady thus sets before us this attribute of the faithfulness of God as the subject of special thanksgiving and praise. It includes the twofold gift of the promise and the fulfilment, the promise, by which the hearts and souls of men are strengthened and elevated, and taught to rely on the Word of God in loving hope and confidence, and then the veracity of God, in bringing out in His own time and way the accomplishment, notwithstanding, as is implied, all the perversity of men, which might tempt Him to change His counsel and leave them to the consequences of their own ingratitude. To our Lady, whose mind was so full of the intelligence of the rights of God, and who knew also so well the miserable history of His treatment at the hands of the people which He had chosen for His own, this attribute of His faithfulness in His promises must have seemed more wonderful than it may seem to us. Perhaps in her own deep humility the close of her *Magnificat* may have had some reference to the last words of her cousin to herself, " Blessed thou that didst believe! because those things shall be accomplished which were spoken to thee by the Lord!" and she may have made it a subject of ths purest joy in her own heart, that she had to be the instrument of the most beneficent counsel of Him Who was not only most mighty, most powerful, most holy, and most merciful, but also most faithful.

We have again in these concluding words of the *Magnificat* an instance of the singular pregnancy of the expressions of our Lady. No one could have drawn out more fully and beautifully the immense copiousness of the redemption of which she is here speaking. But she sums all this great subject up in the simple words, "as He spake to our Fathers." These words refer us to that great and rich field of the prophetic description of the Gospel Kingdom, which was no doubt the daily food of the mind of Mary, as of all the saints of the Old Testament. It includes all the manifold promises, from the beginning to the very end of that system of anticipations of which something has already been said in these volumes. It includes the original prediction to Adam and Eve as well as the glowing details of the picture there sketched, as expanded in the mouth of Isaias and his companions of the great choir of the Prophets. The picture was ever growing on the eyes of the devout students of the sacred writings, and it is there that even the children of the Church have to look for the full revelation of the blessings which they enjoy in her bosom. We must remind ourselves once more of the Providential disposition of God in giving to His people, both before and after the Incarnation, this elaborate description of the blessings bestowed in that great mystery. To our Lady's mind the words used by her represented the whole picture as it was familiar to herself. She must have pondered it from the very first dawn of her life, with that same characteristic intensity of attention and calmness of appreciation, which distinguished her in her contemplations of the fulfilments of the prophecies as they were successively unrolled before her eyes. As she summed up all the misery and degradation of the fallen Angels in two words, so here she embraces all the glories of the Church in this simple formula.

The whole of this great Canticle of our Blessed Lady may be summed up without much difficulty from what has now been said. It begins by the outpouring of two great affections of the soul, the magnifying God and the rejoicing in God her Saviour. We have already explained what it is to magnify God and there can be no difficulty about the affection of joy, the deliberate and careful rejoicing, founded on the grateful considerations of the immense benefits of salvation, one by one. The ground given by our Blessed Lady for the expression of these two principal affections is that God has done great things for her both as her God and as her Saviour. The great things of which she speaks are said to have, as their result and fruit, that all generations shall call her Blessed. The great things themselves are pointed out as the results of the exercise toward her of the three great attributes of God, His power, His holiness, and His mercifulness, a mercifulness which is exercised from generation to generations of those who fear Him. The great things which had been done for her by her God and her Saviour are further connected with the working of His Providence in the government of His creatures, on which He has acted in this case, as in others, according to His rule of the casting down of the proud and the exaltation of the humble, of the filling the hungry with good things, and the sending away empty of the rich. It had been the lowliness or humble estate of His handmaiden that had drawn down on her that loving and gracious regard of God which had led to her exaltation. She sees in the mercy of the Incarnation and all its results the operation of the law already mentioned. The proud rebel Angels have been cast down from their seat, they have been scattered in the very conceit of their own hearts, and the humble have been exalted, first by the exaltation of the Incarnate Son in His Human Nature, the pattern and model and principle of all humility, and then in her own exaltation through Him, and that of the whole race to which she belongs. In the same way is applied the operation of the law by which the hungry are filled with good things and the rich sent away empty. Lastly, our Blessed Lady turns to another great attribute of God as having been exercised in the Incarnation, the attribute of His faithfulness. He had taken up and received, and made His own, in a new way, by the Incarnation, His servant Israel, fulfilling thereby His own promises as made from of old to the fathers of the chosen race. The mercy had been promised to Abraham and His seed, it had been conferred on them by the Incarnation of the Son of God in her womb, a daughter of Abraham.

The large and simple lines of thought which are followed out in the *Magnificat* make it fit for that general and continual use by the Catholic Church for which it has been destined by God. Day after day, in her Vesper service, the Church lifts up the hymn of Mary as the fittest expression of her own dutiful affections, giving glory and thanks to God, and rejoicing in the salvation which He has wrought for all mankind in the Incarnation, and for all His gifts in the order of Providence and the order of Redemption. She calls to mind for her children the three great attributes of power, and holiness, and mercy, which are exercised day after day in the government of the world, but especially in the fruits of the Incarnation—an ever flowing and most abundant stream of graces and blessings of the highest kind. She rejoices and gives thanks for the elevation of the Mother of God, for the glory which thence redounds to her God and her Son, and also for the immense benefits which make generation after generation eager to call her Blessed. The elevation of Mary is the greatest fruit of the Incarnation, and when the Church rejoices over it she sees in it all the elevation of all the saints and all the blessed, by virtue of the Precious Blood. It is the highest expression of that principle of the kingdom of the Incarnation, in consequence of which the King of heaven and earth chooses to surround Himself with a large and countless crowd of princes and potentates, who reflect and share His own greatness. Mary's privilege, like the prerogative of her Son, is unique, but it is reflected in the glory and the power of the saints of God.

The Church finds the rejoicing of Mary over the defeat of God's enemies the natural expression of her own gratitude for His endless mercies, and for the peculiar love and predilection with which He has looked in mercy on the race of Adam, and raised it, even after its Fall, to the thrones left vacant by the rebel Angels, and she can remind herself at the same time of the condition on which the favours of God are given under every dispensation, the condition of humility, and of holy and reverent fear. In the commemoration of the faithfulness of God to His promises to the seed of Abraham, she is again roused to give Him thanks for this instance of His mercy, through which alone it is that the blessings which she possesses are hers. She sees also an occasion of thanking Him, in humble confidence, for the promises which secure to herself, now made the heiress of all to which His faithfulness binds Him, the grace and light, and strength, and indefectibility which are necessary for her position in the world, and which make her able to discharge to the children of men the great office entrusted to her. Her children rest for their own salvation, and protection, and guidance, and perseverance, on the same faithfulness of God, on the continual exercise on their behalf of His power, His sanctifying work in souls, and His mercifulness, as a part of which they reckon the blessings which they enjoy from the patronage and intercession of her whom they are always to have reason to call Blessed, and of all their brethren in Heaven who are already enrolled among the saints and princes of His kingdom.

CHAPTER X.

THE NATIVITY OF ST. JOHN.

St. Luke i. 59—80.   *Vita Vitæ Nostræ*, § 7.

THE Gospel narrative tells us nothing more about the Visitation of our Blessed Lady than that she remained at her cousin's house about three months, and then returned to Nazareth. We must accustom ourselves to these silences in the sacred history, wherein weeks and months and years, about which there must have been so much to tell, about which we shall perhaps have so much knowledge and instruction in the kingdom of our Lord hereafter, are passed over with hardly a word. It is not the object of the Evangelists to give us anything like a complete history. They have been guided to select for us just what it is necessary for us to know, just what it was fitting they should tell when they wrote. And it is very likely indeed, as may be seen by the treatment of the Divine truths and events which have been revealed to us, that if more had been told us, the world would have raged still more furiously against the revelation than it has. These three months, during which the visit of our Lady certainly lasted, must have been a time of wonderful repose, prayer, spiritual profit, close intercourse with God. Our Lord was present in the womb of His Blessed Mother in the house of Zachary, and His presence was known and honoured, both by the Blessed Mother herself, and by her hosts. For it is hard to suppose that St. Zachary did not share the Divine knowledge with his wife and his child.

The presence of our Lord with His Blessed Mother meant a perpetual stream of fresh graces and holiest inspirations to her soul. It meant a continual homage of affections of the most tender love and gratitude on her part to Him. We have seen what it effected in the souls of St. John and St. Elisabeth at the first moment when it began, and we shall see immediately its effects on the soul of St. Zachary himself. It is impossible to suppose that what had so great an effect when it began, and when it was coming or had come to an end, was not equally productive of holy results, in the way of enlightenment and sanctification, during the whole period during which it lasted. Whether St. Joseph was present or not we are not informed. But we must be on our guard, as has been pointed out, against drawing any conclusion from the mere silence of the narrative. In any case, the period of these three months was a time of immense and most rapid spiritual growth, though, like many such times in the history of souls, it was outwardly a period unmarked by any great events which could attract attention.

"And Mary abode with her about three months, and she returned to her own house." It has been thought by some of the Christian commentators, that these words, coming as they do in the sacred history before the account which immediately follows them of the Nativity of St. John, imply that the visit of our Blessed Lady came to an end before the time for the birth of the child of St. Elisabeth. Moreover, some reasons are given by these writers for the departure of our Blessed Lady, before the actual birth of St. John. These reasons are met by others on the part of other authorities, who contend that it would have been most seemly and natural for the visit to have been continued till its natural completion, after the birth of the forerunner of our Lord. In truth, Holy Scripture is silent on this point also, and the reasons on one side or on the other, may have been set aside, in the actual course of events, by some decree of the wisdom of God of which we are ignorant.

But it seems, on grounds of criticism, unsafe to argue peremptorily from the words which have just been quoted that our Blessed Lady was not present at the birth of St. John. It is evident that the narrative is cast in the form which it now bears for the sake of keeping more distinct the two mysteries, the mystery of the Visitation properly so called—that is, of the beginning of the sojourn of our Lady with her cousin, and the marvellous incidents by which her first salutation was followed,—and the other mystery of the birth of St. John, and the marvellous incidents by which that birth, in its turn, was illustrated. It is not at all unlikely that we have here an instance of what is common in the formation of the Gospels, though it is not always so manifest on the face of the narrative. The narrative, as we possess it, is made up of separate short documents, originally distinct, each of which relates the incidents or the sayings of some one mystery, or miracle, or discourse, or anecdote, and each of which therefore, either begins or ends with some few words by way of showing that the particular subject is opened or closed. Then there follows, in the text as we have it, the beginning of another and entirely distinct narrative, opening perhaps with some words which, if taken as in connection with what has been immediately prefixed in the arrangement, might mislead the reader as to the order of the events in point of historical sequence. The Gospel of St. Matthew is full of such pitfalls for the unwary critic.

In the present case we have the arrangement of the Church, which keeps the feast of the Visitation on the day after the octave of the Nativity of St. John, as a kind of guide to us, and this at all events sanctions the opinion that our Lady was present at the Nativity itself. For if there had not been some tradition about the Visitation, which authorised the belief that she was present, as has been said, when St. John was born, it is not likely that the direct words of St. Luke would have been forgotten, which seem to say that she left her cousin before that time. If there had been no such reason for the present order in the calendar, the Visitation would naturally have been celebrated before the Nativity of the Baptist. We therefore may conclude that there was some early tradition on the subject, by which the arrrangement of the Calendar was settled in seeming discrepancy from the Gospel narrative.

"Now Elisabeth's full time of being delivered was come, and she brought forth a son. And her neighbours and her kinsfolk heard that the Lord had showed His great mercy towards her, and they congratulated with her." The fact of the birth of a child at the natural time was nothing that could create wonder, but we are not told that St. Elisabeth had made her state of pregnancy known before the time came for her to become a mother indeed. It is said in the Gospel narrative that she hid herself for five months after her conception. The number of the months is clearly given by St. Luke in connection with the Annunciation of our Lady, for he goes on to say that in the sixth month the Angel was sent to her. It is not therefore certain that St. Luke means us to understand that St. Elisabeth did not keep her holy secret after the five months had expired. But, in any case, the birth of a son was what had been predicted by the Angel to her husband, and this may well have been taken as a fresh confirmation of the truth of the words of St. Gabriel, a large part of which refer to what was still future, the work and office of this blessed child. The birth of a son was always considered a matter for special congratulation, and we find that Anna, the mother of Samuel, had made this particular petition to God that He would grant her a man child. Thus the congratulations of the neighbours and kinsfolk may have been offered, both for the marvellous favour of her being a mother at an age so advanced, and also for the particular gift of the child who might grow up at least to be like his father, the minister at the altar of God. This supposes that they knew nothing, as yet, of the miraculous vision of his father before his conception.

"And it came to pass that on the eighth day they

came to circumcise the child, and they called him by the name of his father Zachary." The rite of circumcisisn, as it seems, was performed wherever it might be convenient, and not necessarily in the synagogue or in the Temple. There must have been some point in the ceremony at which it was the custom to give the name of the child. This it seems to have been properly the office of the father to do. But St. Zachary was still under the affliction which had befallen him as the punishment for his incredulity, and thus the office was undertaken by some other person of his own family. When the text says that they called him by his father's name Zachary, it is meant that they were going so to do, and perhaps the word had been pronounced, when St. Elisabeth interrupted the speaker, saying that her child was to be called John, meaning the grace or mercy of God. She may have learnt this from her husband, notwithstanding his affliction, for it is natural to suppose that they had used some of the ordinary means of communication in such cases of infirmity. But it may be that she knew this also by Divine revelation. The name John was not uncommon among the Jews, and there could be no objection to it on ordinary grounds. These people seem to have thought that the child should be named after some of the family. " And they said to her, there is none of thy kindred that is called by this name." The objection seems to have been divinely prompted, in order that it might give the required occasion for the appeal to the father of the child. "And they made signs to his father, how he would have him called. And demanding a table book, he wrote saying, John is his name. And they all wondered." They must have wondered at the entire agreement between St. Elisabeth and her husband, for the name may not have been a matter of great ordinary importance, and in such cases, there would not have been any reason for the parents to have consulted or agreed together.

But a still greater marvel was immediately to take place. All were aware of the infirmity which afflicted the holy father of the child, and indeed, it had been brought prominently before the minds of all by the discussion about the name of the child. They were therefore prepared to receive with great astonishment the sudden and complete restoration of the gift of speech to St. Zachary. This was what now took place. "And immediately his mouth was opened, and his tongue was loosed, and he spoke, blessing God." The crown was thus put to the joy of this holy pair, and at the same time a providential preparation was made for the discharge by St. John of his future office, for which it was requisite or convenient that those who knew him should look on him as one whose whole history had been marked by God in a way that promised great things concerning him. From his very birth he was thus a remarkable child, even if the full use of his reason, and the other unusual gifts which had been bestowed upon him while yet in the womb, remained a secret from the generality of men. There was something prodigious about his conception, as was evident from the great age of his mother, there was something of a Divine purpose in his coming into the world, as was evident from the circumstances

which had occurred about his name, and there was
also the wonder of the sudden recovery of his father
from the affliction which had been so many months
upon him. These things would be enough to attract
attention, and to account for the general opinion
formed of his lofty destiny.

"And fear came upon all their neighbours, and all
these words were divulged," that is, spread abroad,
"over all the mountainous country of Judea." The
city in which St. Zachary dwelt was on the hills,
which form a considerable part of the inheritance of
the tribe of Juda, and give to its products a different
type from that which prevails in Galilee. In such
a country report would easily fly from town to town,
and the general impression would remain in the
common mind, ready to meet the Baptist when the
time came for what St. Luke afterwards calls his
manifestation to Israel. "And all they who had
heard them laid them up in their heart, saying,
What an one think ye, shall this child be? For the
hand of the Lord was upon him." These last
words seem to signify that there may have been
other marvellous points about the childhood of
St. John, of which we have no direct mention in the
Gospel history.

The joy of the neighbours of St. Zachary and
St. Elisabeth at the birth of their blessed son, and
also at the marvellous recovery of the aged priest
from the affliction which had been so long upon
him, is a feature in the history which is entirely in
keeping with the whole character of this part of
the Gospel narrative. The Annunciation and Visitation are, as far as possible, mysteries of pure joy.

Q

We apply the name "joyous" to other parts of the Holy Infancy, such as the Nativity itself, the Purification, and the Finding in the temple of the Holy Child. But in all these three mysteries there is something of the shadow, indeed, of more than the shadow, of the Cross, and other portions of the history are more distinctly marked with the brand of suffering. There is suffering in the Nativity, suffering in the Circumcision. The Purification includes the first formal announcement of the future Cross made by St. Simeon to our Blessed Lady, as if it were a part of the Providence of God that this prediction should be made by one of His most authoritative ministers in the very temple itself. It is needless to point out how the joy of the Epiphany is dashed with the first fulfilment of the prophecy of Simeon in the massacre of the Innocents and the flight into Egypt. After the Purification, when the soul of our Blessed Lady was already pierced by the sword which was never thenceforth to be absent from her thoughts, there is no incident in the story which has not its share of this element of suffering. But it is not to be found in the Annunciation and in the Visitation. It is as if the good Providence of God had chosen to give to our Blessed Lady at least these three months of unmixed joy, such, almost, as might have been her lot, if she had actually become the mother of the Incarnate God under a dispensation which did not require the Atonement for the sins of mankind.

Thus were fulfilled those words of St. Gabriel to St. Zachary, at the time of the vision in the temple of which we have already spoken, that at the birth of St. John many should rejoice. Perhaps the words of the Evangelist are meant to point out this fulfilment. The whole life and career of St. John were, indeed, full of causes of joy to the whole world, but it seems as if St. Luke had meant us to understand that his birth was, in a special way, a most joyful mystery. Such an occasion would be incomplete, it might be said, unless there had been the marvellous restoration of St. Zachary to the full use of his faculties at the moment of the naming of his holy child. This was a kind of crown to all the spiritual joys and blessings of the Visitation. Our Lord often grants to His servants these temporal blessings as a kind of complement to more important gifts which affect the soul. As was said of Him on the occasion of one of His double miracles, " He doeth all things well." The principle of this tender method of Providence is expressed by Him when He says that the children of the Bridechamber must not mourn when the Bridegroom is with them. The presence of our Lord in the womb of His Blessed Mother had wrought the most wonderful results in the souls of those aged saints and their still more blessed son. It was in a manner right that no element of sorrow should be left unremoved, and that the joyousness of so great a spiritual mystery should spread itself over the whole neighbourhood around the abode in which our Lord had shown, for the first time, His power of scattering blessings on every side.

We need not regard the joyfulness of these early

mysteries of the Holy Infancy, simply as a gleam of sunshine, vouchsafed for the purpose of gladdening the hearts of our Lady and the saints with whom her time was spent. For the effects of spiritual joy, especially on the most saintly souls, are very great indeed. Joy enlightens, and enlarges, and fortifies, and enriches, in a marvellous manner and degree. Our Blessed Lady was already consummate in all perfection of virtue, and yet it may have been the Will of God that she should have this season of intense and unalloyed rejoicing immediately after the accomplishment of the Incarnation, in order that she might grow ever more mightily and swiftly in grace, and He may have had the same purpose with regard to the souls of St. John and of his parents. The discipline of sorrow and suffering may be necessary or convenient for the purpose of bracing and strengthening the souls who are subjected thereto. But God ripens and matures and expands the spiritual energies by other influences as well as those of sorrow, and, indeed, His method of training them to their highest beauty and perfection is usually an alternation of pain and joy. Few souls may be fit for the most intense and continual joy, which yet may be the most profitable of all the measures of grace to those who are already the the furthest advanced in perfect union with Him Whose life is essentially joy, unceasing, unalloyed, unalterable, and ineffable in its brightness.

It is only natural to find that this glorious and most happy mystery of the Visitation should have its canticle of joy and thanksgiving. It gave occasion, as we have seen, to the Canticle of our Blessed

Lady herself, which is the foundation of all the New Testament songs of joy. But that Canticle was uttered at the very beginning of the three months of our Lady's sojourn with her cousin, and expressed most directly the affections of her heart as to the great mystery itself of the Incarnation. It dwelt chiefly on what we may call the heavenly part of the mystery, the casting down of the proud rebels against God from their thrones and the elevation of man in their place by virtue of the humiliation of the Son of God. The earthly issues of the Incarnation are summed up very shortly in the *Magnificat*, as if our Blessed Lady had been divinely guided simply to suggest them, and then leave them for future celebration by the blessed father of the Baptist. This is the chief distinction between these two great Canticles, as we shall presently see. The *Benedictus* grows out of the *Magnificat*, singing the praises of God more especially for the fruits of the Incarnation as unfolded in this life, here and now, in this lower world, before those who reap its benefits pass to the vacant thrones in heaven. If our Blessed Lady gives thanks to God for His gifts through our Lord which are eternal, St. Zachary has the commission of thanking Him for those fruits of our Lord's condescension which accompany and encompass us in the pilgrimage on earth, from our cradle to our grave. Thus the Church has chosen this as the last song of thanksgiving which she sings over the grave of her children, before it finally closes over them, both because no words can sum up more perfectly the gratitude which we owe to God for the earthly privileges of the Christian life, and because the thoughts which these words suggest are so full of the tenderest consolation to the mourners who have, then and there, to leave those whom they have loved until the day of that last meeting which is to know no separation.

CHAPTER XI.

THE CANTICLE OF ZACHARY.

St. Luke i. 67—80. *Vita Vitæ Nostra*, § 7.

"And Zachary his father was filled with the Holy Ghost, and he prophesied." The canticle of St. Zachary, of which we have now to speak, is as Scriptural in its language as that of our Blessed Lady herself. But it does not seem to be so formally arranged after the pattern of any one of the Old Testament canticles as is the *Magnificat*. Just as the blessed Elisabeth, in her greeting to our Blessed Lady, had taken up the last words of the salutation of the Angel, and completed the truth which they enunciated, so also we find that this canticle of the father of the Baptist takes up the last thought of the Canticle of Mary, and enlarges upon it. This last thought in the *Magnificat* is the thought of the faithfulness of God to His promises. It is this attribute of God on which the canticle of Zachary chiefly dwells in its first and longest portion, keeping, as has been said, to those results of God's fidelity which belong to the earthly kingdom of our Lord. The second and shorter division of the canticle is occupied with an address to the holy child himself who had just been born. It speaks of his office in relation to the coming Messias, the giving of Whom to His people is the subject of the first part, that gift being especially considered as the fulfilment of so many prophecies. There is also another peculiar feature in this canticle, the manner in which the holy old man plays, as we should say, on the names of the chief personages concerned in the carrying out of the great work of mercy which has given occasion to the hymn of thanksgiving. We shall speak of this more at length in due time. This will suffice for an account of the canticle in general.

"Blessed be the Lord God of Israel, because He hath visited and wrought the redemption of His people, and He hath raised up a horn of salvation for us in the house of David His servant." St. Zachary thus catches up the last strain in the song of our Blessed Lady, who had spoken of the merciful taking hold of His servant Israel on the part of God. She had left out all reference to the special promises made to her own ancestor David. Now St. Zachary fills up the omission, speaking, as she had spoken, of God as the God of Israel, but adding that He had raised up a horn of salvation in the house of His servant David. It is also to be noted that he uses here, and at the end of his canticle, the word which is rendered "visited," as if he had in his mind some reference to that actual presence of God with him and his household, which was brought about by the Visitation of our Lady. He uses the word in the sense in which it is elsewhere used in Scripture, where God is said to visit, whether for good or for evil, whether in the way of chastisement or of consolation and deliverance, whenever He acts in some special and unusual manner in His Providence, which shows that He is dealing with certain peoples or persons for some great object of His own, with unusual rigour or unwonted tenderness.

As the word "visit" is thus of ambiguous meaning, and may be applied indiscriminately either to punishment or deliverance, the aged saint specifies the manner of the visitation of God of which he speaks, by adding that He hath wrought redemption to His people. The full meaning of the words is that in which they have ever since been used by the Catholic Church, as the *Magnificat* also has been used by her and will be used to the end of time. The visitation of which the Saint speaks is the Incarnation, not the simple dwelling of God for a time among His people, but the making Himself man, one of themselves, in that holy race of Israel which He had chosen. And the redemption which He has wrought is not any temporal deliverance, such as those of the people from the bondage of Egypt or from the yoke of the Philistines and the like, but the spiritual deliverance, of which all those historical deliverances were the types, the deliverance from the bondage of sin and Satan and the hopeless banishment from God and from Heaven, which was the appointed punishment of sin. This is the only true deliverance worthy of the condescension of the God of Israel, and unless we were to be delivered from these spiritual slaveries and enemies, all temporal prosperity and liberty would be of light account. It is the redemption of which the Psalmist sings when he says, "With the Lord there is mercy and with Him plenteous redemption, and He shall redeem Israel from all his iniquities."[1]

Thus we see at once that the canticle of which these are the opening words carries on the strain of rejoicing which our Blessed Lady had begun, by dwelling especially on the benefit of redemption, and the effects of the Incarnation as enshrined in the kingdom of Christ in the Church. Our Lady had spoken of the scattering of the proud Angels in the conceit of their hearts, and the defeat of all their devices, whether to exalt themselves unduly in Heaven or to bring about the destruction of mankind and the disappointment of the good designs of God for their elevation. She speaks of the issue of the enmities originally set between Satan and the Woman and her Seed, and she has only at the close of her song mentioned the earthly portion of the great warfare. Zachary speaks of the kingdom of the Messias as promised to David, to whose throne our Lord was to succeed. "He hath raised up a horn of salvation for us, in the house of His servant David." These words at once give the character of the Son of David to our Lord, the Redeemer of the world, and they imply the fulfilment of all the special promises made about the throne of David. Our Lord is Saviour and also King. For it is a horn of salvation of which the saint speaks as having been raised up for mankind, and in the words which he

[1] Ps. cxxix. 7, 8.

uses the holy name of Jesus is alluded to. The house of God's servant David is specially mentioned as the home of this great salvation. The word horn in Scripture means power, royal authority, dominion and the like. Thus the saint refers immediately to the words of the Angel at the Annunciation about the "throne of David His father, and that He was to reign in the house of Jacob for ever, and that of His kingdom there was to be no end." This is the proper Scriptural account of our Lord's work, that He is not simply a Redeemer, but also a King, as St. Peter says in his address to the chief priests after the day of Pentecost. " Him hath God exalted with His right hand, to be Prince and Saviour, to give repentance unto Israel and remission of sins."[2] St. Zachary says that God has raised up this horn of salvation, because, by the wise Providence of God, the family of David had for many centuries lost the royal power and dignity, and thus the kingdom had to be restored, a most true and spiritual kingdom, the character of which is made very plain in the verses which follow. The same thought is implied in the words of the Annunciation, that God should give to the Child of Mary the throne of His Father David. But the word used by St. Zachary brings out more clearly the feature of the restoration and resuscitation of that throne. This is the first line in the description of redemption.

Thus we find that the first line added by St. Zachary to the short description of the work of God for mankind, as given in the *Magnificat*, brings out two great features in the dispensation

[2] Acts v. 31.

of the Incarnation. The first of these features is that it is distinctly a dispensation of redemption. This essential feature belongs to it from the very first moment of its prophetic history, for it is a part of the original Gospel delivered in Paradise after the Fall. It is implied in the words of our Blessed Lady in the *Magnificat,* more than once. It is contained in what she says about the mercy of God from generation to generations, in what she says about the exaltation of the lowly, and the filling of the hungry with good things. It is especially signified in the last verse of her Canticle, wherein God is said to have taken hold of His servant Israel, to remember mercy, and that this is in accordance with the promises to Abraham and to his seed. But our Lady had left undescribed the Kingdom of the Redemption, she had spoken more directly of the confusion of the enemies of God than of the details of His mercy on the objects of His compassion. S. Zachary tells us that the visitation of the people of God is for the especial and particular purpose of redemption.

He tells us in the second place that this redemption is enshrined in a visible kingdom, settled on the House of David. The Redeemer then, as has been said, is a King, reigning, according to the words of St. Gabriel, for ever in the House of Jacob, a King of whose kingdom there was to be no end. This is something beyond the simple idea of deliverance, or redemption, for these great blessings might be imparted once, and then might conceivably pass away. But in the statement about the "horn" of salvation raised up in the House of David "the servant of God," we have the idea conveyed of permanence and stability as well as of powerful deliverance. For the words themselves seem to sends us back to one of the great prophetic psalms, the *Memento Domine David*, which by many commentators is considered as a psalm of very late composition referring to the times of our Lord, where we have words about making the horn of David flourish, or lengthening the horn of David, and preparing a lantern for His Christ. Thus we may consider that St. Zachary dwells both on the idea of redemption in itself, and on that of the permanent kingdom of the Redeemer in the Church, and that thus his opening words are an expansion of a part of what was contained in the finishing clauses of the *Magnificat*.

"As He spoke by the mouth of His holy prophets who are from the beginning, salvation from our enemies, and from the hand of all who hate us. To perform mercy to our fathers, and to remember His holy testament, the oath which he swore to Abraham our father that he would grant us." This again is a repetition of the note struck by our Lady herself, who had mentioned at the end of her Canticle the promises made to the fathers. St. Zachary specially mentions the prophets who are from the beginning. This expression in Scripture seems to signify the great antiquity of those who are thus spoken of, but it may be taken literally in the present case. For the ordinance of prophecy is one of the institutions of God's government of the world which has been in operation from the very beginning, and the words in which St. Zachary sums up the message confided to the prophets show that he refers to the promise made from the very beginning of the history of man. His words imply that the promise contained the grounds of hope resting on faith in the coming Redeemer, and that this faith was not in any temporal mercy only on the part of God, but such as embraced the remission of sins and spiritual reconciliation with Him. But this was in a special way the characteristic of the promise by which enmities were set between the Woman and the serpent, and her Seed and his seed. The words of the canticle, therefore, imply that the promise of the remission of sins was made at the very beginning, that this promise was renewed in all subsequent promises made later on in the history, and that it was by faith in this promise that the merits of the true redemption were made available to the reconciliation of every soul who inherited this faith.

The words of St. Zachary also imply that the kingdom of the Redeemer had been made the subject, not of one prophecy only, but of a chain of successive predictions, the first of which was as old as the world, while the last may have been of comparatively recent date. A series of prophecies of this kind must of necessity be not simply one in which the original prediction is repeated over and over again, but rather one in which the subject grows and expands and developes, as line after line is added to the picture. We have already spoken of this gradual unfolding of the rich promises of God, contained indeed in germ in the original prediction, but growing upon the eye of the devout student, age after age, until the whole of the glorious design of

God became manifest in its full proportions and beauty. Perhaps it may be said that Jacob, in his words about the sceptre which was not to depart from Juda until the coming of the Messias, gave the first open hint of the kingdom of the latter. The promises made to David and his house at the time of the settlement of the kingdom upon them form another stage in the series, and the language of these predictions can only be verified of the glories of the kingdom of the true Son of David. In the times of the prophets Isaias and Jeremias the house of David had come to be odious to God and to men alike, as Isaias expresses it, and we find the latter of these two prophets commissioned to declare that Jechonias, the occupant of the throne in his days, was to have no successor on the royal throne. The Babylonian Captivity brought about the fulfilment of this prophecy. The throne of David was cast down in the dust by that great calamity and chastisement.

But at the same time, and parallel with these predictions of disaster we find other prophecies of a different kind, such as that of Amos, of the restoration of the tabernacle of David which had fallen, and the more famous passages in Isaias concerning the root and rod of Jesse, and in Jeremias about the raising up to David of a just branch. And, again there are other prophecies, not only of the restoration of the kingdom, but of its immense extension and amplification, so as to take in the Gentile nations, as well of the perpetual continuance of the kingdom thus restored and enlarged. And we may include in the predictions of this class the famous prophecy of Daniel about the empires of the world, at the end of the series of which he places the establishment by the God of heaven of the kingdom which shall never be destroyed. This is the worldwide kingdom of the Redeemer, which is to last for ever. It is the establishment of the kingdom of the Incarnation in the house of David of which the blessed Zachary now speaks. It has been raised up by God, as He had promised by the whole choir of His prophets in successive generations from the very beginning of time.

St. Zachary goes on, in the verses which immediately follow, to describe this kingdom by a twofold note. The characteristic of a well ordered and flourishing kingdom is, in the first place, its security from outward danger and aggression, the absence of any foes powerful enough to threaten it or malicious enough to disturb it. This was one great element in the prosperity, for instance, of the Israelitish kingdom under Solomon. There were no external enemies for him and his people to fear. The other characteristic of a kingdom in a happy state is that there is internal peace and wealth and security, in the abundant means and resources of the citizens, their mutual harmony, their obedience to the laws, their freedom from everything that may breed division, disturbance, discontent. It seems as if the holy father of the Baptist intended to describe the kingdom of which he speaks as distinguished in both these ways. He first speaks of "salvation from our enemies, and from the hand of all that hate us," and then after the remarkable. clauses in which, as we shall explain, he seems to use the meaning of the three names of John, Zachary, and Elisabeth as each containing a reference to some feature in the goodness of God in the new kingdom, he goes on to add the other characteristic note of which we speak, "that we being delivered out of the hand of our enemies might serve Him without fear, in holiness and justice before Him all the days of our life." Thus the promised kingdom is described as possessing the great characteristics of the highest prosperity, external and internal alike.

"Salvation from our enemies and from the hand of all that hate us." The kind of antithesis between our enemies and those who hate us, is taken from one of the Psalms, where we find the same words, "He saved them from the hand of them that hated them, and He redeemed them from the hand of the enemy."[3] We may well understand the words as promising us deliverance from the dangers which beset us from enemies like our own sensuality, the flesh, and the world, which have no personality of their own, and in the second place, from enemies who live by a life of their own, and are full of the most venomous and relentless hatred of us, such as the evil spirits, and the men whom they sometimes make their instruments for the carrying on their warfare against us. Thus we are promised deliverance from these two kinds of foes, internal and external, according to that passage of St. Paul, where he says that "our wrestling is not against flesh and blood," meaning not only or principally against our own sensuality, "but against principalities and powers,"[4] and the

[3] Ps. cv. 10.   [4] Ephes. vi. 12.

rest. Against these twofold foes we are promised salvation by the prophetic message which has been since the beginning of the world. Not that we are to be delivered from the assaults and molestations whether of the flesh and the corruption within us, or of the devils and their agents outside us, but that the merits of the redemption of which he is speaking are sufficient to give us strength to make these assaults on us the occasions of victory and triumph, not of defeat. The enemies who assail us have their forces weakened. We are endowed with new forces, new strength, new light, new courage in our resistance against them.

The words "to perform mercy with our fathers," seem to bear a sense kindred to that which has been explained in reference to the words of our Lady, about the mercy of God being from generation unto generations unto those who fear Him. That is, the Incarnation, in the redemption thereby wrought for the world, is a performance of mercy not only to those who are living at the time when the actual mercy is shown by God becoming man and paying the debt of justice for all mankind. For the effects reach back as well as forward, and are as available for those who lived and died in the earliest ages as for those who live in the latest. The ancient fathers were saved by faith in the coming of the Redeemer, just as the latest generations of men may be saved by faith in the redemption long ago performed. The Incarnation and the redemption by our Lord were the payment of the price of the salvation of the ancient fathers, as well as of that of later generations, and this payment of the price due to the jus-

R

tice of God is an act of mercy to the one as well as to the other.

Again, the fathers, even of the chosen people, and even the greatest saints among them, were still in a state in which they had need of further mercy from God, even though their reward was ultimately assured to them. For no one could enter heaven until the gates thereof were thrown open by the victory and Ascension of our Lord, and the final "revelation," as St. Paul speaks, " of the sons of God," is still future, to take place at the general resurrection. In this sense the mercy of which the canticle speaks was performed to the fathers themselves, and was not merely a mercy promised to them the fruits of which were to be reaped by others. And further, the triumph of the Church, the establishment of the kingdom of heaven all over the world, and other such results of the Incarnation, all of which were the subjects of prophecy, may be considered as the performance of mercy to the fathers, who had been encouraged by the promises in the hope and faith in which they lived and died.

" To perform mercy to our fathers, and to remember His holy testament, the oath which He swore to our father Abraham, that He would give us." In these words it does not seem fanciful to discern a kind of reference to the names of the holy family in which this beautiful canticle had its origin. For the name of John signifies the grace or the mercy of God, and the name Zachary signifies the memory of God, and the name Elisabeth signifies the oath of God. The name of John had been specially given by the Angel at the time of the revelation to

Zachary of the miraculous conception which was to take place of the child, and it had been insisted on specially, by both the parents, when he had to be named at his circumcision. This would give the name a singular importance in the mind of his father, and it is not wonderful that he should dwell upon it in this his canticle of thanksgiving. Having thus begun to apply the meaning of the name of the child, it was natural to him to go on with the allusions to his own name and the name of his wife. The testament, or covenant, of which the saint speaks may be understood generally of all the promises of God. The word is used of the promises made by God to Noe, both before and after the Flood, and at the later time the rainbow was given as a sign of the covenant thus made. But the more precise meaning of the word may be that which applies it to the covenant made with Abraham of which the rite of circumcision was the appointed sign.

The word which signifies the oath of God, in the second clause, is without any direct connection with the preceding in the Greek text, and, as it seems, must be referred back to the former words at the beginning of the passage about the horn of salvation. That is, it appears that the horn of salvation is the fulfilment of the oath which is here mentioned. This oath of God was made to Abraham after he had shown his wonderful faith and obedience in being ready to sacrifice his son Isaac, in whom, notwithstanding, he had been told that the promises made to him were to be fulfilled. "By my own self have I sworn, saith the Lord, because thou hast done this thing and hast not spared thy only-begotten son for My sake, I will bless thee and I will multiply thy seed as the stars of heaven and as the sand that is by the sea shore. Thy seed shall possess the gates of their enemies, and in thy seed shall all the nations of the earth be blessed, because thou hast obeyed My voice."[5] It is on this passage that St. Paul comments in the Epistle to the Hebrews " For men swear by one greater than themselves, and an oath for confirmation is the end of all controversy. Wherein God, meaning more abundantly to show to the heirs of His promise the immutability of His counsel, interposed an oath, that by two immutable things, in which it is impossible for God to lie, we may have the strongest comfort, who have fled for refuge to hold fast the hope set before us."[6]

There is here therefore also a kind of advance and increase, so to say, in the faithfulness of God. He was bound to perform mercy to the fathers, first because He was, as St. Peter calls Him, a faithful Creator, Who would not therefore forget His children in their need. He was bound also by His special promises, and particularly by the promise which He had given when the covenant of circumcision was made with Abraham and his race. And, in the third place, He was bound by His own oath, which added a new confirmation to the faith of those in whose favour it was made. We can thus see that these clauses in the canticle before us are not simply owing to the desire of the saintly priest to find references to the great counsel of God in his own name and in those of his wife and son. It is very likely that we

[5] Gen. xxii. 16—18.   [6] Heb. vi. 16.

have here traces of the habitual dwelling of his mind on the securities, if we may so speak, which God had given to His people as to the execution of that great counsel. They had not only to trust in their general knowledge of the goodness and mercy of God. They had the special privilege of being in covenant with God, a privilege sealed to them by the sacred rite of circumcision, which had just been performed for the infant son of St. Zachary. They had the still further assurance, on which, as we have seen, St. Paul thinks it well to insist, of the oath of God made to Abraham, after he had shown his faithfulness in not withholding from God even his only son, in whom the promises made to him were bound up.

The act of Abraham was a foreshadowing of the act of God in giving to us His own Son, and there may perhaps be some reference to this in the language of Scripture. This consideration of the pledges which God had given for the fulfilment of His design of mercy belongs to that temper of loving and careful reflection on His dealings with men, as manifested whether in Scripture or in His Providence, of which we have so beautiful an example in our Blessed Lady. It is a dutiful acknowledgment and answer to the mercy of God in letting us know so much of His methods. Thus it might have a favourite occupation of the mind of a saint such as St. Zachary, even apart from what we might consider the accident of the suggestions contained in the names here alluded to. Moreover, when we find Scripture or the saints speaking of the fulfilment or performance of mercy to the fathers, it must be remembered that something more is meant than that what was promised to the fathers was performed in favour of their posterity, as if there was any separation and distinction between them. The mercy in the Incarnation is performed to the fathers, not only because it was promised to them, nor only because they lived upon the grace which was given in consideration of the faith in the promised Redeemer. It was performed to them also because they are, in the sight of God, one with their posterity, living to God in the same chosen body of which their posterity are also members, as the Church is one body, not two bodies, in heaven and on earth. All live to God, as our Lord says when He proves the future resurrection from the words of God in which He called Himself the God of Abraham, Isaac, and Jacob, so many years after the death of these Patriarchs. Thus, in acknowledging the faithfulness of God, it was only natural that a saint like St. Zachary should rehearse the distinct and several pledges by which God had bound Himself, declaring that they had all been fulfilled, notwithstanding the unfaithfulness to Him of so many among the inheritors of the promised boon. Thus these clauses, suggested by the names of himself and his family, are in their natural place in the canticle of Zachary.

The next words of the canticle, as has already been explained, at least to some extent, set forth the substance of the great promise, of the testament or covenant, of the oath, the effects and fruits of the gift of the horn of salvation raised up in the house of David. "That He would grant to us that being delivered from the hand of our enemies we may serve Him without fear, in holiness and justice before Him all our days." This, then, is the boon conferred on men by the Incarnation in the Kingdom of Christ. We are delivered from the hand of our enemies, and we can serve Him in holiness and justice before Him, without fear, and this all our days. These words may be considered as summing up the fundamental privileges of the Gospel dispensation. In the first place, the grace of God delivers us from the hand of those enemies, of whom mention has already been made. We have already pointed out that this twofold description seems to cover the chief requirements of a peaceful and flourishing kingdom. The enemies from without are those of whom mention has been made in the Canticle of our Blessed Lady. In that Canticle we are reminded of their discomfiture, their ejection from their state of glory and power in heaven. Here they appear rather as the malignant assailants of mankind, than as the rebels against God in His own Kingdom. We are delivered from their power, not by being altogether removed from the reach of their attacks, but by being strengthened against them after having been set free from the kind of slavery in which men were held by them before the Gospel privileges were brought home to them.

It is needless to enlarge on the results of that most cruel tyranny which was exercised by the evil spirits before their power was broken by our Lord. He Himself describes His own work as that of one who invades the domain and palace of a strong armed man, despoils him of his goods and takes away the weapons in which he trusted. No doubt under every dispensation, and especially under the Mosaic law, there was always at hand the assistance of the grace of God to aid men against their spiritual foes. But this does not in any measure diminish the truth of the picture as drawn by our Lord. Apart from the Gospel graces, Satan and his companions were rulers, though usurpers, instead of simply foes. They had taken possession of the world, and set up their tyrannical sway everywhere over mankind. They had seized on the very instincts of religion aud piety. They had perverted conscience, they had misdirected prayer and worship. It is little, after this, to add the long description of their usurpations in the realms of morality, law, society, and the rest. They are still foes, but foes whose power has been wonderfully weakened and shattered in a thousand ways. It is part of the saintly instinct to recognize their power, their activity, their malice, their presence and their snares on every side. If the language of the sacred Scriptures about these matters sounds strange and exaggerated to any of us, it is because such persons are to some extent under the influence of the world, and of Satan, one of whose prime devices it is to induce people to disbelieve in his activity, if not in his very existence. This then is the first great benefit of the merciful dispensation of the Incarnation, that we are delivered out of the hand of our enemies, words which imply that we should otherwise be practically in their power, and so we are able to follow out our Christian vocation in the service of God.

Secondly, we become in a new manner able to

serve God. Not that God could not be served under the old law, but that His service was more difficult, encumbered by a number of legal and external observances, what St. Paul calls the weak and needy elements. These might have been very useful to those who were in the state of bondage, but they are impediments to those who have the spirit of the children of God, and who serve Him without so many figures and shadows. Again, the fear of which St. Zachary speaks was the fear characteristic of the Law, a servile fear, and as such, a thing to be got rid of and changed for the free loving service and reverential fear of the children. Thus St. Paul says, "You have not received the spirit of bondage again in fear, but you have received the spirit of adoption of sons whereby we cry, Abba Father."[7] Again, the justice and holiness of the Gospel dispensation are far superior to anything that could be ordinarily attained under the Law. For the Gospel graces enable men to practise lofty virtues and live a life which is truly a participation of the Divine life, as St. John says that God has given us so much charity[8] that we are called and are the sons of God, and St. Peter speaks of Christians as being made partakers of the Divine Nature.[9] The justice or virtue which can be reached under the Gospel are truly such, and most heavenly in their perfection. The two words used in the text may be distinguished, the first as signifying interior holiness, according to the precept of the Law, as quoted by St. Peter (1 Ep. i. 15),

---

[7] Romans viii. 15. [8] 1 St. John iii. 1.
[9] 2 Peter i. 4.

"be ye holy, as I also am holy," the second as denoting the perfect practice of all moral virtues, justice, temperance, and the like.

The Saint then adds the two particular blessings which crown this gift of holiness and justice, namely, that these perfections are practised by Christians before God. By this he may mean, either that they are truly such virtues as to be esteemed as such by God Himself, or that the Gospel state of the service of God is a kind of life in His presence, a close familiarity with Him which was unattainable before. This is because our Lord really lives in us, as He says in the discourse in which He promises the Blessed Eucharist, and also because that great mystery itself makes our God present to us in a new way which had no parallel or anticipation in the older Covenant. Finally, the last words of this clause, "all our days," may be considered as involving the gift of perseverance, which is comparatively easier under the Gospel dispensation. There is also an allusion to the permanence of the dispensation itself, which has not to yield and make way for any other to which it is a preparation and an introduction, for it is the final completion of the mercies of God to mankind in the economy which He has chosen for bringing them to heaven.

This, then, is the substance of the Divine promise to the Fathers, as explained by the blessed Zachary in his canticle. Our enemies, who hate us with an inveterate and most intense hatred, because we are God's creatures and highly favoured by Him, are checked and beaten off, their tyrannical power over us is destroyed, and we are fortified against them, not only by the weakening of their forces, but by the strengthening of our own. This is the fulfilment of the first part of the promise made to Abraham by God on the occasion of the oath of which St. Zachary speaks, when it is said to the patriarch that his "seed shall possess the gate of their enemies." Of course this image is to be found repeated in other passages of Scripture, and it is important to see that St. Zachary understands it as of the defeat of the spiritual enemies of mankind. The blessings of which he here speaks as subjects of promise on the part of God must have been in his mind as the matter of a great chain of successive prophecies, rather than of any single prediction. But such promises are usually found to contain, at least virtually, the two elements of the deliverance from enemies and the opportunity and facility of the practice of the service of God. The last part of the commentary of St. Zachary, the serving God without fear in holiness and justice before Him all the days of our life, is the description furnished us by the saint of the Old Testament, illuminated already by the rising light of the New, of the spiritual benefits promised by God by the whole ordinance of prophecy as the especial fruit of the Incarnation. These benefits are expressed in the single passage to which we are referring by the words, "in thy seed shall all nations be blessed." And it would require an endless commentary indeed to exhaust the full meaning of these words, which embrace all the spiritual blessings of the Church, as well as all her influence on society, or human life in all its aspects and phases, an influence ever at work for good even in departments which are not directly spiritual.

We may now pass on to the second part of this canticle. St. Zachary has celebrated the horn of salvation raised up by God in the house of David, in language which shows how entirely spiritual were his conceptions of the kind of deliverance that was to be wrought, and the kind of kingdom that was to be set up. Next he turns to his own child, and speaks to him of the glorious commission which he was to receive in the preparation of this new kingdom. "And thou, child, shalt be called the prophet of the Highest, for thou shalt go before the face of the Lord to prepare His way. To give knowledge of salvation to His people unto the remission of their sins, through the bowels of the mercy of our God, in which the Orient from on high hath visited us, to enlighten them that sit in darkness and in the shadow of death, to direct our feet into the way of peace."

The first words of this last part of the hymn are a kind of paraphrase of the words of the Angel to St. Zachary himself at the time of his vision in the Temple. St. Gabriel had said, "He shall go before Him in the spirit and power of Elias, that he may turn the hearts of the fathers unto the children, and the incredulous to the wisdom of the just, to prepare unto the Lord a perfect people." The words before us show how St. Zachary understood this commission of his holy child. He was to be called, that is, he was to be, the prophet of the Highest. The Highest Himself then was to come, He was already among them, He had visited them, but St. John was to go before His face, and was to be called His prophet. He was to be His precursor, a herald sent before His face. He was to proclaim His near approach. He was to fit the people for receiving Him when He came, especially by his preaching of repentance. For repentance was the one indispensable condition to enable men to receive our Lord when He came, because His mission was one for the remission of sins. But for this repentance is the essential requisite, without which there can be no remission of sins to those who are capable of repenting, and all who are capable of sin are capable of repentance. And when he had prepared the people to receive our Lord by the preaching of repentance, by the baptism which was a profession of the state of penitence, and by the holy instructions which he was to give them for the amendment of their lives, then he was to reveal our Lord personally to them by pointing Him out. In these many ways St. John was to be a prophet, and as our Lord said of him, more than a prophet. He left behind him no prediction, he worked no miracle. His prediction was the pointing out a Person already among them. His miracles were the penitence and the conversion to which he roused the people by the grace of Him Whom he pointed out. His office was as much higher than that of the prophets as he was nearer to our Lord, his work more personally connected with Him, in truth, a beginning of His.

St. Zachary goes on to describe the substance of the message which his son was to have it in charge to deliver. "To give knowledge of salvation unto His people, unto the remission of their sins." The words "knowledge of salvation" may contain another allusion to the holy name of Jesus, as if it were meant that St. John was to make known to the people that salvation was now brought home to them by the advent of our Lord and the preaching of His kingdom. The two things which our Lord lays down as conditions of salvation are faith and repentance, which is included in baptism. His words when He began to preach were, "the kingdom of heaven is at hand, do penance and believe the Gospel." After the institution of baptism, He said, "he that believeth and is baptised shall be saved, he that believeth not shall be condemned." The salvation made known by St. John was thus the repentance from sin, and the faith in Jesus Christ, by means of which they obtained remission of sin. This is what his father here says about giving knowledge of salvation to the people unto the remission of their sins. It is conceivable that men might have their sins pardoned, as by the redemption wrought by our Lord, without knowledge of Him. This is the case with Christian children, in whom original sin is cancelled and to whom heaven is opened, without repentance or knowledge of their Redeemer on their own part, though they belong by Baptism to the body of the faithful, which is His Church. St. John was sent to make known our Lord as the object of faith, the Redeemer, the Lamb of God Who taketh away the sin of the world, and thus his mission is most accurately described in the words of this canticle.

"Through the bowels of the mercy of our God, in which the Orient from on high hath visited us." That is, as it seems, the remission of our sins through Jesus Christ is above all to be traced up to the compassionate love of God for us as its original fountain head and source. It was not simple compassion, but compassion set in motion and urged on to its wonderful excesses by the most tender love for us on the part of God. There was nothing in us by way of merit to bring down on us, more than on the Angels who had fallen, the mercy of God in the Incarnation. It was all because He loved us so much even while we were His enemies. It is to this original fountain of love that the blessed *Zachary* traces the condescension of the Incarnation and of the redemption wrought thereby. For it is in those bowels of mercy that he says that the Orient from on high hath visited us, using once again the word which refers to the presence of our Lord in the womb of His blessed mother in the humble dwelling of himself and St. Elisabeth. That is, he refers to the Incarnation as the special fruit of this combination of love and of compassion. God might have had mercy on us in a thousand ways. But the way He chose was the way of this visitation, for love is not content with mercy. It must share itself the low condition of those whom it loves, and this issued in God becoming man, thus making Himself poor and mean like us, and carrying out His mercy in that way rather than in any other. And thus there is good reason here for speaking of Him in the tenderest way as "our God," for He has showed us unutterable love, and made Himself ours in a new way.

The word in the original, which is rendered here "the Orient," or the dayspring, is in the Greek a word which primarily conveys the idea of springing up, and this may be applied indifferently to anything that can be said to spring up. Of these things there are two of which the word is used in sacred Scripture. These are the light of the dawning day, which shoots up through the darkness overhead, and the shoot or branch of a tree. Either image might be indifferently represented by the Greek word, as if we were to use in English the word upshooting or upspringing indifferently of either. The holy author of the canticle of which we are now speaking did not probably mean to quote directly any one of the many passages which occurred to his memory when he used the word, unless it were that of the prophet Malachias in his last chapter, "unto you that fear My Name the Sun of justice shall arise, and health in His wings."[10] It appears certain that the image before him was that of the dawning light, rather than that of the branch or shoot springing up. But he would be quite aware that there were many other passages in the prophets which would be suggested by his language, which would call up a large range of prophetical statements concerning our Lord. Some of these spoke of Him under the other image of the Branch. "Behold the days come, saith the Lord, and I will raise up to David a just branch, and a King shall reign and shall be wise, and shall execute judgment and justice in the earth."[11] In the prophecy of Zacharias the Hebrew word is the same as that in this prophecy of Jeremias, and it signifies

[10] Mal. iv. 2.   [11] Jer. xxiii. 51.

the branch, not the dawn of light. Yet we have there in the Greek version the same word which is used in other passages where the image appears to be that of the dayspring. "Behold I will bring My servant the Orient,"[12] and again, "Behold a Man, the Orient is His name, and under Him He shall spring up, and shall build a Temple to the Lord."[13] Another passage which would rise to the mind of the devout Jews at this prediction would be that of Isaias, "Arise, be enlightened Jerusalem, for thy light is come, and the glory of the Lord is risen upon thee."[14] There are many other such passages.

It may perhaps be said, in explanation of the use of this twofold image, that the truth which the image represents, and which is the main subject of thought in the mind of contemplatives like St. Zachary, requires both comparisons to represent it fully. The image of a plant springing up, a branch growing and expanding, is admirably suited to represent the gradual progress, whether of our Lord Himself in His manifestations in the Incarnation, or of the kingdom which He came to found. Such an image is required for the economy of the Incarnation, and it is all the more needed, when we take into consideration the extreme humility and hiddenness of our Lord in the beginning as Man, or again, the low and humble estate in which His Blessed Mother was, on account of the decadence and insignificance of the royal line at the time of His Birth. On the other hand, the dawning of light is not, in the countries with which the prophets were familiar, a gradual growth. It is rather a sudden burst of

[12] Zach. iii. 9.   [13] Zach. vi. 9.   [14] Isaias lx. 1.

S

glory, chasing away the shadows and darkness of night. But the idea in the mind of Zachary is, first of all, God visiting His people in His own Person. He comes down from on high first, and then manifests Himself gradually when He has come down. The dayspring visiting from on high is the first part of the Incarnation, the shoot springing up from the ground is the second, the gradual revelation of the Incarnate Son. Again, the growth of the kingdom of our Lord was that of an organised living body, and in this respect the image of the branch is more applicable than that of the dayspring. It may also be questioned whether there is so much difference in the terms used in the original as to enable us to say that the words might not be interchanged. And it must be remembered that St. Zachary is not quoting. He is using, in the same way as our Blessed Lady and St. Gabriel used it, the language of the prophets, without restraining himself from applying it to his own purpose.

"To enlighten them that sit in darkness and in the shadow of death, to direct our feet into the way of peace." Thus does the blessed Zachary sum up the ends and effects of this visitation of the dayspring from on high. The first effect is the dispelling of darkness, and the second effect is the guiding the feet of those thus enlightened into the way of peace. The whole world, Jews as well as heathens, were sitting helpless in darkness and in the shadow of death. The image of sitting implies that they were making no effort to relieve themselves. They were powerless and hopeless. Though the desire of the light may have been there, till the light came they could not move. The desire of the world for God is expressed in the beautiful image used by St. Paul in his address at the Areopagus at Athens, where he says that God had set all the nations of the earth "that they should seek God, if happily they may feel after Him, or find Him," using a word which describes the groping of men in the dark after the way, or the door, or whatever they need. And in his former speech at Lystra the Apostle had said, that God, though He "suffered all nations to walk in their own ways, nevertheless left not Himself without testimony doing good from heaven, giving rains and fruitful seasons, filling our hearts with food and gladness." [15]

But to sit in darkness is, as it were, to give up the search after God, notwithstanding the many instincts and needs of nature which were always prompting men to seek after Him, as we see in the history of the philosophy of the Greeks. At the time of our Lord all the world is described as sitting hopeless and helpless. The Jews had the sacred traditions and the truth about God, they knew what they worshipped, as our Lord said, but they were in darkness and the shadow of death, the former on account of their great ignorance, and the latter on account of their many dominant sins. The Gentiles were in far greater ignorance of God than the Jews, because they not only knew Him not, but they served the devil and their own lusts under the names of a number of false deities, whose worship was connected with intense moral degradation. Thus even the moral law had become largely obscured

[15] Acts xvii. 27, xiv. 16.

among them, as it is now among many nations outside the Christian pale. And thus their ignorance was united to the shadow of death, which is the special image of sin, as distinguished from ignorance, to a degree which was not to be found among the chosen people.

But now, for both of these, the dawn from heaven was shooting far up into the sky, to enlighten both, the Jews first and through them the Gentiles, and the other blessed effect was soon to follow on or accompany the dispelling of the darkness, the guiding their feet into the way of true peace, to enable them to reconcile themselves with God and thus enjoy peace of conscience, to know Him and Jesus Christ whom He had sent, to understand His commandments, to be able to obey them, to wield the whole armament of grace and light which was to be provided for them in the teaching and sacraments of the Church. This may be sufficient as a commentary on these beautiful and soothing words. But they may perhaps also include reference to that peace of which St. Paul speaks more than once, the taking away the wall of division between different peoples among the children of God, and the foundation of the one Church in which all are to be one. This is the more likely, when we consider that the canticle of Simeon takes up the canticle of Zachary, as this last caught up the ending words of the *Magnificat*. It is in the third Evangelical canticle that we shall find the reunion of the Gentiles clearly set forth. But the hint of this is contained in these words of St. Zachary, in which a distinction seems to made between the Gentiles and the Jews.

"And the child grew, and was strengthened in spirit, and was in the deserts until the day of his manifestation unto Israel." These few words sum up all that we are told, on the authority of Scripture, concerning the infancy and early manhood of St. John. Here, again, is a time of silence into which we should be glad to peer, if it was in our power. For the childhood of the saints of God is often very full of wonders and anticipations, in their infantine beauties of character, of their future services to God. In the case of St. John we know that his use of reason was anticipated, and there would therefore probably be many unusually wonderful manifestations of sanctity in his earliest years as well as later on. We are only told that he grew in body, and that, as he advanced in years, the Spirit of God within him grew stronger and stronger. In his case there was a real continual advance in grace, as there had also been in our Blessed Lady, such an advance as could not be in our Lord, Who was full of all perfection possible from the very first. The other thing which we are told of St. John is, that he was in the deserts until the time came for him to come forth to the world as a preacher of penitence. It is likely that his parents may have died not many years after his birth, and the marvellous child may have then taken up his abode as a hermit in the desert, preparing, by continual prayer and intercourse with God, and the practice of mortification and silence, for the great work which was to be committed to him. In this way also he might incidentally have laid the foundations of his great reputation for sanctity, and the great authority which he enjoyed from the very first, when he began his shortlived ministry among the people as the preacher of penitence and the remission of sins.

CHAPTER XII.

THE OPENING OF ST. MATTHEW'S GOSPEL.

St. Matt. i. 18—25. *Vita Vitæ Nostra*, § 6.

SOMETHING has already been said concerning the manner in which God deals with each single soul in the arrangements of His Providence. We have now to deal with a single instance of this beautiful method, in the course followed by· Him in the guidance of the great soul of the saint who stands next to our Blessed Lady herself in the order, as it has been called, of the Incarnation, that is, the blessed Joseph her holy spouse. The course of our work now brings us to the point at which something more must necessarily be said as to this method of God with His chosen saint. We have said that it is most probable that St. Joseph accompanied our Blessed Lady to the house of St. Zachary, when she went thither to visit St. Elisabeth. We do not usually think of him as remaining there the whole time of the three months during which her sojourn lasted. Nothing certain can be determined as to this point. It may be thought most likely that he returned alone to his humble trade at Nazareth, until the time came for him to fetch home his wife from the house of St. Zachary. If he had remained with Mary, it might have been for the sake of being of some use to the holy Zachary, as Mary was occupied in attending on her cousin. But Zachary was dumb and probably deaf, and it might have been some burthen to the holy pair to entertain both. It is therefore natural to acquiesce in the common impression, which supposes that during this time, or the greater part of it, St. Joseph was absent from the side of our Blessed Lady. It may have been agreed among them that he should return to fetch her home at the end of the three months. For the time of the birth of the Baptist could easily have been anticipated from the words of the Angel to our Lady concerning St. Elisabeth. Thus the Providence of God may have arranged external circumstances, in such a manner as to correspond with His designs in working out the great spiritual perfection of a soul so dear to Him.

Before we proceed to speak of the very short passage of Scripture which is all that we have to guide us as to the length of this interval, and what passed during it, it is well also to notice that we now change the guidance of St. Luke for that of St. Matthew. It may be thought that, with two inspired Evangelists, there can be little difference as to the authority of the narrative. There is no difference at all in the authority of the narrative, but there is a very great difference between the object of the two narratives, and this makes it very important to have a clear view of what that object is in each case. We do not speak of the general object, which is kept in view in all parts of the Sacred Scriptures equally, but of the special aim of the writer of the Gospel in each of the cases before us. This special aim gives its shape and form to the narrative, and determines what is to be inserted therein, what is to be omitted therefrom.

The object of St. Luke in his first chapter is, that the Church should possess a simple and clear statement of the facts connected with the carrying out of the mystery of the Incarnation, especially of the two kindred and inseparable mysteries of the Annunciation and the Visitation. St. Luke's narrative is in truth a history, a history, however, which omits everything which is not strictly an incident which it was important to relate, and giving no side explanations of many things which we should certainly have been happy to know more fully. The two stories of the conception of St. John and of that of our Lord Himself are linked together by the appearance of St. Gabriel in each, and by the presence of our Blessed Lady in the house of Zachary. Our Blessed Lady is the most prominent human figure, and it is hardly rash to say that the very words of the narrative may come from her.

In the Gospel of St. Matthew we have a narrative which is a history indeed, but a history the whole shape and design of which is argumentative. The whole Gospel of St. Matthew was put together for use among the teachers of the first Church at Jerusalem and their converts, and the opening chapters especially are just what they are, very mainly because the whole is compiled for this purpose. St. Matthew gives us only two short chapters on the infancy of our Lord. Of course these chapters as they stand in our New Testaments are merely arbitrary divisions. But they contain, in truth, five short sections, which were probably in existence, as separate sections, before they were placed in the Gospel in the order in which they now stand. Each one of them has an argumentative or a controversial purpose, and the whole is therefore far less of a simple narrative than the portion of St. Luke with which we have lately been dealing. But here again we may say there is a prominent human figure, and that figure is St. Joseph. But let us first examine what is the controversial purpose of the first Evangelist in these opening sections of his Gospel.

The first of these sections contains the genealogy of our Lord, tracing His line, apparently through St. Joseph, up to David and Abraham. The second section contains the relation of the revelation, made to St. Joseph by the Angel, of the Divine Conception of our Lord in the womb of His Mother, and this section is strengthened argumentatively by the citation of the prophecy of Isaias about the Virgin who was to conceive and bear a Son, Whose Name was to be Emmanuel, God with us. This section concludes by relating how exactly St. Joseph obeyed the injunction now given to him. The third section contains the account how, after our Lord had been born in Bethlehem, the wise Kings came from the East to Jerusalem to ask for the new born King, Whose star they had seen, and how they were directed by Herod, after careful inquiry from the chief Jewish authorities, to Bethlehem, as the place where the King was to be born. This section, again, is strengthened by the quotation, not so much by St. Matthew himself as by the scribes and priests of Jerusalem in answer to the enquiry of Herod, of the prophecy of Micheas concerning the birthplace of the Messias. A short account of the Epiphany is added by the Evangelist, as an introduction to the next section, which relates the massacre of the Innocents and the flight of the holy Family into Egypt. Here again it is St. Joseph who is warned by the Angel. At the close of this section St. Matthew relates the return from Egypt, which may be considered as in his mind a section by itself, for the reason that here again, as in the case of his narrative of the massacre, he fortifies his statement by the citation of a prophecy in which the incidents of which he is speaking had been foretold. He cites the well-known passage of Jeremias to support the story of the massacre of the children of Bethlehem and the neighbourhood, and he adds the words of the prophet Osee, about the calling of the Son of God out of Egypt. Finally, this Evangelist relates how it came about that St. Joseph, on his return from Egypt, went to live at Nazareth, rather than at Bethlehem, out of fear of Archelaus. And in illustration of this statement, and in explanation of this feature in the early history of his Master, he alleges the testimony, not of any one prophet in particular, but of the prophets in general, that the Messias was "to be called a Nazarene."

Thus St. Matthew treats the history of the holy Infancy in what might afterwards have been called an apologetic manner. He shows to the Jewish Christians, and, through them, to the Jews who might be on the road to conversion, or who might have to be dealt with controversially, that our Lord's early history exactly fulfilled the predictions concerning the Messias. He was to be the Son of David, and He was the Son of David. He was to be conceived and born of a Virgin, and He was conceived and born of a Virgin. He was to be born at Bethlehem, and He was born at Bethlehem. And as to this sign, St. Matthew can bring the fact of the witness of the chief priests and elders themselves, solemnly called together for consultation by the king on the occasion of the arrival of the wise strangers. The other points on which he insists are just those which would strike the Jews, who might be inclined to find some fault with the details of the history. Why was our Lord taken down into Egypt, and why was His birth at Bethlehem so obscured by the fact that He lived all His years at Nazareth, in a part of the country out of which as was once said by them, no prophet sprang? The answer is contained in the facts of the massacre, the flight, the return to Nazareth rather than to Bethlehem. Each of these particulars was no real difficulty, for each had even been made the subject of definite prophecy concerning the Messias. These are the points in the history of the Sacred Infancy which admitted of argumentative proof from prophecy, and it is for this reason that St. Matthew has selected these and left out so many other points in the same history, which did not so readily admit of this kind of argument. This is the simple account to be given of this part of the

Gospel of St. Matthew, who says not a word about any other part of the Holy Infancy.

Without excluding other purposes, which St. Matthew may have had before him in the composition of this part, as of all parts, of the history, it is clear that the contents of these several sections are so arranged and so selected by him as to be at once perfectly accurate statements of the facts related, and also statements so framed as to serve his argumentative object of the defence and explanation of the Christian version of the facts of our Lord's life. Now, the Gospels themselves tell us what were at least some of the objections made to our Lord while alive, and it is not likely that they were much changed after His Ascension. One of the most common objections that we meet with is that He was the carpenter's son. Another was that He ought to have come from Bethlehem, the city of David. Another was that none of the chief priests and scribes had received Him. Another was that He was a Galilean, and more than that, a Nazarene, for it seems that in Galilee itself Nazareth was not held in good repute. This purpose of the Evangelist should be kept in mind in our consideration of each of the several sections of which we have spoken.

For the present, we need only speak of the first of these objections, which may be supposed to be met by St. Matthew in the section of which we are now speaking. No doubt it might be said, that all his life St. Joseph had acted as the Father of the Child of Mary, and had been obeyed by the Child as His Father. It might be inferred from this by some objectors, that our Lord had really been the

Child of St. Joseph, and that the claim that He was the Son of God, conceived by the Holy Ghost, was a later invention of His disciples. As a matter of fact, we know that this was the allegation of many of the earliest heretics. To ourselves the answer to this difficulty would be furnished most satisfactorily by the history of the Annunciation and Visitation. The splendid series of divine communications and manifestations which are related by St. Luke in his first chapter have more argumentative weight in themselves, if there must be a comparison, than the narrative which St. Matthew gives us of the dream of Joseph and the words of the Angel to him in his sleep. It is far more to us to know what Gabriel said to our Lady, and all the incidents of the Visitation, than this dream of St. Joseph. But what St. Matthew has given us is more to the point of his purpose, because it explains perfectly what might have been a difficulty even after the other evidence of the Virginal Conception of our Lord. For the more certain it might have been shown to be, that our Lord was miraculously conceived and born of a pure Virgin, the more would it require explanation how it was that He was always reputed, and passed for, the son of Joseph the carpenter, whose whole life, as far as it met the eyes of men, would have been a contradiction to the claim of that Virginal Conception.

The account given by St. Matthew in his opening chapter is the best of all answers to this difficulty. It shows in the first place that St. Joseph knew of the Virginal Conception. It does not relate that Conception itself, in the manner of St. Luke. It adds the strongest of all human evidences to it, the evidence of St. Joseph. It shows in the second place that he had thought of having nothing to do with our Blessed Lady, after that Conception had taken place. It shows in the third place that he would actually have withdrawn from her in some secret way, but for a special Divine command. This makes it clear that the line of conduct which he always pursued, acting as the father of the Child of Mary, was only adopted by him after the will of God had been intimated to him that so it was to be. This also accounts for the citation of the prophecy of Isaias by St. Matthew. That prophecy contained three distinct predictions, the first of the Conception by a Virgin, the second of the Birth from a Virgin, and the third that the Child was to be the Incarnate God. The first two points are proved in the most ample manner by what is stated of St. Joseph, both before and after the revelation made to him, and the last is left to be proved by the whole history of our Lord.

This being the case as to the purpose of St. Matthew, it cannot be surprising if we find him wording his statement exactly in conformity with that purpose. He produces the witness of St. Joseph to the points which he specially desires to prove beyond cavil. These points are that our Blessed Lady was a pure Virgin, both when she conceived and when she bore our Lord, that St. Joseph knew this perfectly, that he was so well aware of it as to have thought of withdrawing from a position which was not his by right, and which involved immense responsibility, that of the father of the Child who had been so marvellously conceived. But St. Matthew is very careful to tell us further, that St. Joseph thought of doing this in such a way as to avoid any appearance of what would have been contrary to justice, the seeming to cast the slightest slur on the purity of his spouse. He also tells us how he was prevented from carrying out this thought by the warning of the Angel that he was to act as the father of the Child, Who had been miraculously conceived.

This is the direct natural meaning of the narrative of St. Matthew. No other meaning is without some difficulty in his words. But at the same time it is obvious that the history of the trial of St. Joseph, of the manner in which he may have been exposed to doubts, or hesitations, until the revelation was made to him by the Angel, and the like, does not belong to the purpose of the Evangelist. He takes up the history of St. Joseph at the point of his dream, when he was already in perplexity. It is an instance of precisely the same method that the first Evangelist mentions the Divine and Virginal Conception, not directly, though it is the most important feature of all in the history, but only as discovered by or known to St. Joseph, and as a cause to him of perplexity. The doubts and hesitations themselves of this Blessed Saint might have been told in a far fuller way by an Evangelist who had not this distinct purpose before him, in the first instance, of showing how it was that our Lord came to be considered so universally the son of Joseph, and this without any protest on the part either of St. Joseph or his blessed Spouse. This trial of St. Joseph is one beautiful part of God's dealings in the history of the Incarnation, and the testimony borne by St. Joseph, to the Divine Conception of our Lord is quite another part. It follows as self-evident that the perfectly true statement of facts which was the best for setting forth the testimony of St. Joseph, may require some supplementary considerations before it becomes a full narrative of the dealings of God with the soul of His chosen saint, in preparing him for the position he was to occupy in the kingdom of the Incarnation.

This is the simple and critical explanation of the manner in which this narrative of St. Matthew has been dealt with, from the earliest times in the Church, by those who have desired to trace out carefully and devoutly the dealings of God with the great saint of whom we are now speaking, and to explain the simple words before them in a manner most compatible with the very high sanctity which the whole Christian world attributes to St. Joseph. We turn to the narrative of the Evangelist, not simply for the proof of that particular point which he was commissioned to set forth, but for light as to what was to him and all the Apostles an axiomatic truth, the immense sanctity and pre-eminent position of St. Joseph in the kingdom of the Incarnation. It cannot be denied, and no one would wish to deny, that the very high idea which we have of that sanctity throws much light on our interpretation of the words of the Evangelist. It is in strict accordance with the truest principles of the interpretation of Scripture that this should be so. We use the same principle in the explanation of other passages of Sacred Scripture, much in the same way, and with the same reverence for every kind of truth, as when we use the ascertained facts of cosmogony, and our knowledge of natural things, in the explanation of the narratives of the Creation or of the Deluge. Not only it is right to use our knowledge in this way, but it would be most uncritical not so to use it. When we reject, for instance, the Helvidian interpretation of certain passages in the Gospels about the so-called brethren of our Lord, we have not only the simple Greek words to guide us, but the universal feeling of Catholics to support us. And this would be enough for our own judgment, even if it did not happen that, by carefully harmonising the statements made concerning those who are thus called our Lord's brethren, we can arrive at a clear confutation of the Helvidian theory.

The account of the hesitation of St. Joseph, and of the manner in which it was overcome, is thus given in the passage of St. Matthew of which we speak. "Now the birth of Christ was in this wise. When as His mother Mary was espoused to Joseph, before they came together, she was found with child of the Holy Ghost. Whereupon Joseph her husband, being a just man, and not willing publicly to expose her, was minded to put her away privately. But while he thought on these things, behold the Angel of the Lord appeared to him in his sleep, saying, Joseph, Son of David, fear not to take unto thee Mary thy wife, for that which is conceived in her is of the Holy Ghost, and she shall bring forth a Son, and thou shalt call His Name Jesus, for

T

He shall save His people from their sins. Now all this was done that the word might be fulfilled which the Lord spake by the prophet saying, Behold a Virgin shall be with child, and shall bring forth a Son, and they shall call His name Emmanuel, which being interpreted is God with us. And Joseph rising up from sleep, did as the Angel of the Lord had commanded him, and took unto him his wife. And he knew her not till she brought forth her firstborn Son, and he called His name Jesus."

No manner of stating the simple facts could be more perfectly adapted to the object of the Evangelist, while at the same time we shall see that he has carefully selected his words, so as to guard us against any incorrect interpretation of their meaning, such as might lead us to form sinister conjectures as to the state of mind of St. Joseph. St. Matthew says that our Blessed Lady was found to be with child of the Holy Ghost, and there can be no doubt, as St. Jerome says, that the person by whom she is said to have been so found must have been her husband, St. Joseph. He says that St. Joseph was a just man, and he gives his justice as his reason for not thinking of anything that could expose her to public obloquy or suspicion. But St. Matthew does not tell us what the measure was which St. Joseph thought of adopting and which he describes as the "putting her away privately." The original words would be more literally rendered as "leaving her free privately," and they must evidently point to some kind of action on the part of her husband which would leave her honour intact in the eyes of men, while it amounted to a practical separation between them, and a renunciation on her husband's part of all authority over her. The statement seems to amount to this, that St. Joseph thought it more perfect for himself to retire from his position with our Blessed Lady, but that his justice forbade him from doing this in any way that might expose her to hostile remarks.

There is but one feature in the whole passage before us which can seem difficult to understand. The Evangelist says that Mary was found with child of the Holy Ghost, and, as it seems, by St. Joseph, and yet it is a part of the message of the Angel to reveal to St. Joseph that that which is conceived in her is of the Holy Ghost. This has led many commentators to understand the first words as if the discovery of St. Joseph had not gone beyond the fact of the conception in the womb of Mary, and had not yet reached the point of a knowledge that that conception was the work of the Holy Ghost. They think that the words "of the Holy Ghost" are put into the passage by St. Matthew, in order that he may not leave for a moment on the minds of his readers the suspicion that the Conception was the result of any but Divine agency.

This may perhaps have been so. But why should St. Matthew be thought more careful to guard his readers against a misunderstanding, than to show that St. Joseph was free from the same? His words are more naturally understood in the latter manner than in the former. "She was found with Child by the Holy Ghost, whereupon St. Joseph thought of setting her free." On the other hand, the argument against the doubters of the Divine Conception would have been more forcible if he had said, if such was the case, that St. Joseph was not aware of the miraculous character of the Conception until it was told him by the Angel. That is the state of mind in St. Joseph which these commentators think to have existed. If so there was every reason in the world why St. Matthew should have said so. It would not follow that he had come to any unfavourable conclusion, for he might suspend his judgment. This, moreover, is not quite consistent with the epithet which St. Matthew applies to St. Joseph, and which contains the reason for his intention of avoiding all public exposure. If St. Joseph thought of his wife anything less than was the truth, such an intention would have been a measure of mercy and clemency and indulgence, or at least of forbearance of judgment, but not of justice.

But it seems unnecessary to assume that there is any inconsistency in the statement that Mary was found, before the revelation, to be with child by the Holy Ghost, and the revelation made of the same fact by the Angel. We must not assume that this truth was the one point as to which the Angel was sent to instruct St. Joseph. This is not the case. The Angel is sent to St. Joseph to give him practical guidance, not to do what he was thinking of doing, and to do something which he was thinking of not doing. That is, he was to take to him his wife, which it was his intention at the time not to do, and she was to bear a Son, to whom St. Joseph was to give the holy Name of Jesus, because He was to be the Saviour of the world. It is quite obvious that he could not venture to do this, even after the revelation of the Divine Conception which had taken place in her, unless he had been distinctly told to treat Mary in every respect as his wife, and to conduct himself in every respect as the father of her Child.

It is not perfectly certain whether the quotation of the prophecy of Isaias, which follows these injunctions on the part of the Angel, is meant by St. Matthew as his own addition or comment, or whether the words of the prophet were actually quoted by the Angel in his instruction to St. Joseph. But the last verses of the passage of the Evangelist seem to imply that the words were used by the Angel, because they seem intended to explain to us exactly what it was that St. Joseph understood as the injunction of the Angel. He took unto him his wife, he preserved her untouched, that she might not only have conceived as a Virgin but also bring forth her Son as a Virgin, and he called the Child when born by the name which had been enjoined him by the Angel. It would have been very natural for the Angel to be commissioned to bid St. Joseph lay aside his fear of taking his wife, and to give as a reason that she had conceived by the Holy Ghost, even if the Saint had already risen to that conclusion from what he had observed and heard and knew about his Spouse, as St. Jerome supposes. For, in any case, he could not as yet receive the truth on the faith of the direct word of God. But this might be absolutely necessary to enable him to bear the responsibilities laid upon him. And if the words of the Angel had stopped short at the revelation of this truth, he would still have been without the practical guidance of which we speak, and, but for the words about laying aside his fears, he might still have doubted whether or not to carry out his original intention. And it must be remembered again, that St. Matthew had to meet the difficulty created in the public mind by the manner in which St. Joseph had acted from this time to the day of his death, a difficulty only to be fully answered, not by the fact of the revelation as to our Lord's Conception, but by that of the order now given to St. Joseph on the part of God.

CHAPTER XIII.

THE TRIAL OF ST. JOSEPH.

St. Matt. i. 18—25.   *Vita Vitæ Nostræ,* § 6.

HAVING thus explained, as far as is necessary for the intelligence of the sacred text, the purpose of the first Evangelist in this short paragraph, which contains all that we are directly told by him concerning the state of mind and the conduct of St. Joseph at this most important crisis of his history, we may proceed to draw out, as far as may be, the hidden history of this great saint during the interval between the Incarnation and the incident which St. Matthew has here related of the vision in which the Angel appeared to him in his sleep. The workings of God with such chosen souls must ever have a great attraction for the contemplative Christian, although it is very seldom indeed that such subjects are directly touched upon in the Gospel history. It would be almost as reasonable to expect St. Matthew or St. Luke to give us a detailed account, day after day, of all that passed during the long years of the Hidden Life at Nazareth, as to look for an account of this process of divine grace with St. Joseph in the part of the Gospel now before us. But Holy Scripture is enough for us in all our needs, and because it says so few things about these treasures of the secret action of God it by no means follows that it tells us nothing or even little in those few words.

The Visitation of our Blessed Lady closed naturally with the birth and circumcision of the child of Zachary and Elisabeth. As has been said, the time could have been sufficiently foreseen for St. Joseph to have made an arrangement with his beloved Spouse that she should return home after about three months. It is natural to suppose that when that time had arrived he was at hand to fetch her to her own home. We have already seen that it is most reasonable to consider that the formal marriage of this blessed pair, as distinguished from the ceremony of betrothal, had taken place some time before the Annunciation. It could not have been delayed until after the point of time which we have now reached, that is the Nativity of St. John Baptist. That birth took place only six months before the Nativity of our Lord. If therefore St. Matthew speaks of the formal marriage in the passage which we have been discussing, the time of this incident must be put back to a point before the departure of the Blessed Virgin to her cousin's house for the Visitation. On many grounds this does not appear likely. St. Matthew therefore must not be understood as speaking of the formal marriage when he tells us of the hesitation of St. Joseph about taking to himself his wife. As this taking to him of his wife cannot be understood of the formal marriage, it follows that the Evangelist means us to understand him to speak of some other occasion, on which there was a possible opportunity of his acting in one way or the other, as to receiving or not receiving his Spouse in their common home, or remaining or not remaining there with her. For there is some reason for thinking that the little property at Nazareth was the property of her family, not of his. But if this be so, we can find no other occasion so natural for the occurrence of the hesitation of St. Joseph as this of the termination of the visit of our Lady to St. Elisabeth.

If St. Joseph had been absent from his wife during the greater part of these three months, it might be supposed that even naturally he would become aware of the pregnancy of our Lady on his return to her side. Or, if his knowledge of the truth was to be acquired from what he might hear from others, as St. Elisabeth and St. Zachary, or from what he gathered from Mary herself, or from the marvellous incidents of the birth of St. John and the song of rejoicing of St. Zachary, this would be the natural time for that knowledge to be brought home to him. Moreover, this would be the time when some decision must be of necessity taken as to his own conduct. If he was to leave Mary, under whatever impression concerning the nature of her conception, this would be the most opportune moment. She had already been away some months from her home, and separated from him. Thus, if this state of things continued, no new step would be taken to attract attention, and the criticism of the world would be avoided. On the other hand, if she now returned to live with her husband, it would be impossible for him to separate himself after this from her without some new and open act which would look like a rupture. But, when this was followed by the birth of her child, the slur on her purity would have been cast in the eyes of men. She was well where she was, in the holy home of St. Zachary and St. Elisabeth. They were her kinsfolk, persons of consideration, who knew and esteemed her immense graces and were even conscious of her singular elevation in the counsels of God. This therefore seems the most reasonable interpretation of the thought that was in the mind of St. Joseph at the time of which we are speaking, and it seems very difficult—unless we return to the supposition which there are so many grounds for rejecting, that at this time our Lady had not yet been formally married to St. Joseph—to find any other point of the history at which this hesitation of the latter can be placed.

Having said thus much as to the time of the hesitation of St. Joseph, we must now proceed to consider what was its exact character. Here we are met by a considerable difference of opinion among the Catholic commentators. It must be remarked at the outset of any discussion on this subject, that our conclusion must naturally be formed in harmony with what we have already come to consider true concerning St. Joseph and our Blessed Lady herself, and concerning the relations between them. We have seen reasons for thinking that they were both raised already to a very high state of sanctity indeed, that they were both full of devotion to the great mystery of the Incarnation, the accomplishment of which was the subject of their most ardent desires and prayers, and that they were both greatly familiar with the prophecies concerning the execution of that great counsel of God. We must further add that we have reason also for thinking that both our Lady and her husband were bound to maintain the most perfect continence in their married state, that St. Joseph was conscious of and a consenting party to the vow of virginity of which our Lady had spoken to the Angel at the time of the Annunciation, and that he was himself a partner in that holy resolution.

Now it is plainly impossible for those whose ideas of our Blessed Lady and of St. Joseph are such as are here described, to form the same conclusion as to any such subsequent portion of their history as that now before us, as those whose usual thoughts concerning this holy pair are altogether different. We must be consistent in our conclusions concerning all the parts of this history, and it will not be reasonable to forget, when we come to one point of the story, what we have already seen grounds for thinking certain on another. Yet we very commonly find even Catholic critics who seem not always to remember who St. Joseph was, and what were his ideas concerning his blessed Spouse, when they have to interpret the passage of the Gospel now before our minds. We must avoid this mistake, and endeavour to make our conceptions of the thoughts and intentions of these holy souls uniform and consistent. With this principle to guide us, it will not be very difficult to see our way to what may reasonably be supposed to be the truth as far as we can ascertain it.

The time in the history of which we are now speaking, was a time of immense glory to God, and of delight to the holy Angels, who watched from heaven the gradual unfolding of the great plan for the redemption of the world. But the incidents of that wonderful time were mainly interior. The greatest thing that had ever happened in the history of creation had taken place in silence, when the Eternal Word of God became Man in the womb of Mary. Then began that marvellous existence of the Word made Flesh, which was from that moment the chief delight of the Eternal Father. Then began the life of the Sacred Heart, with all its rich fruits of the most beautiful and intense acts of virtue. Then began that close companionship between the Heart of the Son and the Heart of the Mother, which, next to the communing with God of the Sacred Heart Itself, was the most wonderful and glorious thing in the spiritual world that had ever been in existence. Then began with fresh impetuosity and intensity, that ever-increasing perfection of the interior life of Mary, open only to God in its fulness, but to some extent revealed to the celestial citizens, which, next to the human Life of our Lord, was the most precious thing that earth had ever produced, or ever could produce, in the sight of its Maker. As each day passed over the head of Mary and of the Divine Babe in her womb, it gave occasion to the most beautiful worship and obedience to God that had ever been rendered, and the prayers and affections of these two Sacred Hearts rose up in a perpetual column of incense, so to say, before the Throne on high.

Even if we suppose that St. Joseph had no part in the Divine secret at first, it does not follow that he too was not at this time an object of the highest pleasure to God, on account of the manner in which he bore himself under the new circumstances in which the Holy Family was placed. God derived great glory from the homage paid to our Blessed Lady by her cousin St. Elisabeth. He was greatly glorified by the exultation of the holy Baptist in the womb of his mother, He was honoured by the Canticle of the *Magnificat* revealing the highest devotion to Him, and by all the incidents of that blessed stay of our Lady in the house of her kinswoman, which were crowned and summed up, as it were, in the canticle of Zachary. All these things were most glorious to God and in the eyes of Heaven. It is not much to think that at this same time God was receiving the homage of very noble and precious virtues from the pure and humble soul of the holy Spouse of Mary. We have already said that the fact that no revelation had been directly made to St. Joseph, at the time of the Incarnation, does not of itself prove that he had no other knowledge or surmise of what had taken place. There is good reason for thinking that St. Joseph may have witnessed the reception of his blessed Spouse at the hands of her cousin. This would not be inconsistent with the supposition that he was, even after that, not a partaker in the fullest sense of the Divine secret of the Incarnation. He may have heard and witnessed all that passed, and yet he might have had of it no more than human knowledge. Then we may suppose he left the house of Zachary, though even this is not certain, and that it was arranged that he should return and fetch his Spouse after the time of the birth of the child of Elisabeth.

It is at this point then that it seems most natural to suppose that the hesitation and trial of St. Joseph took place. He would come to that trial prepared for it by all the graces which we have seen it reasonable to think that he had already received, by his own considerations of what he might have already noticed in his holy Spouse since the moment of the Annunciation, what he might have heard while present, if he was present, in the house of Zachary, as well as all the prayers which it cannot be doubted were poured forth for him by our Blessed Lady. It was most difficult for her to speak even to him of the great privilege which had been conferred on her, at least it would have been most difficult, without some direct injunction from God. Her own perfect humility might have been shocked at having to speak a word. She had to commit the matter, so tenderly affecting both her and him, to the Providence of God, awaiting in heroic patience and confidence, and in great indifference to external consequences, the issue which God would decree. But if she could not speak, that would be all the greater reason for her prayers. Moreover, if she must be silent, it does not seem necessary to suppose that silence was incumbent on St. Elisabeth, nor could anyone fail to observe the singular deference and homage paid to the Mother of God in the house of her cousin. All these things must be taken into consideration in our estimate of the probable effect on St. Joseph's mind of the knowledge, whenever it was that he acquired it with certainty, that his pure and most holy bride had conceived a Child and was about to be a Mother.

There ought not to be any difficulty in understanding the distinction which is here implied, between knowledge on the one hand, however certain, which rests upon the highest human evidence, or on the conclusions which a devout mind may make for itself from the study of prophecy or from theological considerations, and the certainty, on the other hand, which follows on the word of God communicated to the soul in any of the many ways in which it pleases God to reveal His acts or His intentions. It is the difference between the light of the sun and any other ordinary light whatsoever. And it is moreover characteristic of a true revelation, to leave on the soul so much certainty as to make any doubt impossible. Thus if the blessed Spouse of Mary had every kind of ordinary certainty concerning the Conception by the Holy Ghost, it would still have been a very different kind of certainty from that which he possessed after the revelation had been made to him. But something more must be added before we are able to look at this question with perfect clearness. What has hitherto been said supposes that the hesitation or doubt of St. Joseph would have been entirely removed, if he had at once had a Divine certainty concerning the truth of the Divine Conception. This is far from being the case. That the Child of Mary was divinely conceived by the operation of the Holy Ghost was one truth, and that St. Joseph was to perform for Him the part of a father was quite another. It must be remembered that no amount of certainty on the first point could shed any light upon the second. God might have chosen Mary for His Mother, without choosing Joseph for His earthly father and protector. It might have been conjectured that it would be so, it might have seemed likely from certain points in the system of the prophetical predictions that it would be so. But this was pre-eminently a point as to which a certain guidance from heaven was necessary. Moreover, the inspiration under which Mary had acted in going to visit St. Elisabeth was given to her and not to her husband. She must have submitted it to him, as her own thought. After the revelation to St. Joseph, all the movements of the Holy Family are made in consequence of revelations to him and not to her. But this method of the Divine guidance had not yet begun. Thus, even if we were quite certain that St. Joseph knew the mystery of the Incarnation as fully as, or more fully than, St. Elisabeth and St. Zachary, the further question whether he was to assume any position of authority or protection over the Divinely chosen Mother remained perfectly unsolved until the time came for God to solve it. We may now return to the simple words of the Evangelist with which we are dealing.

The Scripture narrative informs us that when he found that Mary was with child by the Holy Gholy, St. Joseph did not know at once what it was right for him to do. He was a just man, and therefore did not wish to expose her to any public discredit. It was thus that he conceived the half-formed

.resolution of "putting her away privately." It must be remembered, again and again, that these simple words of the first Evangelist occur in a narrative which has been drawn up, not with the purpose of explaining to us the interior history of St. Joseph, but with the purpose of adducing him as the one most unexceptional witness to the supernatural conception of our Lord in the womb of His Mother. In this light, the words amount to a statement that the husband of Mary was so utterly without any part in the conception of her Child, that he was even about to separate himself from her in the best way which was consistent with his justice and charity, both of which forbade him to do anything that might be construed into a slur on her purity or her faithfulness to himself. This state of mind in the holy patriarch is consistent with more than one hypothesis as to the actual amount of his knowledge concerning what had taken place, and the form the doubts in his mind took, as to that, or as to his own conduct.

Though St. Matthew has not thought it his business to explain exactly which of several alternatives is the true one in fact, yet it is fair to think that here, as in other places in his Gospel, where his great brevity, and other characteristics, have left a difficulty for his readers, he has been at some pains to give them a hint as to the solution of that difficulty. In this place we consider that he has left such a hint in the words in which he has spoken of that which was manifested to St. Joseph, and which was the cause of his difficulty, namely, the words in which he says of our Blessed Lady, "she was found to be with child of the Holy, Ghost." These words seem to imply that he who found her with child, that is, St. Joseph, knew that the Child was conceived by the Holy Ghost. As has been said, they are like other words which St. Matthew puts in here and there in his Gospel, just when he has said something which might perhaps raise a difficulty in the minds of his readers which the Evangelist does not stop to explain further. But however that may be, let us see what are the possible states of mind which are consistent with the language of St. Matthew with regard to St. Joseph. These possibilities will be found to correspond to the various interpretations which are adopted by the Fathers as to the words before us.

It is possible, in the first place, that St. Matthew may mean that St. Joseph found that his wife was with child, but did not know the secret of the Conception bp the Holy Ghost. In this case the words "by the Holy Ghost" are added by the Evangelist, as it were, before their time, probably for the sake of not waiting a single moment without a protest in favour of the truth, and for the more perfect honour of the Blessed Mother. This state of mind, however, might admit of various phases of opinion or surmise or conjecture or decided judgment. St. Joseph probably knew that the Messias was to be born of a pure Virgin, in some marvellous way, without having any clear idea of the manner in which His conception was to be brought about, whether it was to be by the direct action of the Holy Ghost, or whether some supernatural power was to enable her to conceive without any other agency than her own. The prophets had said nothing about the action of the Holy Ghost. St. Joseph might have surmised that something marvellous had taken place, but he would have no suspicion or fear of anything that could be blameable in Mary.

We must add a second hypothesis, for the sake of exhausting the possibilities of the case—that he might have had some undefined fear, which did not amount to a certain judgment, that she had in some way which he could not conjecture, or explain, conceived in the natural manner. But it seems inconsistent with the character of this glorious saint, as well as with the knowledge which he must have had of the holiness of his wife and of her vow of virginity, that he could have formed the thought that she could have violated her vow, and that she was to blame and worthy of dismissal from his home, on the one ground on which our Lord afterwards allowed separation. Here it is only right to insist on what has been already said, that on the simple grounds of reason and criticism, we must not allow ourselves to forget the conclusions which we have already formed as to the lofty sanctity both of Mary and of Joseph, which would be of themselves enough to make it impossible for an injurious suspicion to enter his mind.

In the next place, if it be asked what is meant, in accordance with this supposition, by the fear of St. Joseph and his resolution or design of putting our Lady away in private, we can only think that he meant to withdraw in some manner from her company, perhaps leaving the place of his abode for some place unknown, so that it might not be obvious that he had entirely and for ever left her to herself. His fear would be that of living any longer with her, and this fear, in the hypothesis before us, would be simply grounded on his ignorance of the manner of her Conception. He was not reproached for his fear by St. Gabriel, as Zachary had been blamed for his slowness of faith. He was bidden by the Angel to have no fear of "taking to himself" his wife, and he is said after the vision to have "taken to himself" his wife. These twice-repeated words, then, require to be explained in some way consistently with the hypothesis adopted as to his hesitation. They cannot be understood, as has been shown, of any ceremony of marriage as distinguished from betrothal, for the simple reason that, at the date of the termination of the visit of our Lady to her cousin, there were less than six months before the Nativity of our Lord. But it is quite evident that the moment when St. Joseph took to himself his wife could not have been earlier than the end of the Visitation, though it might not have been later. Nothing that could be done, at so short a distance of time before the birth of our Lord, could be of any avail in preserving the honour of our Lady from suspicion, if it was anything that bore the appearance to the world of their first union in marriage. The taking her to himself of which the Evangelist speaks must therefore have been something the contrary of the course on which, if he had been left to himself, he might have determined. This was to separate himself from her in some way which would not make her the object of public animadversion. The direct contrary, therefore, to this course must have been his continuing to act towards her as he had done ever since their marriage, and remaining her husband in the eyes of the world, as much after the Visitation as before the Annunciation.

The words of the Evangelist are equally consistent with other suppositions as to the state of mind of St. Joseph. They are consistent with the supposition, which is suggested by St. Jerome in the lesson which the Church has selected to be read on Christmas Eve. This is, that seeing her to be with child by the Holy Ghost, he did not think that it was for him, without further authority, to act as her husband in the bringing up of the Child to which she was to give birth, and that therefore he thought it well to retire and leave the work of God to His own good providence. This hypothesis makes St. Joseph fully conscious of the Divine mystery, but afraid to mix himself up with its execution without authority. It is not easy to exaggerate the importance of the difficulty which is here supposed to have weighed with this blessed Father, but which is so often left unconsidered by writers on the Gospels. It surely might well appear most presumptuous, on the part of one in his position, to seem to the eyes of the world to be the Father of the Divine Child, unless it were quite certain that it was the will of God that so it should be. It might even seem to St. Joseph a kind of sacrilege, to present himself to the world in such a light. He might have seen something of those reasons of theological convenience in this Divine arrangement, after it was made, which are dwelt on by the Fathers of the Church in their explanations of this passage. That is one thing. But it would have been quite another, to assume without authority that he might so act as to give to the world the impression that the Divine Child was his own son. It might have seemed to him that such a course might be bearing a false witness in this great economy of the Incarnation, and giving to future enemies of the truth a ground for denying the very Divinity of our Lord. It may be considered as absolutely impossible that St. Joseph, with all his humility and spiritual discernment, could have thus thrust himself into the mystery of which not a word had yet been said to him on the part of God. This hypothesis is further confirmed by what St. Chrysostom has remarked, that it was the office of the father to give the name to the child at circumcision, and that the words of the Angel to St. Joseph enjoin on him to perform that office, thus appointing him, once for all, as the father of our Lord.

It is this hypothesis which seems to be the most reasonable explanation of the history before us. It seems almost impossible to think that, however certain St. Joseph might have felt that his holy Spouse was in truth the Mother of the promised Messias, the Virgin spoken of in the prophecy of Isaias and in those of Jeremias and Micheas, as well as in other predictions of the redemption of the world, he could have gone on acting as the father of her Child without a special Divine commission so to act. If it had been possible for him to have been present at the Annunciation as at the Visitation, if he had received from Mary herself the full narrative of all that had passed in her, if St. Elisabeth had told him all that she knew by Divine revelation of the mystery of the Incarnation, still until the words of the Angel to himself, bidding him act as he was to act, it does not seem possible to think that he could have taken on him the office which God intended for him, without having that office specially conferred upon him. Nothing had been said to Mary, nothing had been said to Elisabeth, nowhere was it written in the prophecies that he, as the husband of Mary, was to take the place of the father of the Incarnate God. It might appear, to an enlightened spiritual discernment, unlikely that God, the author of marriage, would unite two most highly favoured saints in that sacred bond, and then work anything in one of them, even the very elevation of that person to the grace of the Divine Maternity, without leaving intact and unimpaired the rights and relations which marriage created and implied. The Holy Ghost could not undo what He had done in making Mary the wife of Joseph, even when He wrought in her the Conception of the Son of God, and this meaning may even be contained in the words of the Angel. But the relation in which St. Joseph was to stand to our Lord was to be so unique, that it naturally required nothing short of a revelation to establish it.

It is moreover, not difficult to see that the delay in this revelation to St. Joseph, may have served many purposes in the order of Providence. For it enabled him, as we shall see, to be tested by God as to his fidelity, before he assumed the great office destined for him. It also enabled him to be adduced, as he mind not to act without them. We conclude then with perfect confidence, that the perplexity of St. Joseph was not about his wife's condition, but about his own conduct considering that condition. It was not whether Mary had conceived by the Holy Ghost, but how he was to act in consequence of her Divine Conception.

We may turn from these considerations to that of the very beautiful and glorious virtues which must have been exercised by St. Joseph under this Providential trial. And it is very important to observe that the virtues which were elicited by this probation were almost alike and equal; whichever may be the supposition as to his state of mind which we adopt as the most probable. Let it be supposed, for instance, that he was ignorant altogether of the Divine character of the conception of Mary. In that case he would have had a very severe trial as to charity of judgment, for the fact of her conception would have been made evident to him, in whatever way, and he would have had no evidence to lead him to the conclusion that she was as pure as the snow notwithstanding appearances. If this were so, then we should have in this great soul a singular and most marvellous triumph of heroic charity of judgment. With all the temptations before him, he would still have foreborne in any way to give assent to a suspicion contrary to the perfect virtue of Mary. This would have been a wonderful triumph of grace, and it would have secured for him a wonderful return of further graces from God, Who is above all things pleased with charity. St. Joseph could not but know that the Mother of the Messias was to be a pure Virgin, and it would not have been beyond the reach of supernatural charity that he might have said to himself that he would rather believe that the great miracle had taken place in her, than form a judgment adverse to her in his own mind.

In the same case his withdrawal from the position of her husband in the eyes of the world, would also have been a measure of the greatest charity as well as of great humility. Then again the prompt manner in which, on this and on other occasions, St. Joseph obeys a command of God no more formal than such as is conveyed in a dream, shows us that he was conspicuous for an immense and most perfect docility, as well as for charity and humility. He could not have obeyed the Angel's commands with more unquestioning docility, if the injunction given to him, and the revelation made to him, had been of the most simple and ordinary kind, as if he had been commanded to do something of the commonest character in the service of God, and to accept as true something in itself antecedently quite probable and easy to believe. But the truth which the Angel revealed to St. Joseph was no less a marvel than the miraculous conception of the Son of God in the womb of a pure Virgin. And the injunction which was conveyed to him at the same time was no less than a command to act for the rest of his life as the father of that Incarnate God.

Again, even though a Saint, it might have been expected that he would have asked for some sign, or have made some difficulty, as Zachary did. But instead of this he is perfectly satisfied with the

simple intimation of the truth and of the will of God, given in a dream. If he be supposed to have divined, whether with certainty or obscurely, the great wonder that had come about in his Blessed Spouse, we cannot help seeing how full he must have been of true spiritual discernment, how ready to believe great things of God, how well instructed in the prophecies, and at the same time how wonderfully full of the deepest and truest humility, so as to shrink with all his heart from the great position, which some men might have claimed without further doubt, of the head of the family of which the other members were Jesus and Mary. He did not grasp or clutch at this honour, when it seemed to be within his reach, as it is implied by St. Paul of Satan, that he clutched eagerly at what seemed to him to be a chance of being equal with God. With the simplest and deepest humility, St. Joseph thinks of hiding his own unworthiness in flight, thus declining all part in the execution of that one most glorious mystery of which his heart had so long been full. But by that very reluctance, he made himself all the more worthy to be as the father of the Child, and so he won, so to say, by his humility, the great position which, in a kind of way, belonged to him by right. For, as Mary was his true and inseparable wife, so the Child of Mary must have been to him as a Son. So he won, by the exercise of heroic virtue, the position in the Kingdom of God which might have been deemed to belong to him naturally.

That St. Joseph should have conceived the thought of leaving our Blessed Lady in some way which would not attract notice cannot be wondered at, for such was the most natural and the most humble as well as the most charitable resolution that he could come to, by the unassisted use of reason and prudence. Thus he neither exposed her to any discredit, nor put himself forward unduly and without authorisation. But the course that God had designed for him was far more perfect, as soon at least as he had come to know that God so willed it. It was the most perfect, because God had made him the Spouse of Mary, and there was no reason, in her selection as the Mother of God, for the separation of this holy tie. God does not interfere with what He has already sanctioned, except for some most sublime purpose. In this case, the purpose of God for the sanctification of St. Joseph in the very highest rank of sanctity, for the protection and also for the more rapid progress even of Mary in the course of her own sanctification, His purpose for the execution of His designs on the Infant Jesus, which required that He should have an earthly father and ruler, and be commonly called and thought the Son of the carpenter, all these required the presence of Joseph by the side of Mary in the carrying out of the counsel of the Incarnation. There were higher ranges of sanctity here, than there might have been if St. Joseph had been allowed to listen to his own humility, and take no part in the future life of our Lord and His Mother. His humility led him so far, and then there came the command of God, another call on his humility in the form of the most immediate and unhesitating docility, and the whole of the beautiful history of the Holy Family became possible, because the father of the family was there as well as the Mother and the Child. There would have been a great gap in the holy home of Nazareth, if it had been otherwise. And if there had been a page in that beautiful history left unwritten, so also would there have been left unwritten a most beautiful and glorious page in the history of the Catholic Church in heaven and on earth. We should have missed all the prodigies of love and power contained in the exercise of the patronage of St. Joseph. But it by no means follows from all that is here said, that the collation of his destined position on this blessed father was not, in the Divine counsels, dependent on the perfection with which he met the trial of which we are speaking. Just as the humility and the purity of our Blessed Lady were the divinely appointed foundations of her dignity as the Mother of God, so, on the docility and the humility and the charity of St. Joseph were to be built the other great virtues, the beauties of which his presidency of the Holy Family unfolded before God and the Angels. And thus he rose ever higher and higher in the favour of God. The virtues practised in his absence from the side of Mary at her Visitation became the sources to him of the ever increasing richness of his grace, and won for him the firmness, the courage, the patience, the endurance, the marvellous prudence, the immense faith, the unexampled charities, of which the rest of his life was the constant display.

We may thus see, in this trial of St. Joseph, considered in the view which is here taken of it, something very analogous to what may be called the trial of Mary herself at the time of her Annunciation. We cannot imagine that our Blessed Lady could have failed at that moment, when the whole execution of the counsel of God depended upon her receiving, in the manner in which it was received, the message of the Angel. And yet it was not, in the abstract, impossible that a maiden chosen for the high privilege of the Divine Maternity might not have risen to the full height of perfection expressed in the whole demeanour and conduct of Mary. For this cause we say that her perfect faith won for her that transcendent grace, and this thought seems to be contained in the words of St. Elisabeth, " Blessed thou who didst believe." So we can hardly imagine that St. Joseph could have failed under his great and unique trial, and yet we can see that his perfect correspondence to grace in every particular under that trial may, as has been said, have been required for the bestowal upon him of the great dignity which was destined to him. We add a few considerations in illustration of what has already been said, which may not be exactly such as to be recognised by all as having the power of direct argument, but which are still not such as can be altogether discarded.

In the first place it will certainly seem to many minds a great illustration of the view which is here taken of the nature of the hesitation of St. Joseph, that it appears fairly certain that, though absent from the side of Mary during the greater part of the three months, he must have accompanied her to the house of her cousin, and have come back, at the time of the Circumcision of St. John, to fetch her again to their home. This implies that he must almost certainly have heard his blessed Spouse utter the *Magnificat*, and that he was probably present while Zachary carried on the strain of thanksgiving in his own glorious canticle. Now if this was so, it is not easy to see how the truth of the Incarnation in all its fulness could have been hidden from him. Any one who had heard the salutation of Elisabeth, who had listened to the Canticle of Mary, and to the canticle of Zachary, must have been dull indeed in spiritual preception, if he did not grasp the fundamental truth without which these canticles must have seemed a tissue of unintelligible or even foolish words. The Canticle of Mary fixed in her one person the execution of the mightiest works of God's mercy and sanctifying power, and the canticle of Zachary is utterly unintelligible and purposeless unless it testifies to the actual visitation of the people by God, in the raising up the horn of salvation in the House of David, of which St. Joseph was the representative, and in the illumination of the darkness and misery of the whole world by the dayspring from on high. How could such strains as these ring on the ears of any one even moderately conversant with the prophecies and the ways of God, without awakening or intensifying the thought that the great mystery of the Incarnation had been accomplished in Mary? Canticles such as these imply that those in whose ears they sound are living in an atmosphere of the highest faith, and rejoicing in the fulfilment of the very highest promises of God. If the whole household of Zachary, so to speak, were living in this atmosphere of grateful glorification of

God for His mercies, it is not easy to suppose that it was not also breathed by the blessed Spouse of Mary. We have to strain our minds, if we imagine that he could have been ignorant of what was so familiar to those with whom he was most closely and in so many ways united.

We may see also that it may be most truly said that the Providential position of St. Joseph, both in the Holy Family and in the Kingdom of God, might be secured to him and made firm to stand all trials and to meet all exigencies, by this period of preliminary silence as to the Will of God. As regards the first of these two points, it has already been said that the words of the Angel to St. Joseph, in the dream in which the great revelation was made to him, conveyed the express injunction that he was to act as the Father of the Child as soon as He was born. We are in the habit of speaking of St. Joseph as the foster father, the putative father, and the like, of our Lord. These expressions are rightly used of him, because, in the ordinary sense of the word, our Lord had no father on earth. But it must not be forgotten that, as St. Joseph had all the rights of a husband over our Blessed Lady, so had he all the authority and rights of a father over her Child, as soon as it was settled by a distinct decree of God that he was to discharge to each his natural office as the Head of the Holy Family. The gain in this respect is immense. It would be a great loss to all who are bound together in Christian marriage, if they could not look to the marriage of St. Joseph and our Blessed Lady as the perfect type and pattern of all such unions, and this would not be possible if the

V

relations between them were only, so to say, honorary and not true, kept up for the sake of appearance before the world, and not for the sake of the exercise of all virtues and duties which such relations imply, as far as was consistent with that consecration of each to God of which we have already spoken. That consecration in no way interfered with or cancelled the authority of St. Joseph. It did not do this before the Incarnation, and the revelation to St. Joseph showed that it was not to do this afterwards.

In the same way, it would be an immense loss to the Christian home, if we were to consider the condescension of our Lord in taking the place of the Child in that blessed Family to be a mere appearance and not a reality. Everything in the subsequent history of the Holy Family testifies to the perfect reality of the obedience of our Lord to both His parents, as they are called in the Gospels. Even at the time when He left them, that He might stay in the Temple, as we shall see, what He then did was in no ways derogatory to the natural authority either of His Blessed Mother or of St. Joseph. The circumstances of the Incarnation made it a question which the Angels might have asked themselves, whether the God made Man would subject Himself to the ordinary laws in general, and in particular, to the law of filial obedience and duty. But, if the answer was ever in doubt, it was sufficiently given, once for all, in the course of the revelation to St. Joseph.

We may say just the same as to the great position of St. Joseph in the spiritual kingdom. Here also that position is secured by the trial through which he had passed. It would have been different if there had been no such phase in the internal history of this most exalted soul. The years that were to follow, with all their troubles and joys, their dangers and their deliverances, might have brought many a time of doubt and difficulty to the head of the Holy Family which it would have been less easy to meet, but for that knowledge, how solid was his position and how certain his commission, which was the result in his soul of those weeks of anxiety and prayer. In the same way, as to that other office of which we speak. We are accustomed in the Church to venerate and have recourse to this great Saint, as having in a special manner the gift of guiding souls in spiritual perplexities, and in the exercises of the interior life. But it is a law of God's Providence that the saints who have special powers and offices of this kind, are those who have themselves passed through the experience of the dangers and trials, out of which they are able to help others to make their way in safety. In this way the office of St. Joseph in the spiritual kingdom, is founded on the experience of his own soul, and his power, in the same way, is the reward and fruit of his own faithfulness.

The few weeks of the Visitation period were soon passed, but it may be that they cut very deeply into the soul of this glorious sufferer, as the iron in the prison of Egypt cut into the soul of his great prototype, the son of Jacob. The experiences of the spiritual life are sometimes acquired in a long course of time, sometimes they are gained in a few hours, into which are contracted the pains and the anguish of years. It may well have been so with St. Joseph. His trial was in itself unique, and cannot ever be in all its features the trial of any one else. But it may well have included in itself a very deep and penetrating experience, and it may have been the Providential preparation of his soul for the great office which he was to fulfil in the spiritual kingdom. He had abundant lessons afterwards, in the perpetual communion which he enjoyed with Jesus and Mary, but he could never after this have had trials and doubts of this particular kind. One short period of trial and disturbance may, in this way, often add more to the spiritual enlightenment of a soul in the path of perfection than many long periods of comparative tranquillity and peace. This then is another feature in the mystery before us, of which it is not easy fully to understand the immense significance.

A further noticeable element in the Providential arrangement of this epoch in the history of the Holy Family may be found in the new relation in which it placed these two most beautiful souls of Mary and Joseph one to the other, as well as in the intimate communion which must so soon have sprung up between the soul of the appointed Father and that of the Divine Son in the womb of Mary. Very beautiful indeed must have been the relations between Joseph and Mary before the Incarnation. As far as earth went, they were all in all one to the other, and they were souls of the most transcendent sanctity and, on that account, souls between whom the most tender and perfect union could be formed.

It is one of the miseries of earth, that there can be so little of perfect communion between soul and soul. But the fact is arranged by the mercy of God, because there are so few souls of which those who love them best could bear to see the whole without any concealments. All these concealments will be done away in the Kingdom of Heaven, for there every soul will be perfect in its degree, and there will be nothing in any that can displease or disappoint any one else. It is reasonable to believe that, in some measure and degree, between souls that are very closely united to God even here, there may sometimes be the anticipation, in part at least, of the perfect openness and communion of the kingdom of bliss. And if ever there were two souls of whom this might be thought to be the case, those two souls would have certainly been the souls of Mary and of Joseph.

That which had come between them, as it were, at the time of which we are speaking, was not so much a cloud of misunderstanding as a threat of separation. Mary had been most wonderfully elevated, and the immensity of her dignity was enough in itself to place a distance between her and all the world. We see how this dignity of the Mother of God was recognised at once by the blessed Elisabeth and her holy Spouse. It is not easy to think that it was not recognised with equal veneration by St. Joseph himself. Up to this time, during the short period of their married life, there had not only been between them the closest union of hearts and purposes and desires, but there had been the most beautiful exercise of their mutual duties, the guidance and ruling of the husband and the obedience and reverence of the wife. And now she had become the Mother of God, and there had been no word of intimation from Heaven whether this was to interfere with the relations which had hitherto existed between them. The elevation of the Blessed Virgin thus raised of itself questions which must sooner or later be settled, and which, until they were settled by some divine intimation, must of necessity cause a certain kind of perplexity. Moreover, the new condition of this Blessed Bride, as we have seen, implied a further question as to the future relations between her husband and her Child.

As long as St. Joseph was absent from her side, as we suppose him to have been during the three months of the Visitation, these questions might remain in abeyance as to their practical solution, though they could not but be continually present to the mind and heart of each. And then, in God's good time, there came the blessed moment when all shadows of this kind were chased away by the message of the Angel to St. Joseph, which determined his position in the new kingdom as plainly as the former message at the Annunciation had determined that of Mary herself. It was not a mere removal of doubt or anxiety. It was the elevation of St. Joseph, as the Annunciation had been the elevation of Mary. It was the bestowal on him of a dignity second only to hers. There was to be no separation. The bond which God had once made fast was not to be unloosed. They were to be to one another far more than they had ever been before. Their union was made more than ever indissoluble by that tie which had not before existed between them. If Mary was to become a Mother, Joseph was to become as a Father. The new bond of union between them was nothing less than the presence of the Incarnate Son of God, the Child of Mary, and all the duties in each which that presence involved. St. Joseph was to "take to himself" his wife. Their union was consecrated, not divided. He had a new office both to her and to her Child. She could see in him, not simply the Spouse who was to be the guardian of her Virgin purity, but the guide, and head, and provider, of the Holy Family, now made complete and perfect in its kind by the presence of the Divine Infant in her womb. A new cluster of relations and duties had sprung up between them, every single exercise of which would make them dearer the one to the other, as well nearer to God and higher in the most consummate sanctity, and more intimately familiar with the most divine mysteries.

The trial was over, and its termination brought the full reward of the beautiful faithfulness in which it had been met. There was nothing to retract, or to ask pardon for, no misunderstandings or misconceptions to be explained, no complaints of anything that might have been otherwise. The severest test had been applied by the good Providence of God to both these great souls, and in each case the result had been the most perfect practice of the virtues for which the occasion gave scope. Mary had acted with the utmost perfection, both in the Annunciation and afterwards. She had followed the inspirations of

God, and by so doing, had helped in the most efficacious way the blessed Spouse to whom God had united her. St. Joseph had been tried with the opportunities of a thousand judgments and surmises, and doubts and difficulties, whether as to himself or as to his Spouse, and out of all the swarm of possible imperfections he had given in to none. More than that, there had been a period of Divine silence as to what were to be their relations in the future. This, too, had been borne with admirable patience. With what joy, and with what increased love and confidence in each other must they have met, after the period of trial had passed away! What must have been the beauty and sublimity of their mutual converse, as soon as Mary could speak without reserve to Joseph as to the great mystery which had taken place! However great we may imagine the pain to have been which may have fallen on these two tender souls during the time of darkness, such as it was, it is certain that far greater in proportion must have been the joy and delight of their reunion, and the happiness which must have inundated them when each could see in the other an appointed instrument for the execution of the greatest work that God could do, and know that in this great work they were to labour side by side.

It is only natural to add to these thoughts the further consideration of the immense supplies of new graces which must have come down, both on our Blessed Lady and on St. Joseph, after the completion of the trial of which we have been speaking. It is the way of God, as we have seen, especially in the case of St. Joachim, St. Anne, St. Zachary, and St. Elisabeth, to delay the bestowal of His favours, in order that those on whom they are to be conferred may be prepared for them in His Providence, especially by the discipline of adversity and the exercise on their own parts of patience, humility, and other virtues. This principle runs through the whole of the sacred history on which we are now engaged, and it certainly had its place in the Providential dealings of God with St. Joseph and our Blessed Lady. What must have been a trial to him could not be without its anxieties and troubles to her. And we may surely suppose that one of the reasons for this method in the Providence of God, is that He desires thereby to call forth from the saints the exercise of these beautiful virtues, not simply for its own sake, but in order that their co-operation with the graces which they already possess may win for them higher and higher favours.

God might have declared His will to St. Joseph, as to his part in the economy of the Incarnation, at the same time that He declared it to Mary as to her part. But in that case the workings of grace in the heart and soul of St. Joseph would not have been so exquisitely meritorious as they were in consequence of his trial. The time had not come for the exercise on his part of any act of his new dignity, and in the meanwhile he was preparing for himself an increased treasure of grace by the perfect manner in which he met his trial. And we may gather as a corollary from this that, now that the time at last came for him to undertake the work committed to him in the guardianship and guidance both of the

Mother and the Child, God bestowed on him very bountifully indeed the special graces which belonged to this new and most glorious office. It is from this time, as has been said, that we begin to hear of his acting as the chief and head of the Family. The new dignity brought with it new duties and responsibilities, and these implied, on the part of the infinite goodness of God, abundant ministrations of grace to enable him to perform them.

Lastly, we may see in this mystery a great instance of what is continually taking place in the dealings of God with His saints, though it can never take place on so large and magnificent a scale as in this instance of Joseph and Mary. It is not the way of God, in His ordinary dealings with His most beloved and faithful servants, to let them see beforehand what it is that they are to do for Him, though this may sometimes be the case, as it seems to have been the case with St. Paul, of whom our Lord said, "I will show him how great things he must suffer for My Name's sake."[1] Even those words do not necessarily imply that this knowledge was to be communicated to the Apostle immediately on his conversion. However that may have been, it is not the common way with God to let the saints see what it is that is before them, either in the way of joy or in the way of suffering. Joseph and Mary had perhaps planned out a life for themselves, a life of most close service to God in prayer, of the most perfect practice of the interior virtues, of the most ardent longings for the coming of the Messias, and of great charity to their neighbours, and the like. They

[1] Acts ix. 16.

might have intended to live as Joachim and Anne lived before the conception of Mary, a hidden life in their own quiet town, a life known only to God. Such, at least, might have been their plans for the future, if, indeed, they dreamt of any plan at all, and did not rather leave themselves, with perfect abandonment to the guidance of God day after day.

This would have been very beautiful, but the dreams, even of saints, are not so beautiful as the realities which God prepares for them in His Providence, for His thoughts are not as ours. Now they were to change all their plans, and to enter on a new and most marvellous career, a career full of the most terrible crosses as of the most heavenly delights. How far above all their conceptions was the path which God had marked out for them! How immensely greater the occasions of sanctification, how immensely more magnificent the spiritual gifts and blessings and glories which He had prepared for them! How utterly different, and yet how much more splendid, the thoughts of God for them, than their thoughts for themselves! And finally, if we ask what was the one foundation on which all this great edifice of sanctity was to be raised both in the one and in the other, we can find no other answer than that which our Lady uttered in her *Magnificat,—Quia respexit humilitatem ancillæ suæ.* The trial of Mary was one, and the trial of Joseph was another. But the virtue which raised them both to the thrones prepared for them was the same, the virtue of humility.

CHAPTER XIV.

THE EXPECTATION OF THE NATIVITY.

St. Luke ii. 1—15.   *Vita Vitæ Nostræ*, § 8.

IF, as is most reasonable, we suppose the Incarnation to have taken place on the day which we now keep as the feast of the Annunciation, and the Nativity of St. John Baptist to have occurred three months later than that time, it seems naturally to follow that the end of the visit of our Blessed Lady to her cousin St. Elisabeth is to be fixed at the beginning of July. That would leave a space of between five and six months before the Nativity of our Lord Himself. We may suppose, further, that as much as a week or more may have elapsed between the time at which St. Joseph and our Blessed Lady left Nazareth for their journey to Bethlehem, and the first Christmas Day. The intervals of time between the several mysteries of which we are speaking would not be made less certain to us, even if we could not think that our Lord was born on the 25th of December. He was born nine months after the Annunciation, and at that last-named time St. Elisabeth had entered the sixth month of her pregnancy. Further, if we are right in thinking that the revelation as to the mystery of the Incarnation was made to St. Joseph just after the Visitation of our Lady, we have this space of something more than five months, of which no account is given us in the Gospels, but during which St. Joseph and our Blessed Lady were living together in the utmost happiness at Nazareth, in preparation for the moment when the greatest event in the world's history was to take place in the birth of our Lord.

There are blank spaces in our maps of the heavens, spaces in which there are no stars on which human eyes can gaze, even with the aid of the most powerful instruments. But it would be foolish for us to think that, because our powers are limited, and can find nothing for the eye to rest upon in those unfathomable depths of the heavens, therefore it is certain that there are not, in those same unoccupied fields, many bodies of great magnitude and brilliancy, to those who can discern them, surpassing even what we see with our eyes or our telescopes. Few of us think much of those five or six months in the existence of Jesus, Mary and Joseph. And yet it cannot be doubted by any reasonable Christian, that every moment of this space of time was filled up by each of them, in his or her degree, with actions and affections most delightful and most glorious to God. It was a time of the deepest peace, the most perfect silence, the most fervent occupations and love, a time, the records of which, as far as they were manifested to the eager eyes of the Angels, must have opened to them wonders of the Divine condescension and wisdom such as they had never before conceived, and revealed beauties of the workings of grace in the human hearts and souls which were conscious of the great mystery, at which even those insatiable students of the great works of God must have sunk back in astonishment and awe. The world went on as usual outside that sacred home, which was now the sanctuary of the Incarnate Lord. The busy crowds in some central thoroughfare of a great seat of commerce and government dream even less of the sacramental Presence, the adoring Angels, the unceasing human worship, the active converse of our Lord with His chosen souls, which are going on in some quiet humble Carmelite convent close at hand, than did the inhabitants of Nazareth dream of what that cottage contained in front of that cave. Let us try to sum them up shortly for ourselves.

The first thing that must strike us, in our considerations of this wonderful time, is the presence of God on earth in a new way, brought about by His union with our nature in that Sacred Humanity which was never from that moment to be separated from Him. To do honour to that special presence of God in which He vouchsafed to dwell, in a certain sense, with His chosen people, there had been ordained a Tabernacle on which the tribes of Israel had lavished all their treasures, and certain families had been set aside by a special consecration for His service there. There, by a whole elaborate system of holy rites and sacrifices, by continual praises and propitiations, honour had been done to Him Who vouchsafed to dwell between the Cherubim. The Holy of Holies, in which the Ark of the Convenant was kept, was open to no one but the High Priest alone, once in the year, and the sanctity of that secret shrine spread its wings over the whole of the fabric of which it was the centre. Later on, the Temple had been designed by David and built by Solomon, and no holy place on earth was enriched so munificently, or guarded so reverently, no place ever drew to itself to so large an extent the homage and devotion of the most enlightened and holy among men. We see traces of this extreme reverence, in the love of the Apostles and of the early believers in Jerusalem for that holy place and the rites by which the presence of God was honoured. But now, that He had really come upon earth, now that the Word had become Flesh, and "tabernacled" among men, the temple in which He was enshrined was nothing but the Sacred Body and Soul of Jesus Christ in the womb of Mary. There was that awful Presence, around which is gathered the trembling adoration of the Angelic host, there was its shrine, its temple, its throne, and it had no earthly worshippers but Mary and Joseph.

Another consideration that strikes us on this subject is that of the immense spiritual gifts which this Divine Presence would shed around it. Many indeed and great may the gifts have been which fell on the unconscious neighbours, on the relatives and friends and helpers of the parents of our Lord. But the gifts of sanctification are usually by far the greatest to those who can best understand them, who know whence they proceed, and who can best correspond to them by their own co-operation. They are usually greater by far, when they are given to those who have already received most, and been most faithful to what they have received. Who, then, can be surprised at anything that the saints have said about the heights of holiness to which our Blessed Lady and her Spouse were raised during this period of their silent dwelling with our Lord? They were dwelling, as it were, in Heaven itself, for they had Him with them Whose presence makes Heaven what it is. Mary was, in truth, the living tabernacle in which the Incarnate God was enshrined. She moved about and seemed to outward eyes to be like other holy women, and no difference in the simplicity of ordinary home life marked her out as consecrated to the highest service of God that ever fell to the lot of a purely human being. And yet she carried about with her her God as her Child, as the priest carries the Blessed Sacrament, in countries where no external honour can be done to It on account of the unbelief of their inhabitants. We call her in her Litanies the Tower of David, the Tower of Ivory, the House of Gold, the Ark of the Covenant, and these and the like titles belong to her in an especial manner on account of her privilege at this period in the history of the Incarnation. But, if the tabernacles in our churches had soul and spirit, if they could understand the Presence within themselves and venerate It, if they could pray and love and honour It by interior acts of the highest virtue, they would become holy in a sense in which they cannot be holy now, and there would be no limit to their growth in sanctity. And yet such was the privilege of Mary, such, as we may surely believe, the rapidity and intensity of her sanctification.

It is easy to see, also, how, from the moment when St. Joseph, at the bidding of the Angel, laid aside his hesitation as to his own position with regard to the Blessed Mother and her Child, he also must have had opportunities of advancing in holiness second only to hers. He was living day and night in the sanctuary. He was tending, serving, providing for, and communing with the Incarnate God and His Mother. Even if he had been but little instructed in the prophecies and in the Scriptural doctrines concerning God and the coming Messias—and this we can hardly think, if he had devoted himself in a special way, like our Lady herself, to the mystery of the Incarnation—yet even if this had been so at the beginning, we cannot doubt that his perpetual homage and prayer and meditation must have enriched his mind with wonderful illumination as time went on, and, as it is only reasonable to think, as our Lord spoke secretly to the heart of a Saint so dear to Himself. The Christian commentators understand that, when we are told that St. John Baptist leapt in the womb of St. Elisabeth at the salutation of Mary, the Scripture signifies to us that the mind of the Precursor was immensely enlightened, and that his was no childish joy, but the full intelligent delight of a richly-endowed soul at the contemplation of the great mystery. It is not much to suppose that when St. Joseph, not a child in his mother's womb, but a well-tried and highly-trusted Saint, was allowed to know the Presence of his Lord so close to him, not for a moment or a passing visit, but for the long months which were to elapse between the Visitation and the Nativity, and to know also his own most intimate relation and office in the mystery, he too was enabled by God to enter into the heavenly marvel, to understand what it was that had taken place, Who was the Child in the womb of Mary, to adore His Divinity, to venerate the gifts of His Humanity, and to see in them the ever-flowing and inexhaustible source of blessings and graces for the whole human race.

The contemplation of the Divine mysteries connected with the Incarnation must have been an occupation which absorbed all the thoughts and affections of our Lady and her blessed Spouse during the interval between the Visitation and the Nativity. They might have said, like the Apostles on the mountain of the Transfiguration, that it was good for them to be there. The days passed rapidly on, and there was no lack of food for the soul in the considerations which the mystery suggested, while the beautiful tranquil happiness which shed itself all around the Holy House must have been enough for that blessed pair. If others guessed at the mystery which had taken place in the womb of Mary, they knew it, and the knowledge had been imparted to them for the highest purposes in the counsels of God. Among these purposes we may reckon as the first the continually advancing sanctification of those glorious souls. If they increased, day after day, in their intelligence of the works and intentions of God for the salvation of the world, it is not rash to think that their intense growth in grace had its accompanying manifestations, however occasional and hidden from the greater part of that little world of Nazareth, in the way of holy influences and charitable helps in favour of all those around them. That Mary was about to be a Mother would become known in due time, and even if their nearest relations did not dream of the possibility of her giving birth to the promised King of the House of David, it is reasonable to think that her evident sanctity and the ineffable charm which hung about her home may have made her relatives ask themselves, as was said about St. John after his birth, "what a One shall this Child be?"

But our Lady and her blessed Spouse were deeply read in the Sacred Scriptures, and it is most natural to think that they had received unusual illumination from the understanding of the prophecies. The place of the birth of the promised Child had been as clearly foretold as His birth of a Virgin, or His descent from David and Juda. When the Wise Kings came to Jerusalem to ask for the King of the Jews, there was no doubt on the part of the official representatives of the Jewish Church as to the answer which they ought to give to the question of Herod, Where the Christ was to be born? If it was so well known to the learned men at Jerusalem that Bethlehem was the appointed spot, it is not likely that Mary and Joseph were ignorant of the same truth. And yet the months rolled on, and they were still at Nazareth. Our Lady must have known the very time at which the Divine Birth would take place, and St. Joseph must have had the knowledge from her, if not before, at least after the revelation made to him by the Angel as to the part which he was to take in the administration of the Divine mystery of the Incarnation. Yet the autumn waned and the winter was nigh at hand, and no sign came to them as to any change of residence.

Here again we see the characteristic abandonment of themselves to the Providence of God, which has already met us in the lives of these glorious Saints. Mary had left herself in His Hands as to the great question of her marriage and her virginal vow, and again, she had abandoned herself entirely to the same Providence in her silence as to the mystery of the Incarnation when it came about. St. Joseph had been guided at once by the word of the Angel, though only conveyed to him in a dream, in the great matter of his perplexity after the Incarnation. And now, how was the Child, over which he had been appointed to watch, to be born at Bethlehem? Was it to be his duty to anticipate any heavenly direction, and take on himself to secure, by an act of his own, the fulfilment of the prophecy? If he asked his blessed Spouse, it is not likely that he would have found in her any encouragement to independent action. It was enough for them to leave all these things to God. So their simple preparations for the expected birth were made as if they thought it might take place at Nazareth.

The solution to the difficulty was brought about in God's own way. The hearts of Kings and of the rulers of the world are all in His hand, and while they think they are carrying out their own schemes of wise policy, so often fraught with cruelties and hardships to those who are placed under them by God as their subjects, they are in truth only bringing about the wise purpose of their Master and Judge. There was a great fitness, as has so often been remarked, in the arrangement of Providence, whereby, just at that time, Augustus had decreed the enrolment and possible taxation of all the subjects of the Roman Empire, and whereby also, as far as human causes are concerned, it came about that our Lord was born in the city of David, at Bethlehem. He Who was to be born was the true King of all the world, for nowhere could He be without being King, and moreover, His inheritance of the throne of David could not be more signally attested than by His birth in the holy city. He was, even as Man, an independent Sovereign by right, and could owe no allegiance like other men to the Sovereign of the world at Rome. And yet it was to be a maxim of His religion, and the constant rule of His Church, that subjects were to obey their rulers, for the sake of conscience, as having authority from God, the Author of human society. This principle was to be wrestled against in numberless ways and on numberless pretexts, whether the ground of natural right, or the ground of the tyranny of the ruler, or the ground of ancestral independence, or the ground of difference of race or of religion. No more complete answer to all these sophistries of the petty minds of men could be furnished than that contained in the fact that the place of the birth of our Lord was practically fixed by the decree of a foreign ruler, one of an alien and usurping race, one of a different religion, one whose laws were tyrannical and his decrees hard to obey. Nor, on the other hand, could there be a more evident proof of the truth that the temporal rulers of mankind are but carrying out God's behests, even in the details of their policy, than the subservience of Augustus and his counsellors at Rome to the designs of Providence in bringing about the Divine Birth at Bethlehem.

"And it came to pass in those days there went out a decree from Cæsar Augustus that the whole world should be enrolled. This enrolling was first made by Cyrinus the governor of Syria. And all went to be enrolled, every one into his own city." It cannot fairly be doubted that the authority of St. Luke would be sufficient for the facts which he thus states, even though there were no traces in secular history of the measure which he here attributes to Augustus. That Emperor was a careful administrator of the vast dominions over which he was practically sovereign, and, among other characteristics of such a ruler, we find in him a fondness for statistics of the population of the various countries of which these dominions were composed. The most natural way of explaining the statement of the Evangelist, in harmony with what is otherwise known on the matter, seems to be to suppose that the circumstance mentioned by Josephus, as having taken place not long before the death of Herod the Great, refers to this census, as it would be called in our own days. Josephus tells us that the King exacted an oath of fidelity to the Emperor from all his subjects, and that this led to the refusal of a large body of the Pharisees to take the oath. This would be exactly the kind of edict—for there seems to have been an Imperial edict at the same time, which caused the order from Herod—which would suit the words of the Evangelist. He adds that this enrolling was "first made by Cyrinus, the governor of Syria." Here again we have some difficulty, not in receiving the statement of St. Luke, but in finding its confirmation in secular history. Quirinus was governor of Syria some years later than this date. But this does not make it impossible that he should have held the post at an earlier time also, especially as there are distinct statements about his presence in the East just about the time which would suit the most probable date for the birth of our Lord. It is most likely that the Evangelist has added the adjective, "first," to show that this enrolling was followed at a later date by another of the same kind, as if he had meant to say, this was the first of the enrollings, and it was made by Quirinus when he was governor of Syria. There was another and later enrolling mentioned in the Acts as having been referred to by Gamaliel, in his speech, advising toleration for the Apostles and their followers.[1]

St. Joseph and his blessed Spouse read the will of God, and the solution of their difficulties in the decree of the distant Emperor, as put into execution in the province of Syria by means of his officer Quirinus. There was some hardship in a decree which obliged them to a long journey, to a place where they may have had relations, but to which they were practically strangers, and at that time of year. But the hand of God was in this decree, and they obeyed it with the utmost joy. It was, indeed, a confirmation to them of the unsleeping care of God over His servants, and for the fulfilment of His own counsels and prophecies. We are quite ignorant of the distance of time between the announcement of the edict of the Emperor and the first Christmas

[1] Acts v. 37.

Day. It would take some time for the tidings to reach every little town in a remote province, and the amount of confusion and inconvenience must have been great indeed to simple households like that of St. Joseph. It would be hard enough to secure the execution of such an edict in our own times, if there were many on whom it would fall in the shape of an obligation to take a long journey for the purpose of registration, not for any civil privilege or benefit, but only to secure the means of imposing a tax. But Bethlehem and its neighbourhood were haunted with the memories and legends connected with the childhood of the great King, whose Son was to reign on his throne for ever. It was a holy place, the shrine especially of the royal race, and the attachment which the members of so privileged a family had to it would not be diminished, but rather enhanced, by the fact that they had fallen into obscurity and comparative insignificance. But above all, the birth at Bethlehem was to them the beginning of a fresh stage in the unfolding of the counsel of God in the dispensation of the Incarnation.

It must be remembered, also, that not even the tranquil and intense joys of the nine months which were now drawing to their close, could satisfy the tender and overwhelming longing with which Mary and Joseph must have desired the moment of the Divine Birth. All mothers naturally long for that moment of joy, which, as our Lord says, makes them forget all the pangs of their travail, the moment when they know that a man is born into the world, their own child. These natural longings for the birth of their children in the daughters of Eve are the faintest reflections of the yearnings of Mary to see the birth of our Lord. It was not a man, but the Saviour of men, that was to be born, it was her Child Who had been for so many months her joy and delight, with Whom she had for so long held the sweetest interior conversation and communion, the Child Whose presence, when made known to the Baptist by the sound of her salutation to St. Elisabeth, had sanctified him in her womb, filled him with grace, given him the use as well as the possession of all his faculties of intelligence and will, and made him leap with joy. If our Lord's presence in the womb had made the unborn Baptist leap for joy, what must have been the desire of Mary to take her own Child in her arms and press Him to her heart ? The whole history of the world, since the fall of man, had been a history of longing, on the part of the saints of God, for the moment of the Birth which was now about to take place, and the Fathers speak as if the desires and prayers of those saints had helped on the arrival of that blessed time. But no one of the Patriarchs or Prophets, no one of the kingly line of our Lord's ancestors, or of the holy women who had been, under the Old Testament, the types of our Blessed Lady, could have prayed so fervently or longed so earnestly for the first Christmas as our Lady herself. Her long communing with the Sacred Heart had made her own heart its copy and reflection, and she could enter into the desire of our Lord to begin the work of the Redemption and the instruction of the world, as no one else could understand it.

And with St. Joseph also it was the same as with Mary. He, too, most ardently desired to see the Holy Child over Whom he was to watch, more ardently even than the aged Simeon, who was so soon to hold Him in his arms in the Temple. To Mary and Joseph the time of the Nativity was to be a fresh beginning of their work, for then was to begin His manifestation to the world, in which manifestation they were to be as His ministers and official servants. The great work had, indeed, already begun, but it was as yet known only to few, and so could affect, consciously, only few. It would be as the sunrise of the new Creation, the breaking of the clouds which enwrapped His Infancy by the light of the Sun of Justice. It was a moment awaited with eagerness by the Angels, who were ready to hang over the lowly crib and fill heaven and earth with their songs of joy. All over the world there was a hush of peace, as on the eve of some wonderful renovation, and the crowds of blessed souls in Limbus and in Purgatory were expecting the shock of light and joy which would announce to them the coming of Him who was once more to open the gates of Heaven to mankind.

At whatever interval, before the actual moment for leaving Nazareth, Mary and Joseph became aware of the decree of the Emperor, their preparations for the necessary journey would not take long to make. It must have cost their affectionate relations more pain than it cost to themselves, unless, at least, their cousins knew something of the Divine mystery which had already taken place. The blessed pair must have endeared themselves immensely to all their kinsfolk and townsfolk, even if no one but themselves were aware of the Incarnation. If any one shared the secret, it must have been a pang to lose the hope of being present at the birth of the Infant. The Nazarenes, in general, were not, if we are to judge by the indications of their character in the Gospels, a population on whom it would have been well to confer so great an honour. It would have heightened their pride and their contempt for our Lord afterwards, if He had been born among them as well as brought up. There is no trace, in anything that is recorded as said by them of Him, that they laid any claim to this. He is the Son of Joseph, and His Mother is called Mary, but they never say that He was a native of their own town. But it would naturally be a joy to our Blessed Lady if those cousins or 'sisters,' whom she must have loved so much, could have shared her own happiness, and the leaving them must have been another sacrifice which she willingly made to the decrees of Providence. Although it is very likely that a particular day or number of days, may have been fixed for the enrolment, we are nowhere told that it was so. But even if it had been so, we have no evidence that any of their Nazarene relatives were obliged to go to Bethlehem at the same time for the same purpose. And so Mary and Joseph set out alone with their God, full of joy and desire.

Our meditations on the journey to Bethlehem usually dwell on the hardships and sufferings of the day, on the possibilities of inhospitable reception on the road, as well as at Bethlehem, on the anxieties of St. Joseph, on the gentleness, patience, and charity of our Blessed Lady. These things are all true, but they represent only one side of that beautiful picture. Even to ordinary human hearts, which are full of the prospect of some very great joy, some blessing intensely desired and now, at last, in sight, the anticipations of the coming happiness are wont to overwhelm all feelings of difficulty, or delay, to make all obstacles seem as nothing, and turn all suffering into joy. The holy pair may not have perfectly divined beforehand all the circumstances of humiliation and mortification which, in the Providence of God, were to surround the Infant Saviour on His first entrance into the world. But they were already full of heavenly light as to the immense condescension of God in becoming a Child in a Virgin's womb, and to those accustomed to the contemplation of such condescension it would not seem much more if He were indeed to choose the utmost poverty and privation for His companions from the very first. The Christian priest, as he carries the Blessed Sacrament secretly to the sick, is too much wrapt up in the humiliation which our Lord's love has imposed on Him, to think much of any accidental circumstance of want of preparation and of dignity in the room into which He is being carried. The minds of Mary and of her Spouse must have been too much occupied with the event that was about to take place, to care very much about the minor incidents of the journey.

St. Paul has a wonderful passage in the Epistle to the Romans on the expectation of the whole creation for what he speaks of as the manifestation of the sons of God, which will not be perfected until the day of the general resurrection, when the bodies of the saints will be reunited to their souls in the state of glory. He tells us of the whole physical creation groaning and being in labour, awaiting, as it were, that time with impatience, because the manifestation of the sons of God in their appointed glory is to be the signal for the renovation of the creation itself, which now shares the degradation which has come on mankind, and on all that belongs to mankind, in consequence of the Fall, and which is to be finally exchanged for a new state of incorruptibility and freedom from decay, even in the lower creatures, when man himself is elevated to the glory which has been won for him by our Lord. St. Paul speaks of this yearning of the physical universe for a better state, and then he adds that we ourselves, even in the state of grace and regeneration to which we are now raised, groan within ourselves, waiting for the adoption of the sons of God, that is for the full measure of glory which belongs to us by virtue of that adoption, as we now have it, that is the redemption of our body. And then he adds that the Holy Ghost Himself helps us in this yearning, asking for us with groanings unutterable, as if the Holy Ghost was the Author of feelings of desire and yearnings in the children of God which they could not form of themselves, but which He, as the great master of prayer, forms within them. Thus there is the instinctive yearning of all the world, even of the physical creation, for the consummation which is to be, there is the conscious and the intelligent desire of the saints and of all thoughtful men for something better, and there is the inspired prayer and groaning of the saints, guided by the Holy Ghost to hasten on as it were the day of that great renovation and deliverance.

Although the presence of our Lord on the earth began, as we know, at the moment of the Incarnation, still the eve of the Nativity was a moment at which all the expectations and longings which awaited Him and in a certain sense, hastened His appearance, must have been intensified and renewed. The needs of the world were as great or greater then than now, for now the work of God has been more than half accomplished, for the Atonement has been made, the sacrifice of the Cross has been offered, the Church has been set up all over the world, and thousands of saints are already in the possession of the fulness of beatitude in the Vision of God, though not as yet in their glorified bodies. The perfect redemption is more certain than it was, and it is already begun by a beginning the consummation of which is certain, in the case of millions on millions of the children of Eve. The language of St. Paul shows us that the longing for its completion grows almost more intense as the process towards that completion proceeds. And this is but natural, for expectation grows in proportion to the strength of hope, and the hope of those who have already received a part of a great boon that they will possess the remainder is stronger than that of those who have as yet received no part of it at all. Thus the desire of a soul in heaven for the consummation of its bliss may be tempered by its present happiness and by its perfect union with the will of God, but in itself it must have a keenness of appetite which is greater than any it has formerly felt. In this sense the possession of our Lord in any degree whets the appetite for this posession of a further degree, as the Scripture says, "they that eat Me shall yet hunger, and they that drink Me shall yet thirst." And thus in proportion as the minds and hearts of men were aware of the boon which had been conferred on the world by the Incarnation they would long all the more for the next step in the process of Redemption in the Nativity, and if they were not aware of the Incarnation, they would long for our Lord's appearance with all their original desire for the redemption for which they waited.

There are legends concerning the prodigies which occurred in various parts of the world, a fountain of oil flowing at Rome, flowers and vines budding and bearing fruit at E'.gaddi, and others of the like kind. Although the stories do not appear to rest on any certain evidence, and may be accounted for in other ways, we may take them as signifying the universal expectation of the world, and even of inanimate nature, according to the passage of St. Paul, before the coming of our Lord. It is natural to think that there may have been some manifestations of this kind, but whether this was so or not, there is no doubt that the event which was about to take place, was the dawn of an unexampled renovation and elevation of the whole world. This being the case, it would not have been wonderful if prodigies of this kind had happened. It is certain that the whole race of mankind yearned for its

Saviour. Those who were the highest in the spiritual life, the chosen souls guided and enlightened by the Holy Ghost, who were the best acquainted with the promises of God, the needs of man, the importance of the soul, and its almost boundless degradation under the weight of sin and the penalties which were the consequences of the Fall, would now yearn with a longing which may well be called "unutterable" to use the words of the Apostle, all the more as they felt the time to be nearer and as their minds were illuminated from time to time by flashes of the light of prophecy, written and unwritten. Even those who were not so highly elevated in the scale of spiritual intelligence might well feel their pulses quickened and their hearts moved by strange desires, for our Lord had already been on earth for many months, and He Who is the light of the world might well kindle with joy at His Presence any who shared in the partial possession of the illumination that came from Him. And if St. Paul could speak as we have seen, of the whole physical universe as conscious and alive to its own needs, and their coming satisfaction, on account of its endless capacities of greater beauties and more perfect organization in the new kingdom of incorruption, it is not much to think that even in that lower universe there may have been some witness vouchsafed to the advent of the Desire of the whole world. Our Lord had come at the Annunciation, but it had been as the seed which is hidden in the earth. Now the time was at hand for the appearance of the little blade, so to speak, which is the first manifestation of the life and fruitfulness of the seed, and which, as such, causes more joy in the heart of the anxious husbandman than even the ear and the full corn which afterwards follow. The old poet tells us that some men do not know "how much the half is more than the whole," meaning that there is a peculiar joy in the first grasp of an object much desired, which is not equalled by the secure and full possession of which the gaining of the half is the earnest.

This was the peculiar joy of the first Christmas, and we must add this characteristic to the desire of our Blessed Lady on the journey of which we are now speaking. Her presence at Bethlehem had now been brought about in a marvellous and providential manner, and thus the last hindrance to the perfect fulfilment of the prophecies was removed, just as the day approached for the natural termination of the first stage of our Lord's human existence in her sacred womb. This evidently divine arrangement must have filled her heart with joy, and quickened the wonderful might and clearness of her hope. Her desires might now be let loose, and their full force and intensity might fall on the long-expected moment when she should be able to clasp our Lord to her heart and gaze upon His face, and claim as her own all the sweet joys of complete motherhood. The inconveniences of the journey were little indeed in comparison. The time had come, and she was fast approaching the appointed spot. Could she have foreseen, as she entered Bethlehem, the reception she was to meet with from the inhabitants of the city of David, she might have sorrowed tenderly for them, but she would have felt very little for herself.

X

But Mary bore within her womb One to Whom the full import of the event which was about to take place was more clear than even to herself. The Heart of our Lord gathered up in His own affections all her yearnings and desires, the yearnings and desires of the whole human world, and of the universe itself. He could understand the perfection of which the Creation which His hand made was capable, what was designed for it in the eternal decrees of its Maker, how glorious was to be that renovation which was to have its source in Him. He could see in everything He had made, and which had been subjected to vanity, as the Apostle says, by the Fall, the want of that greater perfection, and the craving for that more true and abiding beauty. All natures were open to Him, what they were, and what they might hereafter be, while the harmony and balance and mutual interdependence which bound them together in so marvellous an order, was to His eyes only the promise and foreshadowing of a nobler universe yet to come. He had made the human world His own by becoming Man, and in the human world He had already summed up the various orders of existence to which He had given the life which they possessed. All was to be renovated and elevated, and the principle of the renovation and elevation which were to come lay in His own Humanity.

Over that human world the eyes of the future Saviour fell with unutterable love. It was a wild and a tangled maze of degradation and misery, of ignorance where there should have been knowledge of God, of darkness where there should have been light, of foulness where there should have been purity, of cruelty and hatred where gentleness and charity should have reigned. To the Heart of the Saviour of mankind there was nothing, even in all that wilderness of abominations, which did not move the most intense and tender pity. He saw, in all the aberrations of men, the mischief which they generated rather than the guilt which they involved. He read in their most lowering passions, in their most wanton and barbarous excesses, only their need of the redemption which He came to bring them. The louder the cry of sin and pride and hate rose before the throne of heaven, the more deeply did it pierce His Heart as an appeal for help and light and healing and mercy. The maddest ravings of insolence and blasphemy sounded to Him as the most piteous appeals for mercy and relief. On the Cross He was to say of His murderers, "Father forgive them, for they know not what they do!" and now the whole world of sin and crime was crying out to Heaven for the enlightenment of its ignorances and the pardoning of its sins. He fastened, now as then, on every element in the misery of man which could be pleaded as man's excuse.

In the most perverse will He could discern the instinct for good which was wasting itself on a false object. He took account of all the influences of corrupt tradition and evil examples, of the tyranny of the unregenerate world forcing men on to excesses the character of which they did not know. In the depths of moral degradation He read only the need of redemption. His eyes sounded all those depths, and they did not quail before the frightful glare of the Hell to which they led. He would fain have quenched it for them entirely in His own Blood. He could count over also all the struggling elements of good which were lost amid this sea of evil. His eye fastened on natural virtues, on half efforts to follow the law of conscience, on devotional impulses diverted to usurping objects, on every faint and secret homage ever paid to truth or virtue or honour, every sacrifice of self-love, every resistance to licence, every courageous persistence in right against the sneering world or the clamouring crowd. All over the world He saw the evil in a clearness of deformity and a nakedness of malice which would have appalled any but the Saviour. And He saw also good where no one but Himself could have distinguished it from the overlying mass of evil. He saw the evil only to compassionate it, He rejoiced in the faintest good that He might foster it and strengthen it. He came now not to judge but to save, and He took into His Heart with infinite tenderness every single feature in the moral condition of mankind as it lay before Him, which called for healing, or which gave the faintest promise of a welcome to His efforts and devices for the accomplishment of the work of salvation.

Our Lord also knew perfectly all the workings of the good Spirit in the souls of men, from the simplest breathings of a desire for the rewards of virtue, and of a life led in obedience to the interior admonitions of conscience, to the most powerful workings of the Holy Ghost in all the divine love and fervour of the highest prayer. He understood all that had been from the beginning of the world of heavenly conversation and of holy aspiration, and especially He delighted in discerning and confirming the work of the Holy Ghost, Who had moved the hearts most favoured by Him to longing, and petition, and obsecration, and supplication, for the advent of the promised healing of man. All these He took up into His own perfect supplication before the throne of His Father, along with the prayers of Mary and Joseph and the living saints of the holy people, who were then more than ever prompted by the Holy Ghost to pour out their hearts in "groanings" ever more intense as they recognised, from the scroll of prophecy, that the appointed time was at hand. But it was not only that the prayers of the saints who were then to be found among the chosen people were then, as it were, collected in the Sacred Heart and enforced by the strength and might of His own intercession. He was the Lord and Head, not of one generation or nation only, but of all mankind, those who had passed already through the gates of death, and those who were hereafter to enter by the portal of life. Millions of souls were awaiting in the world beyond the grave the consummation of their redemption by His sacrifice, and the supplications and yearnings of the ancient saints, still praying in Limbus, the vast crowds with whom Purgatory was filled, and the infants without number who had passed away with the sign of the covenant upon them, all were included in the great ocean of supplication which broke continually before the throne of the Majesty on

High. All these prayers and desires were present to the Heart of the Redeemer, as well as the needs of the numberless generations who were to pass through the scene of man's probation after the Redemption had been fully wrought.

Each onward step in the progress of the great mystery towards its perfect accomplishment was foreordained, and well known in all its circumstances to the Sacred Heart. Each such step was to our Lord a subject of special and intense prayer, as the moment of its accomplishment drew nigh. When He went forth from the Cenacle, as we are told by St. John, He paused awhile to pour forth that great prayer for the Church of which that Evangelist has given us the record. That prayer was at once the summing up of what He had already done, and the application of what He was about to do to the purposes nearest to His own Heart. He had finished one part of His work, and He was about to take up another. For everything that our Lord did was done with the utmost tranquillity, and in the most perfect order. He looked back over what He had accomplished, and He looked forward to what He was next to do. Now also when the time had arrived when this new great step was to be taken of the Birth into the world at Bethlehem, it may be thought that He would sum up and make perfect, so to say, what had been His work while in the womb of Mary, and offer it to His Father with His the most tender and reverential love, so to take leave of this the first stage of His existence on earth.

The obedience and humiliation of the Nine Months were on the eve of their accomplishment. His

Sacred Body was formed perfect from the very beginning, and the glorious existence to which it had a right, had already been laid aside for the time, in order that it might be the fitting Body of Him Who was to be like us in all things, sin only excepted, and Who was to suffer on the Cross, for the salvation of the world. The Life which He had led in the womb was a Life of intense self-abasement. This had enabled Him to make Himself more completely nothing in the presence of His God and Creator, and thus had added a new beauty to the homage which He had paid to Him. It was this worship of God on the part of the Sacred Humanity which had added a fresh dignity to the whole creation from the first moment of His Incarnation. God had at last been honoured by a worship perfect in its kind, worthy of Himself, and rendered to Him by a created Human Nature. A Human Mind had received all that could be known of God. All His revelation of Himself in the universe, in the several natures whose marvellous harmony and order added its beauty as a whole to its beauty in every part, His teaching concerning Himself in His own Providence and in the inspired books, all had been adequately grasped and appreciated and understood, and a Human Heart had given back to the Creator the homage of a perfect love and a gratitude equal to His gifts, honouring Him as He deserved to be honoured, praising Him as He deserved to be praised, and making to Him the joyful sacrifice of the perfect surrender and oblation of Itself to His glory, and for the accomplishment of His particular decree and will in whatever He should ask of it. All the great attributes of the Creator were now severally and fully honoured, His Power, His Goodness, His Beneficence, His Holiness, His Justice, His Mercy. The intelligent worship of God is the highest and noblest occupation of creatures capable thereof, and to those who know what it is it is the most perfect joy of which their nature can partake. This had now begun in the Sacred Heart, and it was never to cease. It was to spread from Him all over the human race, heart after heart was to catch the flame, which was to fill the whole universe for ever.

The Sacred Heart had now been filled with another great and overwhelming passion. The eternal counsel of God for the redemption of the world by His own sufferings had been presented to Him at the first and accepted, as has been said, most willingly and obediently. All the details and particulars enfolded in this counsel and this commission had been made the daily food of the contemplations of the Sacred Humanity. The offence to God, the mischief to man, the triumph to Hell involved in sin, not only in general, but in each particular transgression of all that ever were to be, had been fully counted up. So also it was with the particular sufferings, interior and exterior, by which all were to be expiated. So also it was with the provisions of grace, the methods of carrying home reconciliation to one soul after another, the ways of winning the perverse, of arousing the languid, of overcoming the obstinate, of fortifying the weak, how to save even the bruised reed, how to keep alive the sleeping fire in the smoking flax. All the arrangements of the Church were rehearsed in the Sacred Heart in its retirement with God, her government, her administration, her ways of dealing with the world, nation after nation, generation after generation, her hierarchy, her Sacraments, her weapons of preaching, of catechising, of prayer, her religious rules, her devices of piety and inventions of devotion, the throne of Peter, the queenly reign of Mary. Our Lord was to come forth, when He did come forth, with His work and its instruments all prepared in His Heart beforehand, all steeped, if so we may speak, in the prayers of the Nine Months.

Nor had He left Himself without a work of most intense actual perfection in the souls most near to Him. The Baptist leaping in the womb of St. Elisabeth witnesses to the truth and efficacy of this activity of our Lord. This opens to us a whole world of the operations of grace which followed on His Presence in the womb of Mary. She herself was of course the greatest recipient of His grace, the most intelligent and faithful in her correspondence to the mighty blessings which that Presence brought home to her in an ever increasing stream, and her sanctification during this time was a work of His which had no parallel in all that He had done in heaven or on earth. He had perfectly fitted her for her great office, as far as its duties had yet come into play, and prepared her for all that was yet to be. In the same way, He had brought about the sanctifications next to hers in their magnificence and beauty, of St. Joseph and St. John, and all around, on those who had had any contact with Him in any way, any communication with His Mother, any intelligence of or share in the mystery,

He had shed profusely and lovingly the gifts of grace which fitted them for the work they might have to do. Who, indeed, can tell how large His bounty may have been in the preparation and sanctification of souls during this sacred time?

And now all was prepared. The Sacred Heart was burning with His own intense but tranquil fire of love for God and man, and for the next onward step in the advance of His work. The appointed days were drawing to their close. He had breathed into the heart of His Mother a longing, even more forcible than before, for the moment of the Nativity, and her prayers had long been rising up to Heaven for the accomplishment of the mystery. The world was at peace. The hearts most dear to God were full of unwonted cravings, inspired by the Holy Ghost, the great master of prayer. In the far East, the pious Kings, if the Star had not appeared to them at the date of the Incarnation itself, were watching the Heavens for some sign of what they had so much reason to expect. Bethlehem, indeed, was not ready. Its people had no thought of who the strangers were who were drawing near its gates. But the place of which "the Lord had need" was ready, for no one would have thought of disputing with St. Joseph for the tenancy of the cave and the stable. Our Lord lay tranquil and obedient in the womb of Mary, waiting only for the moment appointed by the will of His Father, to step forth into the world of which He was the King, leaving to her, as a parting gift of His Power, the unsullied and untouched Virginity which His Presence had consecrated for ever.

HARMONY OF THE GOSPELS.

PART I.

The Holy Infancy.

§ 4.— *The Conception of our Saviour Jesus Christ.*

St. Luke i. 26—38.

(26) AND in the sixth month the Angel Gabriel was sent from God into a city of Galilee, called Nazareth, (27) to a virgin espoused to a man whose name was Joseph, of the house of David and the virgin's name was Mary. (28) And the Angel being come in, said unto her, Hail full of grace, the Lord is with thee, Blessed art thou among women.

(29) Who having heard, was troubled at his saying, and thought with herself what manner of salutation this should be.

(30) And the Angel said to her, Fear not, Mary,

St. Luke i. 31—35.

for thou hast found grace with God. (31) Behold thou shalt conceive in thy womb, and shalt bring forth a son, and thou shalt call His name JESUS. (32) He shall be great, and shall be called the Son of the Most High, and the Lord God shall give unto Him the throne of David His father, and He shall reign in the house of Jacob for ever, (33) and of His Kingdom there shall be no end.

(34) And Mary said to the Angel, How shall this be done, because I know not man?

(35) And the Angel answering, said to her, The Holy Ghost shall

St. Luke i. 36—38.

come upon thee, and the power of the Most High shall overshadow thee. And therefore also the Holy which shall be born of thee shall be called the Son of God. (36) And behold thy cousin Elisabeth, she also hath conceived a son in her old age, and this is the sixth month with her that is called barren, (37) "because no word shall be impossible with God."[1]

(38) And Mary said, Behold the handmaid of the Lord, be it done to me according to thy word. And the Angel departed from her.

§ 5.—*The Visitation of the Blessed Virgin Mary.*

St. Luke i. 39—56.

(39) AND Mary rising up in those days, went into the hill country with haste

St. Luke i. 40—45.

into a city of Juda. (40) And she entered into the house of Zachary, and saluted Elisabeth.

(41) And it came to pass, that when Elisabeth heard the salutation of Mary the infant leaped in her womb. And Elisabeth was filled with the Holy Ghost, (42) and she cried out with a loud voice, and said, Blessed art thou among women, and blessed is the fruit of thy womb. (43) And whence is this to me, that the mother of my Lord should come to me? (44) For behold as soon as the voice of thy salutation sounded in my ears, the infant in my womb leaped for joy. (45) And blessed art thou that hast believed, because those things shall be accomplished that were spoken to thee by the Lord.

---

[1] Gen. xviii. 41. (Said to Sara in the prophecy of the conception of Isaac.)

St. Luke i. 46—53.

(46) And Mary said, My soul doth magnify the Lord,

(47) And my spirit hath rejoiced in God my Saviour.

(48) Because He hath regarded the humility of His handmaid, for behold from henceforth all generations shall call me blessed.

(49) For He that is mighty hath done great things to me, and Holy is His Name.

(50) And His mercy is from generation unto generations, to them that fear Him.

(51) He hath showed might in His arm, He hath scattered the proud in the conceit of their heart.

(52) He hath put down the mighty from their seat, and hath exalted the humble.

(53) He hath filled the

St. Luke i. 54—56.

hungry with good things, and the rich He hath sent empty away.

(54) He hath received Israel His servant, being mindful of His mercy.

(55) As He spoke to our fathers, to Abraham and to his seed for ever.

(56) And Mary abode with her about three months, and she returned to her own house.

§ 6.—*The Revelation made to St. Joseph by the Angel.*

St. Matt. i. 18—25.

(18) Now the generation of Christ was in this wise. When as His Mother Mary was espoused to Joseph, before they came together, she was found with child, of the Holy Ghost. (19) Whereupon Joseph her husband, being a just man, and not willing publicly to expose her, was minded to put her

St. Matt. i. 20—24.

away privately. (20) But while he thought on these things, behold the Angel of the Lord appeared to him in his sleep, saying, Joseph, son of David, fear not to take unto thee Mary thy wife, for that which is conceived of her, is of the Holy Ghost. (21) And she shall bring forth a Son, and thou shalt call His Name JESUS. For He shall save His people from their sins.

(22) Now all this was done that it might be fulfilled. which the Lord spoke by the prophet, saying, (23) Behold a Virgin shall conceive, and bring forth a Son, and they shall call His Name Emmanuel, which being interpreted is, God with us.[2]

(24) And Joseph rising up from sleep, did as the Angel of the Lord had

St. Matt. i. 25.

commanded him, and took unto him his wife. (25) And he knew her not till she brought forth her firstborn Son, and he called His Name JESUS.

§ 7. — *The Nativity of St. John, the Forerunner of our Lord.*

St. Luke i. 57—80.

(57) Now Elisabeth's full time of being delivered was come, and she brought forth a son. (58) And her neighbours and kinsfolks heard that the Lord had showed His great mercy towards her, and they congratulated with her.

(59) And it came to pass, that on the eighth day they came to circumcise the child, and they called him by his father's name Zachary. (60) And his mother answering,

---

[2] Isaias vii. 14.

St. Luke i. 61—67.

said, Not so, but he shall be called John. (61) And they said to her, There is none of thy kindred that is called by this name. (62) And they made signs to his father, how he would have him called. (63) And demanding a writing-table he wrote, saying, John is his name. And they all wondered. (64) And immediately his mouth was opened, and his tongue loosed, and he spoke blessing God. (65) And fear came upon all their neighbours, and all these things were noised abroad over all the hill country of Judæa, (66) and all they that had heard them laid them up in their heart, saying, What an one, think ye, shall this child be? For the hand of the Lord was with him.

(67) And Zachary his father was filled with the

St. Luke i. 68—74.

Holy Ghost, and he prophesied saying,

(68) Blessed be the Lord God of Israel, because He hath visited and wrought the redemption of His people.

(69) And hath raised up an horn of salvation to us, in the house of David His servant.

(70) As He spoke by the mouth of His holy prophets, who are from the beginning.

(71) Salvation from our enemies, and from the hand of all that hate us.

(72) To perform mercy to our fathers, and to remember His holy testament.

(73) The oath which He sware to Abraham our father, that He would grant us,

(74) That being delivered from the hand of our enemies, we may serve Him without fear.

St. Luke i. 75—78.

(75) In holiness and justice before Him, all our days.

(76) And thou child, shall be called the prophet of the Highest, for thou shalt go before the face of the Lord to prepare His ways.

(77) To give knowledge of salvation to His people, unto the remission of their sins.

(78) Through the

St. Luke i. 79—80.

bowels of the mercy of our God, in which the Orient, from on high hath visited us.

(79) To enlighten them that sit in darkness, and in the shadow of death, to direct our feet into the way of peace.

(80) And the child grew, and was strengthened in spirit, and was in the deserts until the day of his manifestation to Israel.

APPENDIX.

HEADS OF MEDITATION ON THE LIFE OF OUR LORD IN THE WOMB.

I.—*Formation of the Body of our Lord.*

1. Mary's desire to minister her substance for Its formation.
2. It is formed by the operation of the Holy Ghost.
3. Her immense increase in grace and sanctification.

II.—*Qualities of the Sacred Body.*

1. Its littleness, to be like ours.
2. Great beauty and delicacy of temperament.
3. Its right to immediate glorification foregone for our sakes.

III.—*Creation of the Soul of our Lord.*

1. It was a soul like ours.
2. Its immense dowry of graces.
3. It was the object of the immense complacency of God.

IV.—*Union of Soul and Body to the Person of the Word.*

1. It was instantaneous on the formation of both.
2. It was the greatest of all God's works.
3. In what way the Father and Holy Ghost also are united to the Sacred Humanity.

V.—*Excellence and perfection of the Sacred Humanity.*

1. It was raised by the Union above all creatures, past, present, future, and possible.
2. The Divine perfections communicated to it.
3. Its great beauty and attractiveness, for the work it was to do.

VI.—*Holiness of the Sacred Humanity.*

1. Fulness of sanctity, admitting no possibility of increase.
2. Substantial and essential sanctity of the Person of the Word.
3. Sanctity by virtue of the Union with the Divinity.

VII.—*Impeccability of the Sacred Humanity.*

1. The Soul always guided by the Divine Person.
2. Free from all sin, because conceived by the Holy Ghost.
3. It was the Source of all purity to all mankind.

VIII.—*Fulness of grace.*

1. It received grace without measure.
2. It was full of grace for others also.
3. Great joy of our Lord on this account.

IX.—*It was adorned by all virtues.*

1. Virtues given to correspond to the greatness and excellence of our Lord.
2. Virtues never sterile but fruitful in others.
3. Fragrance of our Lord's virtues delighting Heaven.

X.—*Fulness of knowledge.*

1. It knew all things past, present, and future.

2. It knew the thoughts, desires, and affections of all Angels and all men.

3. All its knowledge directed to the glory of God.

XI.—*Gifts of the Holy Ghost.*

1. Wisdom, in the loving comprehension of all Divine mysteries.

2. Understanding, of all that related to His own office and work.

3. Counsel, as to all that He had to do and suffer.

4. Fortitude, for the embracing all and executing all perfectly.

XII.—*Gifts of the Holy Ghost* (2).

1. Knowledge, of all created things and of God's purpose concerning them.

2. Piety, a dutiful love to God, His Mother, and all creatures.

3. Fear, a most reverential and loving respect to God.

XIII.—*The joy of the Eternal Father.*

1. For the revelation of His love in the gift to us of His Son.

2. For the elevation of Mary as Mother.

3. For the glory and graces imparted freely to all.

XIV.—*Joy of the Eternal Word.*

1. For the satisfaction of His everlasting desire to become Man.

2. That the Sacred Humanity was to be for ever the recipient of all His perfections.

3. For the accomplishment of the Will of His Father.

XV.—*Delight of the Holy Ghost.*

1. For the accomplishment of the decree of the Most Holy Trinity by His operation.
2. For the creation of the Sacred Humanity, on which He was to pour out all His graces and gifts, for Itself and all.
3. For His own future Mission, as an issue of the Incarnation.

XVI.—*Beginning of the Life in the Womb.*

1. A Life most precious and most perfect, a Divine life, ordered to the glory of God.
2. Meritorious enough to save a thousand worlds.
3. A Life led not for Himself but for us.

XVII.—*Joy of the Sacred Humanity.*

1. At seeing Itself infinitely enriched and united for ever to the Person of the Eternal Word.
2. At seeing the great graces and favours to Mary by communication from Itself.
3. At the gifts It was to communicate to all other creatures.

XVIII.—*Beginning of our Lord's activity.*

1. He began at once and in every way to work for God.
2. With the greatest possible fervour.
3. With the greatest perseverance.

XIX.—*Purity of intention.*

1. Our Lord worked for the end of the glory of God.
2. That all the fruit might be for our benefit.

3. For the highest and noblest end of each particular action.

XX.—*Soul of our Lord seeing God.*

1. The immediate vision of God imparted to the Soul of our Lord.
2. It saw God before anything else, and never ceased to enjoy the vision of Him.
3. More perfectly than all the Angels and Saints.

XXI.—*Beatitude of the Soul of our Lord.*

1. It was flooded with an immensity of joy at the possession of the Beatific Vision.
2. All our Beatitude depends on and flows from that of the Soul of our Lord.
3. Our Lady's Womb became as Heaven, by the beatitude of the Soul of her Son.

XXII.—*Adoration of God.*

1. The adoration of God by our Lord followed immediately on the Vision of God.
2. It was founded on the most perfect intelligence of the excellencies and beauties of God.
3. And also on the most perfect knowledge of His own nothingness as a creature.

XXIII.—*Love of God.*

1. Love of God, generated by knowledge of His infinite goodness.
2. Our Lord loved all creatures in God, as depending on Him and belonging to Him.
3. He loved also all men as His brethren committed to Him by God.

XXIV.—*Gratitude to God.*

1. The knowledge of Its own elevation producing gratitude in the Sacred Humanity.

2. It embraced at once every gift, past, present, and future, and all the circumstances, of the greatness of the Giver, the excellence of the gift, the love with which it is given, the lowliness of human nature to which it is given.

3. It included also all gifts to creatures as given to Itself.

XXV.—*Blessing God.*

1. With a most perfect and universal benediction.

2. Not of affection only, but with the service of a most holy life.

3. Exciting also His Blessed Mother to bless and magnify God, as in the *Magnificat*.

XXVI.—*Our Lord looking on Mary.*

1. As a Lily of wonderful perfection and purity, free from all sin and capable of serving God perfectly.

2. With special joy in her sanctity.

3. With joy that He was the Source of all her gifts.

XXVII.—*Our Lord looking on other creatures.*

1. He compassionated their miseries through sin and their loss of heaven.

2. Their sins as offences against God, with desire to repair them.

3. Also the immense number of their actual sins, their ingratitude, their loathsomeness and their mischievousness.

XXVIII.—*Our Lord offering Himself to the Father.*

1. An oblation founded on His knowledge of all that He had received from God.

2. A perfect oblation, because the offering of what was most pleasing to God, and with an affection of conformity to the will of God which was of infinite value, embracing all His designs and decrees.

3. Animated by a desire of the pure glory of God.

XXIX.—*Renunciation of Beatitude of His Body.*

1. The decrees of redemption and of satisfaction for sin made a life of glory in the Body incongruous, and our Lord renounced it.

2. He also accepted willingly all the sufferings and humiliations of His Life.

3. And all other decrees of God concerning His Life and Death.

XXX.—*Merit of our Lord's actions.*

1. As God and Man, all of infinite merit.

2. He merited the glory of His Body and the exaltation of His Name, although these were due to Him from the first.

3. He applied the merit of His works to all His elect.

XXXI.—*Occupations of our Lord in the Womb of His Mother.*

1. Considering His dependence on God for everything.

2. The gifts natural and supernatural which He had received, and the weakness of the Human Nature which had received them.

3. Arranging the course of His Life, the economy

of the Church, the manner of the Redemption of the world, and His particular Providence over each soul.

XXXII.—*Our Lord's obedience in the Womb.*

1. His Conception flowed immediately on the obedience of His Mother to the message of the Angel.
2. He remained during the Nine Months out of obedience.
3. He obeyed His Mother and others, for the sake of God.

XXXIII.—*Humility of our Lord in the Womb.*

1. In entering the Womb of the Blessed Virgin—*non horruisti Virginis Uterum.*
2. Humbling Himself at the sight of His own exaltation.
3. Resolving on all the subsequent humiliations of His Life.

XXXIV.—*Meekness of our Lord in the Womb.*

1. He begins the practice of meekness which He was to continue to the end.
2. Thereby to appease the wrath of God to men.
3. Resolving on all the meekness of His conversation with men.

XXXV.—*Love of poverty in our Lord in the Womb.*

1. An entire renunciation of all things, though He was possessed of infinite riches.
2. Dependence on His Mother for His Flesh and Blood and sustenance.
3. The exercise of poverty to be continued through His whole Life.

XXXVI.—*Patience of our Lord in the Womb.*

1. Accepting the circumstances of His dwelling in the Womb with perfect intelligence.
2. With the prevision of all the sufferings of His Life and Passion.
3. And of all that He was to suffer in His Blessed Mother and all the martyrs and saints.

XXXVII.—*Sufferings of our Lord in the Womb.*

1. Far more than those of other infants, on account of His full consciousness.
2. From His having the full use of His senses.
3. Our Lady suffering with Him on this account, causing also fresh suffering to Him.

XXXVIII.—*Exercise of prayer in the Womb.*

1. Contemplation of the mysteries of God.
2. Without any pause or distraction.
3. Also of our miseries and faults.

XXXIX.—*Silence taught by our Lord in the Womb.*

1. He chose midnight for His Conception to show the preciousness of silence for union with God.
2. He kept silence for the Nine Months to glorify God and make satisfaction for faults of speech.
3. His silence was the origin of the silence of the cloister.

XL.—*Religious retirement in the Womb.*

1. He chose to remain shut up in the Womb of His Mother for the love of retirement.
2. Our Lady herself was most retiring.
3. This retirement the origin of that of the cloister.

XLI.—*Our Lord in the Womb King of Kings.*

1. He was King of heaven and of earth, by nature, by the appointment of the Father, by purchase, and other titles.

2. He is the particular King of each one of us.

3. He exercises His royal power at once, choosing His servants and preparing for them the graces by which they may serve Him faithfully, and to their own good.

XLII.—*Our Lord in the Womb the Head of men.*

1. We are all His members.

2. We must look to Him for all graces and benefits.

3. He governs us also by means of those whom He sets over us in His place.

XLIII.—*Our Lord in the Womb the Divine Lawgiver.*

1. All authority to command and legislate now given to Him.

2. He not only gives laws and precepts, but also power to observe them.

3. The rules and laws under which we live come from Him.

XLIV.—*Our Lord in the Womb as Priest, Mediator, and Redeemer.*

1. He was anointed with the Divinity Itself.

2. He began at once to negotiate the affair of our reconciliation.

3. He resolved then to redeem us at the price of His own Blood.

XLV.—*Our Lord in the Womb the Sanctifier of men.*

1. He began His office at once, first with the soul of Mary.

2. He went on to sanctify St. John and others by means of her.

3. He looked forward to the many conversions and sanctifications He was to bring about in His Life among men.

XLVI.—*Our Lord in the Womb the Light of the world.*

1. Darkness of the world when our Lord became Incarnate to enlighten it.

2. His enlightenment of His Blessed Mother, which was never hindered by any ingratitude.

3. All the light concerning God and the manner of serving Him which is now in the world, comes from Him.

XLVII.—*Our Lord in the Womb the Prince of Peace.*

1. He offered Himself entirely for the making of peace with the Father.

2. The peace which He brings implies war with ourselves.

3. The law of charity taught, as the great means of peace among men.

XLVIII.—*Our Lord in the Womb our Spouse, Pastor, and Example.*

1. Our Lord espoused not only the Sacred Humanity, but also His Mother, the Church, and all devout souls.

2. His commission to be the Shepherd, Guide, and Guardian of our souls.

3. To be our great Example.

END OF VOL. II.

www.ingramcontent.com/pod-product-compliance
Lightning Source LLC
Chambersburg PA
CBHW020741020526
44115CB00030B/725